# THE SKY IS FALLING

## Also by Peter Biskind

*My Lunches with Orson: Conversations Between Henry Jaglom and Orson Welles*

*Star: How Warren Beatty Seduced America*

*Gods and Monsters: Thirty Years of Writing on Film and Culture from One of America's Most Incisive Writers*

*Down and Dirty Pictures: Miramax, Sundance, and the Rise of Independent Film*

*Easy Riders, Raging Bulls: How the Sex-Drugs-and-Rock 'n' Roll Generation Saved Hollywood*

*The Godfather Companion: Everything You Ever Wanted to Know About All Three Godfather Films*

*Seeing Is Believing: How Hollywood Taught Us to Stop Worrying and Love the Fifties*

# How Vampires, Zombies, Androids, and Superheroes Made America Great for Extremism

THE
NEW
PRESS

NEW YORK
LONDON

# THE SKY IS FALLING

# PETER BISKIND

Requests for permission to reproduce selections from this book should be mailed to: Permissions Department, The New Press, 120 Wall Street, 31st floor, New York, NY 10005.

Published in the United States by The New Press, New York, 2018
Distributed by Two Rivers Distribution

LIBRARY OF CONGRESS CATALOGING-IN-PUBLICATION DATA

Names: Biskind, Peter, author.
Title: The sky is falling : how vampires, zombies, androids, and superheroes
  made America great for extremism / Peter Biskind.
Description: New York : The New Press, 2018. | Includes bibliographical
  references and index.
Identifiers: LCCN 2018017585| ISBN 9781620974292 (hc : alk. paper) | ISBN
  9781620974308 (ebook)
Subjects: LCSH: United States—Civilization—21st century. | Popular
  culture—United States—History—21st century. | Popular
  culture—Political aspects—United States—History—21st century. |
  Radicalism—Social aspects—United States—History—21st century. |
  Radicalism—Political aspects—United States—History—21st century. |
  Political culture—United States—History—21st century. | Right and left
  (Political science) | Polarization (Social sciences)—United States.
Classification: LCC E169.12 B57 2018 | DDC 973.93—dc23 LC record available at https://lccn.
loc.gov/2018017585

The New Press publishes books that promote and enrich public discussion and understanding of the issues vital to our democracy and to a more equitable world. These books are made possible by the enthusiasm of our readers; the support of a committed group of donors, large and small; the collaboration of our many partners in the independent media and the not-for-profit sector; booksellers, who often hand-sell New Press books; librarians; and above all by our authors.

www.thenewpress.com

*Book design and composition by Bookbright Media*
*This book was set in Garamond Premier Pro, Impact, and Oswold*

Printed in the United States of America

10 9 8 7 6 5 4 3 2 1

To Betsy and Kate, with love, as ever, and to Richard Brick.
I only wish I was still able to take advantage of his street smarts
and laugh at his wiseass antics.

# CONTENTS

# THE SKY IS FALLING

# BEYOND THE FRINGE: AN INTRODUCTION

Are things getting more simplistic, and therefore more right
and more left? Yeah!
                              —*Joss Whedon, writer-director,* The Avengers

This book is about American popular culture in the age of extremism.
"Extremism" is a broad-stroke term that covers a myriad of sins—or
virtues—depending on your point of view. "Extremist" has long been a dirty
word in the national lexicon, particularly over the course of the two-decade-
long summer that lasted, give or take a few interruptions, from the end of
World War II to the mid-1960s. Those who dissented from the prevailing
ideology of American exceptionalism—that is, America is special, better,
greater than any other nation on the planet—or who called attention to
the discrepancy between our leaders' lofty rhetoric and the conduct of one
administration after another were branded with the "e" word.

Extremists came in two flavors, right and left. Both were routinely vili-
fied, the former as the lunatic fringe with their tinfoil hats and tales of alien
abduction, the latter as un-Americans, laying the groundwork for Uncle Joe
Stalin's imminent takeover of the United States. But right or left, they were
excluded from the mainstream—from its practices, its discourse or, as we
now say, the national conversation.

Today, the battered centrists who are still walking and talking continue
to use the term as a derogatory epithet, along with cognates like "divisive"
and "controversial," or, more colorfully, "wackos," as Senator John McCain
called Donald Trump's supporters during the 2016 presidential primary.

As the subsequent election suggested, however, the joke was on them. "Extremism," as it turned out, had been undergoing a makeover since long before the results were in. It had been invested with a tangy sizzle of daring and excitement, become the go-to term for characterizing whatever was new and different, ahead of the curve, cooler than cool, more—what? Everything. Extremists were praised as "disrupters," "envelope pushers," "out of the boxers." A random sampling turns up "extreme combat," "extreme medicine," "extreme rendition." Extreme products abound, from flash drives (SanDisk Extreme) to toothpaste (Aquafresh Extreme Clean). The Showtime Extreme channel specializes in martial arts, boxing, and thrillers, that is, "action that never, ever stops." Seeking eyeballs that have wondered elsewhere, even today's "reality" shows have scrambled aboard the extremist bandwagon. According to the *New York Times*, "Reality television, in recent years, has submitted participants to extreme emotional interrogation, extreme physical assault, [and] extreme isolation." Even YouTube's search algorithm guides its 1.5 billion users to extreme content.

Rather than an epithet, "extreme" has become an accolade, while "mainstream" has become "lamestream." Witness Trump's usage of "extreme" to tout the deep background checks he advocates for immigrants from "terrorist countries." "Extreme vetting," he cried. "I want extreme."

On the opposite end of the political spectrum, here is actor Joseph Gordon-Levitt, who plays Edward Snowden in Oliver Stone's film *Snowden* (2016), commenting on his character's real-life avatar: "I consider him the most extreme of patriots."

It is no secret that the age of extremism has arrived. By 2015, the slice of Republicans who saw themselves as "very conservative" had jumped nearly twofold over the previous two decades, skyrocketing from 19 percent to 33 percent. The election of Donald Trump, of course, is the result. Where once, extremism would have been tamed, defanged, co-opted, as was most often the case when outsiders with their noses pressed to the glass became insiders, now the extremes are dictating the terms of the transaction. Those who thought that the majesty of the office would smooth Trump's sharp corners were wrong. Rather, the mainstream is being transformed into what was formerly considered the fringe. What was once inhibited is now exhibited.

A long time ago, in what seems now like a galaxy far away, the rude alarums of rancorous partisanship that roil today's politics were barely audible. After half a decade of brutal world war and relentless ideological struggle against European fascism and Japanese imperialism, not only had foreign enemies been vanquished, but on the domestic front, the ogres of the 1930s had been slain as well. On the left, Henry A. Wallace, the most radical of Franklin Roosevelt's serial vice presidents, had been soundly defeated in a bid to oust Harry Truman in 1948, while the Communist Party USA— which only a few years earlier had been basking in popularity thanks to the prestige the Soviet Union had earned during World War II—was on the run, the remnants mopped up by a decade's worth of witch hunts fueled by the furious outburst of anticommunist hysteria that swept the country from the late 1940s to the late 1950s.

At the opposite extreme, the isolationist America First Party, which had tried to prevent our entry into the war, as well as the neo-Nazi German-American Bund had become no more than footnotes in the history books, while the remaining right-wing movements, soiled by the stain of fascism, found it hard to get traction.

After the election of Dwight D. Eisenhower in 1952, the government fell into the hands of a bipartisan coalition composed of center-right liberals and center-left conservatives, that is, Cold War Democrats and East Coast Republicans whose visions of postwar America were similar enough that they could see eye to eye on basic principles. For their part, Democrats agreed to join their partners across the aisle in vigorously rooting out subversives at home and containing the Soviets abroad. They pursued Wall Street–friendly policies, although they insisted on mild regulation of business because they had little faith that the "invisible hand" of the market, as imagined by Adam Smith in *The Wealth of Nations*, a text sacred to many Republicans, could convert the pursuit of private interest into the general good.

Holding up their end of the bargain, Republicans consented, albeit grudgingly, to accept New Deal programs like Social Security and unemployment insurance, labor's right to organize, and they even paid lip service to the United Nations. From this consensus among moderates, the postwar welfare state emerged, a.k.a. the "center" or the "mainstream," administered by the "establishment," that is, the Ivy League–educated elite entrenched in places like the State Department who were insulated from the electoral tides. With Europe and much of the rest of the world in ruins, Americans could look forward to a decade and more of unprecedented prosperity. Staring into the blazing sun of the flourishing middle class, no less a luminary than *Time* magazine publisher Henry Luce proclaimed the "American Century."

Nevertheless, defying the political winds, a handful of hardy extremists soldiered on. While Reds read and reread their dog-eared copies of *The Communist Manifesto* in prison, the right looked to Ayn Rand's *The Fountainhead* as its bible, Friedrich Hayek's *The Road to Serfdom* as its Fodor's, and William F. Buckley Jr.'s *National Review* as its bathroom reading.

In 1954, however, when the right's standard-bearer, Joe McCarthy, was slapped down in the Army-McCarthy hearings, the anticommunist hobbyhorse he had ridden so successfully stumbled and fell. Bereft of their fearless leader, right-wing extremists stumbled and fell as well. Robert Welch, head of the John Birch Society, who claimed that Eisenhower was a "tool of the Communists" and accused him of "treason," was reduced to an object of ridicule. Barry Goldwater supplied the last hurrah, campaigning for president against Lyndon Johnson in 1964 on a platform of small government. When he defended himself against the charge of extremism by famously saying that "extremism in defense of liberty is no vice," he was all but carted off to the loony bin, and Johnson won by a landslide.

Today, the American political landscape looks starkly different than it did in the post–World War II era, when this country was at the height of its power and the future seemed bright. Jobs have been exported, information technologies have replaced heavy industry, service has trumped manufacturing, capital accumulation has superseded capital creation at the same time that the infrastructure is crumbling. Despite the economic uptick during the early months of the Trump presidency, our so-called hourglass economy has ravaged the out-of-work class and even squeezed the middle class. In the run-up to the 2016 presidential race, the phrase "middle class" was conspicuous by its absence, as aspirants acknowledged the vacuum by avoiding the term. It morphed into "everyday Americans" (Hillary Clinton), "hardworking men and women" (Ted Cruz), or "working families" (Bernie Sanders). The postwar consensus has foundered on the rocks of globalism, ballooning inequities of wealth, and cultural alienation.

As consensus gives way to division, Goldwater and Welch would be right at home in today's GOP, among our militias, birthers, truthers, Promise Keepers, antichoicers, intelligent designers, climate change deniers, last daysers, creationists, stem cell resisters, tax refusers, evangelical exceptionalists, white identitarians, and anti-vaxxers. Bedrock principles written into the Constitution like the separation of church and state are under relentless attack as fundamentalism undermines secularism. The ill-conceived, expensive, and failed military adventures in the Middle East have made the limits of American power all too apparent. As pessimism replaces optimism, democracy has all but dissolved in the acid rain of money. Now, only the wealthy can afford to dream the American Dream.

Barack Obama took office promising to bridge the ideological abyss separating the two parties, as if, to quote Strother Martin in the 1967 cult classic *Cool Hand Luke*, "what we've got here is . . . failure to communicate." But communication wasn't the problem; common ground no longer existed. The polarization of the electorate had been turbocharged by, among other things, what Eli Pariser called the "filter bubble," a phrase describing Google's customization of information to fit the viewpoints of its users. That, added to the multitude of new entertainment providers—cable TV, streaming services like Netflix, Amazon Prime, and Hulu, as well as internet sites like Facebook and YouTube—and devices on which to display them, disrupted the consensus entertainment provided by the studios and the networks. Obama discovered that the GOP had moved so far to the right that his efforts were doomed to failure. As Wisconsin Republican congressman Paul Ryan happily observed in 2009, "It's as if we're living in an Ayn Rand novel."

As an agent of change, culture has often been treated shabbily, as no more than a secondary or even tertiary factor, well in the shadow of the featured players: economics, politics, demographics, whatever. But it's a mistake to underestimate the power of culture to inflame our emotions. To choose just four examples, *Uncle Tom's Cabin*, published in 1852, pushed the nation toward civil war; the release of *The Birth of a Nation* sixty-three years later kick-started the moribund Klan; while in 1949, George Orwell described our contemporary topsy-turvy America with chilling prescience in his dystopic novel, *1984*. Then there was *The Manchurian Candidate* (1962), an almost uncanny example of the ability of the imagination to anticipate events. It envisioned Russian intervention in U.S. elections fifty-four years before it happened.

Ronald Reagan was perhaps the first movie-made president, promiscuously quoting lines from old films and using their plots as a lens through which to view contemporary politics. He was so taken by George Lucas's first *Star Wars* trilogy (1977–83) that he named his antimissile system after it, adding, "the force is with us." Daring Congress to pass a tax increase, he quoted Clint Eastwood, saying, "Go ahead. Make my day." Following Reagan, Donald Trump, of course, was the first TV-made president. Both chicken and egg, culture enhances or inhibits phenomena that may have their roots elsewhere, especially today when the so-called culture wars, fed by economic insecurity and the backlash against the progressive advances of the 1960s, can be so skillfully manipulated that "values voters" act against their own class interests.

As visible as the steel and concrete cities in which most of us live, but just as often invisible as the air we breathe, popular culture is saturated with politics. Far from mere escapism, movies and TV reflect the arguments that agitate the waters of our political life. Unlike the rhetoric of speechifying politicians and bloviating intellectuals that puts people to sleep, telling stories affects them directly, touching their hearts and engaging their minds. Pundits said Hillary Clinton lost the 2016 presidential election because, among other things, she didn't have an appealing story to tell.

Historically, the three networks, with their lowest common denominator programming, shunned politics like the plague, while Hollywood disingenuously tried to shield itself from moralistic or politically motivated attacks by wrapping itself in the conventional wisdom that held that movies are apolitical, carrying no ideology whatsoever. As Sam Goldwyn famously quipped, "If you have a message, call Western Union."

One thing that the witch-hunters of the 1950s, who were busy blacklisting Hollywood talent for smuggling communist propaganda into movies understood very well was that this is patently untrue. Ironically, thanks to cultural Cold Warriors like President Eisenhower's ambassador to Italy Clare Boothe Luce (Mrs. Henry), who threatened to boycott the 1955 Venice Film Festival unless it withdrew its invitation to *Blackboard Jungle* because (she claimed) it aided and abetted our enemies by projecting a sordid image of America, we learned that Goldwyn was wrong.

Not only are Hollywood films and TV full of messages, most often conscious, although sometimes not, but it is those pictures that appear to be totally innocent of politics—sci-fi, westerns, thrillers—that are the most effective delivery vehicles for political ideas, precisely because they don't seem to purvey them. Edgar Wright, who directed and co-wrote satirical hits like *Shaun of the Dead* (2004) and *The World's End* (2013), compared his movies to Trojan horses: "[I] smuggle in other themes under the auspices of a zombie or a sci-fi film."

It's no exaggeration to say that values, and therefore politics, are embedded in the very fabric of movies. Jean-Luc Godard once famously said, attributing it to D.W. Griffith, "All you need for a movie is a girl and a gun," which, looking back at the long history of movies, seems to be a truism, but of course, Godard (and Griffith) is a male describing a male-dominated medium. Now, the #MeToo movement and Parkland, Sandy Hook, et al., have helped us see that girls and guns can be contested, enabling us to imagine movies without either.

In 1930, the studios adopted the Motion Picture Production Code, guaranteeing that American movies would convey mainstream values. It stated that "no picture shall be produced that will lower the moral standards of those who see it. Hence the sympathy of the audience should never be thrown to the side of crime, wrongdoing, evil or sin." The networks would follow suit in the postwar era with their Standards and Practices divisions.

The lessons movies teach us are by no means confined to content. Marshall McLuhan's "the medium is the message" didn't become the mantra of cultural critics until the mid-1960s, but Hollywood was there first, with the lush studio movies of the 1950s that stood in stark contrast to the spare black-and-white films that emerged from war-torn Europe. Those magic Technicolor carpets were testimonials to the wealth it took to produce them. Whether it was Gene Kelly singin' in the rain in Paris, Marlon Brando falling in love in Japan, Jennifer Jones doing the same in Hong Kong, or David Niven traveling around the world in eighty days, the movies that conveyed them to foreign climes not only showed us the lavish production values that American dollars could buy but demonstrated that no place on earth was beyond the reach of Hollywood, and by extension, Washington.

Ideological policing has been around ever since humans learned to string sentences together to make stories. In modern America, it used to be the province of the center, but Reagan-era right-wing watchdog groups like the industrious trolls at Accuracy in Media learned the lessons of the 1950s to such a degree that the pendulum has swung so far in the opposite direction that today's audiences are often more alert to the messages than to the movies themselves. The entertainment industry's perceived liberal bias has made it a perennial target of the right, which at one time or another has gone after subversion in *Sesame Street* and *SpongeBob SquarePants*, while Fox Business commentator Charles Payne singled out *The Lego Movie* (2014). Recently, an Alabama exhibitor refused to show *Beauty and the Beast* (2017) because it includes a gay character, and the alt-right called for a boycott of Disney's *Rogue One: A Star Wars Story* (2016) citing tweets from its writers describing the Empire as a "white supremacist (human) organization" pitted against a "multicultural group led by brave women." Disney chief Bob Iger, trying to get ahead of the controversy, channeled Sam Goldwyn by saying that *Rogue One* "is not a film that is, in any way, a political film."

The fact that our habit of enlivening dull evenings by watching TV and movies exposes us to political ideas is not exactly breaking news. This is not to say that they are entirely consistent or lacking ambiguities or even glaring contradictions. Studies of the electorate starting in the 1960s have called Americans "ideologically innocent," that is, lacking in ideological fervor. Their positions on specific issues have as much to do with group benefits (who gains, who loses) as with abstract political beliefs. It would thus be foolish to look for any sort of ideological rigor in popular entertainment. As bastard children born of the uneasy marriage of art and commerce, moreover, movies and television shows are a fractious bunch. On the one hand, they are riddled with the personal tics and idiosyncrasies of those who create them; on the other, they are subject to the imperatives of the corporate entities that finance them.

What is not yet generally acknowledged, however, is that the ideological dimensions of these entertainments display a surprising degree of internal cohesion. On the basis of these regularities, we can group content into left, center, and right. In sci-fi movies, for example, aliens from outer space are often a flashpoint. In right-leaning shows, they are hostile, invariably invading Earth and zapping us with their disintegrator rays, as they do, say, in *War of the Worlds* (1953, 2005). In a movie in which intruders from outer space wish us ill, we need protection, and therefore that show is likely to favor the police or the military and display a weakness for strong leaders and authority in general, like the *Independence Day* franchise.

At the opposite end of the spectrum, in *The Day the Earth Stood Still* (1951, 2008), the alien is trying to save us from ourselves. A movie in which little green men from Mars are benign or even friendly is likely to portray the military as the enemy—brutal and stupid. Generally speaking, the left welcomes these arrivals, while the right prefers departures.

If we choose to be more granular, this taxonomy can be refined further. Among today's right-wing shows, for example, we can distinguish between those that speak the language of traditional conservatism and those that are colored by populism, libertarianism, white nationalism, or evangelicalism.

One or another of these ideologies may prevail in a given era, but generally, content with clashing points of view battle one another for the widest audience, and therefore the biggest box office. In the postwar era, for example, the big, A-list films like *Giant* (1956) with the largest budgets and the brightest stars—in this case Rock Hudson and Elizabeth Taylor—resided comfortably within the mainstream and dominated the movie landscape. They bought into the idea of consensus; avoided divisive, controversial subjects; and tried to please everyone. Nevertheless, these pictures recognized that no matter how appealing the center made itself, some people were just going to say no and make trouble.

Responsibility for guaranteeing order lay with the authorities, that is, docs and cops, soldiers and scientists. Although the bipartisan coalition of moderate Democrats and Republicans leaned center-right, studio "product," despite the blacklist, leaned center-left. These two competing ideologies squabbled with each other over how best to enforce consensus.

The center-left liberal pictures like *Panic in the Streets* (1950), Elia Kazan's film about the outbreak of plague in New Orleans, favored docs over cops, scientists over soldiers. Docs and scientists preferred the therapeutic model of social control that treated dissenters like patients instead of criminals. Even criminals weren't treated like criminals but were considered sick, not bad. Force was replaced by consent. Citizens did the right thing not because they had to but because they wanted to. *On the Waterfront* (1954) detached Marlon Brando from his mob pals by convincing him—instead of forcing him—to testify before the crime commission, thereby separating the baby from the bathwater instead of just draining the tub. Dissenters who were susceptible to argument or inducements were lured back into the fold with the carrot, in this case, Eva Marie Saint. In divide-and-conquer westerns, Cochise could always be depended upon to return to the reservation because the allure of our society was so powerful that he couldn't say no, but extremists like Geronimo, considerably more disaffected and intransigent, were thrashed with the stick, that is, hunted down and slaughtered. (Whoever dubbed the mission to kill Osama bin Laden "Operation Geronimo" was clearly a fan of 1950s westerns.)

Leading with the carrot and hiding the stick made it possible for mainstream shows to maintain the fiction that power as such was so diffused in America that effectively it didn't exist, and therefore, unlike the Soviet enemy, our democracy was genuinely consensual. And once the witch hunt had done its work, to a large extent it was.

Center-right conservative films, on the other hand, like *The Thing from Another World* (1951, 1982, 2011), though still firmly within the magic circle of consensus, preferred cops and soldiers to docs and scientists. Less averse to the use of force, they spurned the carrot in favor of the stick. In *The Man Who Shot Liberty Valance* (1962), directed by John Ford, Hollywood's cinematic poet of the Old West, James Stewart, a liberal law graduate who arrives in Shinbone, falls victim to a nasty beating at the hands of outlaw Liberty Valance (Lee Marvin), and tries to use the law to put him behind bars. The only man who can whip Valance is John Wayne, the tough guy who believes in force. Throughout the film, liberal Stewart and conservative Wayne spar over the best way to deal with Valance. Still, despite their differences, they share the same assumptions, so they can talk to each other. There's no talking to Valance, though, because he's an extremist and has to be killed.

Republicans and Democrats fought over this issue across many films in many genres, punishing or curing their way to happy endings. The real drama was not whether the "Injuns," as they were known in those days of political incorrectness, or mobsters, or delinquents, or Reds would destroy the American way of life—because they couldn't—but rather, who was going stop them, the cops or the docs, the soldiers or the scientists? And by what means, force or persuasion? In other words, these films agreed on ends but clashed over means.

Extremist movies like *It Came from Outer Space* (1953), in which harmless aliens are set upon by belligerent humans, utilized the same conventions employed by mainstream films but, to put it simply, in the one, the white hats were heroes and black hats were the villains, while in the other, the white hats were villains and the black hats were heroes. They simply traded hats. With movies like *High Noon* (1952) and *Invasion of the Body Snatchers* (1956, 1978), it was difficult to distinguish left from right because the two extremes shared a common animus toward the mainstream and agreed on the necessity of using force. Disdaining moderation, they embraced polarization. They presented worlds that were mirror images of the mainstream. What was bad for the center was good for the extremes, and vice versa. Extremist shows saw the world in black and white and expected their characters to make either/or choices, one or the other: Us or Them.

Extremists knew what they didn't like, but finding themselves on the wrong side of history, at least for the moment, it was difficult for them to figure out what they did like. Consequently, these movies largely defined themselves through negation. If the center was X, they were Y.

The most striking difference between the extremes was that the goal of left-wing movies was to disarm, rather than alarm. They were sympathy-for-the-devil movies that appreciated difference and welcomed the Other, because leftists identified with victims. They had been there themselves. As J.K. Rowling put it many years later, "My heroes are always people who feel themselves to be set apart, stigmatized, or others." Beneath their green, scaly skin and lidless saucer eyes, They were just like Us. If these shows were paranoid, they feared the center and the right, not the Other. Or rather, the center or the right was the Other, dramatized as domestic monsters created by radiation released by nuclear testing or plagues started by rogue viruses, both the products of military or/and corporate research.

Right-wing movies, on the other hand, were xenophobic and paranoid, terrified of alien invasions. They feared invisible enemies, the kind that hid in plain sight, as much as they feared visible ones. Red scare movies like *My Son John* (1952) or Samuel Fuller's *Pickup on South Street* (1953), were shrill and alarmist. They tried to awaken us from the torpor of complacency to the dangers that threatened us. Considerably more sophisticated than their predecessors, today's right-wing shows are liable to be more dismissive of the Other than alarmist. Witness *Roseanne* (2018– ), wherein John Goodman, having fallen asleep in front of the tube, says, "We missed all the shows about black and Asian families," referring to ABC's *Blackish* (2014– ) and *Fresh Off the Boat* (2015– ). Hip to centrist shows, Roseanne Barr replies, "They're just like us. There, now you're all caught up."

Left or right, films that went against the grain were rare in the postwar period. For the most part, they were shoestring productions, B-movies, on the margin of the margins. Extremist shows barely registered on the Richter scale that the entertainment business uses to calculate profits. No more. The most conspicuous development in the second decade of the new century has been the emergence of the comic book epics that now dominate not only American screens, but screens worldwide as well. These shows feature superheroes with extreme powers employing extreme measures to deal with extreme situations. Let's face it, we have learned to love extremism.

How did pop culture become pulp culture, B-movies get A-movie budgets? How did the bottom of the double bill become the top of the double bill, and then the only bill?

With the collapse of DVD sales at the beginning of the second decade of this century, and the competition theatrical distribution has faced from alternative delivery systems, foreign markets have become the studios' most important source of income, exceeding—even doubling—domestic grosses. The Chinese box office is expected to overtake the American market by 2020.

Action travels best, which means that character-driven stories that are deeply American in texture and context are at a disadvantage. Hence, comic book superheroes. As each blockbuster seeks to top the previous one, budgets skyrocket, and studios play it safe by turning to sequels to protect their investments. With superheroes behind masks or under hoods, no Tom Cruises or Ben Afflecks are needed. Interchangeable Chrises (Evans, Hemsworth, Pratt, or Pine) serve instead, as high-priced stars are replaced by brands (*Harry Potter*, *Transformers*, *The Hunger Games*) that in turn evolve into complex universes with ongoing, interlocking stories so that audiences don't have to wait two years for the next *Iron Man* movie but can see Tony Stark's thread picked up in the next *Captain America* sequel. These megabudget narrative daisy chains have come to resemble cable or streamed series more than standalone movies, not to mention providing cradle-to-the-grave welfare for actors who are virtually guaranteed a steady income throughout their working lives. As the difference between movies and TV blurs, becoming one of duration—movies are no more than truncated TV series, as opposed to TV characterized as extended movies—we'll refer to specimens of both as "shows" or "content."

In superhero series, as Ben Fritz explains in *The Big Picture*, old themes are remixed and recombined to provide the illusion of newness, while die-hard fans take comfort in their familiarity. In politics, this is called playing to the base. As the distinctive flavor brought to roles by rich characterization and the tics of the actors who play them are drained away, the superheroes themselves increasingly resemble mythic avatars that transcend national boundaries, perfect fits for the brave new world of globalization wherein they are easily merchandized into action figures and theme parks.

Extremism has defined today's entertainment culture to such an extent that no one gives it a second thought—certainly not the studios—save for exceptions like *New Yorker* reviewer Anthony Lane. In 2015, two of that year's most violent pictures were released on Christmas Day, which would have been unheard of in the past: Quentin Tarantino's *The Hateful Eight* and Alejandro González Iñárritu's *The Revenant*. Lane wrote, "Five hours and thirty-eight minutes of malice and mistrust, in which the characters—mostly men—are trapped in extreme weather conditions and settle their differences with extreme violence. So much for peace and good will."

For the most part, however, extremism passes under the radar, not only earning big bucks at the box office but ecstatic praise from the mainstream. On the far right, pitting Us against Them is Christopher Nolan's much-admired, albeit script-challenged, *Dunkirk* (2017), which falls just short of being a pro-Brexit morality play. As military historian Max Hastings has suggested, if you wanted to shift the blame for England's exit from the European Union from Us (the Brits) to Them (the Europeans), the evacuation of Dunkirk is just the thing. Instead of choosing to leave the Continent, the Brits have been unceremoniously kicked out by an adversary. Of course, to make Dunkirk a stand-in for Brexit, it has to be detached from its historical context, which is exactly what Nolan does, conspicuously refusing to identify that adversary as German. Within the first five minutes, there are four titles flashed on the screen referring to the "enemy," who is not named. Later on, the British briefly mistake a French soldier for "German," but that's it.

On the far left, we have *Avatar* (2009). Perhaps it's just that its obscenely exotic flora poking their 3-D petals out of IMAX screens dazzled our eyes, but James Cameron's movie has become the biggest grosser of all time, with four sequels in the works. As such, it has an outsize significance. As François Truffaut once put it, "When a film achieves a certain success, it becomes a sociological event." Unlike the enemy Other in *Dunkirk*, the aliens in *Avatar* are not only the good guys, but American ex-marines are the bad guys, and this at a time when GIs were fighting hot wars in Iraq and Afghanistan.

The old left/right political spectrum may be bruised and battered, but it still provides a rough roadmap of the ideological landscape in which we find ourselves. In the pages that follow, we shall try to define and describe extreme culture, using postwar mainstream culture as a baseline and taking the election of George W. Bush in the year 2000 as the jumping-off place for the age of extremism, although of course its antecedents go back at least as far as Ronald Reagan.

We will try to show how the movies and TV shows examined in this book inflect the key themes and fiercely held beliefs that have become counters in the culture wars to the left or to the right, and beyond that, how these shows have normalized the extremes so that they have become the new mainstream. The shows discussed were selected on the basis of their popularity and/or their pertinence in illustrating the thesis of the book. The following is divided into four parts comprised of three chapters each.

The first three parts focus on different themes, and proceed from the center to the left and to the right, describing how the particular theme is characterized by the respective ideologies.

In the following pages, we will take a walk on the wild side, becoming intimately acquainted with end-of-the-world scenarios, because extreme culture is apocalypse culture, for the simple reason that the apocalypse provides a laboratory in which we can experiment with extreme attitudes, behaviors, and measures. We will examine how the fictive worlds of pulp culture have been refashioned by extremism, how mainstream authorities have either been delegitimized or just packed their bags and gone home in the face of overwhelming odds. Reason and science are on the defensive, while behavior that was once beyond the pale—violence, lying, revenge—have become the new norm as the public good is replaced by self-interest. We will see civilization ravaged by its discontents, the god-fearing crushing the godless, Us slaughtering Them, and Them returning the favor. Finally, we will witness humans abandoning the human altogether attempting—fruitlessly or not—to attain a higher level of being. Along the way, we'll embrace or flee from a carnival of freaks who have moved from the sideshow to the center ring. We'll be chased by zombies, drained by vampires, stalked by cyborgs, and thrown back into harsh, primitive conditions with which we are ill-equipped to deal. Sounds like fun, doesn't it?

# PART I
# WINTER HAS COME

# 1
# Apocalypse Now

*The end of the world stalks the center, threatening its values—diversity, inclusion, and faith in the authorities—by creating extreme circumstances that call for extreme measures.*

> When the snows fall, and the white winds blow, the lone wolf dies, but the pack survives.
> —*Sansa Stark,* Game of Thrones

The wall—a vast thus far impregnable barrier made of ice and stone some three hundred miles long that appears to rise to the sky—heaves into view. It is the only thing that stands between the Seven Kingdoms and the White Walkers to the north. We're watching the finale of the seventh season of *Game of Thrones* (2011– ). Ominously, a flock of coal-black ravens fills the stormy sky. The camera rises over the wall to reveal Tormund Giantsbane, dressed in furs, his flowing red beard crusted with ice crystals, manning Eastwatch, where he and his men guard against an attack by the Walkers, and their army of the dead, known as wights. It is snowing, which is to say, winter, long feared and foretold, has come.

Tormund makes his way to an observation post high atop the wall, from which he can view the desolate landscape stretching north as far as the eye can see. As he looks down, he sees a solitary figure riding toward the wall. It is joined by another and another and another until the numberless army of the dead, armed with spears, is massed at its base, standing dark against the snow-swept waste. Tormund grabs a horn and blows a warning blast.

Suddenly, the silence is rent by the screech of a dragon. As if from nowhere, Viserion appears, flapping its mighty wings, gracefully swooping and wheeling through the dark skies. Dragons are an endangered species in this show, and Viserion is one of only three remaining specimens, all of which belong to Daenerys Targaryen, a fierce, if diminutive, conqueror who has her heart set on reclaiming the Iron Throne, which once belonged to her family and is now occupied by the evil queen, Cersei Lannister, who rules the Seven Kingdoms of Westeros. The only trouble is, Viserion is no longer alive, having been killed and "turned" by the White Walkers in a previous episode. In other words, it's a zombie dragon, and instead of the fiery red breath exhaled by its siblings that incinerates everything within their path, it shoots jets of hot blue flame suitable for melting ice.

Riding the spiky back of the dragon, the Night King rises and falls to the rhythm of its beating wings and directs its blazing breath at the wall, opening up a breach through which the wights pour. Tormund may be fearless, but he's not dumb. He yells, "Run!" and he and his men abandon their perch amid an avalanche of falling ice and stone. When Viserion is done, all that remains of the wall that once stood tall and proud is a jumble of ice cubes. The wights descend on the Seven Kingdoms.

This episode of *Game of Thrones* presents as bleak a rendering of the apocalypse as we're likely to find, but it has plenty of company. Nothing entertains like disaster, according to the conventional wisdom, but now it seems as though nothing entertains but disaster. It is nearly impossible to go into a movie theater without seeing one or another version of world-ending black swan events, for our purposes starting at least as far back as 1998, a year that gave us three iterations of the end days: a fender bender with an asteroid in *Armageddon*, an "extinction level event" with a comet in *Deep Impact*, and an unpleasant encounter with an oversize reptile trailing a track record of urban abuse in *Godzilla*. More recently, we have had a perfect storm in *Into the Storm* and Vesuvius erupting in *Pompeii* both in 2014, the mother of all earthquakes shaking and baking in *San Andreas* the following year, and the end of the world yet again in *X-Men: Apocalypse* (2016). Aliens from outer space were up to their old tricks as well, making mischief in *The World's End* (2013), *Edge of Tomorrow* (2014), and *Independence Day: Resurgence* (2016), where they return to finish the job they bungled in its predecessor, to name only a (very) few.

CGI has made disasters of epic scale easier and cheaper to render realistically, so it's not surprising that these scenarios are not only everywhere, but they have vastly increased in scope and severity. Forget the tsunamis, raging forest fires, killer freezes, howling tornadoes that flip over cars like june bugs—we can see these on the Weather Channel. To find out what's really firing up our collective fears, we need only click on one of the shows in which it's not merely a city that's in jeopardy, like Chicago (and Hong Kong) in *Transformers: Age of Extinction* (2014), Metropolis in *Man of Steel* (2013), Gotham in *The Dark Knight Rises* (2012), Los Angeles in *This Is the End* (2013), or New York in *The Avengers* (2012); nor an entire country, as in *District 9* (2009); nor even the planet, as in *Melancholia* (2011), wherein a rogue heavenly body speeding toward us in our lane threatens Earth with a head-on collision.

Forget Earth, or our galaxy, for that matter. The fiendishly inventive *Fringe* (2008–13), produced by Steven Spielberg protégé J.J. Abrams, upped the ante, giving us a universe—nay, two universes—in trouble, afflicted by a series of bizarre events that threaten to unravel the very fabric of each. The sky is split by ugly rips and tears that throb like wounds and create a variety of unsettling phenomena ranging from anomalies that scramble time and space to supersize swarms of locusts to humans disfigured by extra rows of teeth, dual irises, and twin faces.

As if that's not bad enough, portals to other worlds, also called wormholes, have become more common than potholes in the streets of New York City. Take the Mr. Big of the vampire world in *Buffy the Vampire Slayer* (1997–2003); he enters our world through Hellmouth. In Fox's *Sleepy Hollow* (2013–17), someone carelessly leaves ajar the "gateway to the world between worlds," that is, our world and purgatory. These vortices, rifts, and black holes are turning our reality into a Swiss cheese. Shock and awe, here we come, only it's not They who are quaking in the bunkers of their imaginations, it's Us, Americans, compulsively relishing and rehashing our own destruction.

No longer are we fighting for our way of life or, as Superman put it, for "truth, justice, and the American way." Now, the stakes are considerably higher. We're fighting for life itself. In the original *Independence Day* (1996), the president explains that instead of battling against "tyranny, oppression, or persecution," the danger has escalated to "annihilation." "We are fighting for our right to live," he exclaims, "To exist." And it is not just Americans whose right to exist is in jeopardy, but the entire human race. Even the size of the alien hardware has increased exponentially. The mother ship in *Independence Day* is 340 miles in diameter, making the flying saucer in the original *Day the Earth Stood Still* look little bigger than a nickel.

Life on Earth wasn't always so dismal. Our planet used to be the envy of the universe, a lush green world that was repeatedly set upon by aliens from shithole planets who had carelessly burned through their raw materials and were trying to help themselves to ours. They wanted what We have, or had. Now the traffic is going the other way, and it's no longer enough for survivors to escape from New York, like the hardy band in John Carpenter's 1981 movie of that title; they need to escape our world. More like it was Ridley Scott's classic *Blade Runner*, released the following year, wherein a future Earth has turned into something resembling a Hieronymus Bosch painting: a noirish hell shrouded in smoke, strewn with garbage, and overrun by thuggish predators. Thus, its people flee to "off-worlds," like the real-life humans who have signed up with private companies such as Elon Musk's SpaceX or the Dutch-owned Mars One, for one-way tickets to the red planet, where they hope to settle or, more likely, die trying. An index of the pessimism that pervades these shows is that the dystopias they picture are not sited in the indeterminate future, but only a few years off. In 2017's *Blade Runner 2049*, a crisis occurred in 2022, the year my driver's license expires.

In Neill Blomkamp's *Elysium* (2013), white flight has taken on a lunar dimension. Earth has been reduced to a ruined husk, ravaged, as a title card tells us, by "disease and pollution." In the opening shot, an airborne camera skims the rooftops of a devastated Los Angeles, chockablock with hollowed-out buildings that look like broken honeycombs, the vestiges of human colony collapse. The 1 percent have fled to a so-called ring-world, an orbiting Malibu that hangs in the sky like a glistening Mercedes hood ornament.

If characters can't put some physical distance between themselves and Earth, retreating to satellites or ring-worlds orbiting our planet, in shows like *Fringe* they jump back in time, to an era before everything went sideways. As the future looks darker, what used to be looks brighter. In 2011's *Terra Nova*, produced by Spielberg, humans from the year 2149, when the planet is beggared by too many people and too little food, choked by pollution and starved of natural resources, transport themselves to the prehistoric era, where they find that living cheek by jowl with raptors is preferable to their life in the future. But not by much. Indeed, the humans in these shows find that the past, far from a utopia of abundance, can be full of nasty surprises.

It's no secret that as the number, magnitude, and gravity of the threats to life as we know it have multiplied, apocalypse porn has become the coin of today's pulp culture. Gone are the villains of yesteryear who entertained fantasies of world domination, the Dr. Nos and Goldfingers of the James Bond franchise. Except for the naïve megalomaniacs who haven't gotten the news, no one wants to rule the world; it would be like aspiring to be governor of Fukushima Prefecture in Japan or president of Syria, in victory ruling over a country reduced to rubble.

Our narratives have gotten so dark that the lucky ones are those who died during the run-up to the apocalypse, while their less-fortunate comrades are left to struggle in the aftermath, as we see in the blackest of these tales, like *The Road* (2009), *Oblivion* (2013), *After Earth* (2013), and *Mad Max: Fury Road* (2015), wherein the battle is lost and disaster has already struck.

These shows pick up the story when the worst has already happened. The asteroid has hit, the infection has gone viral, the ICBMs have found their targets. If civilization has either been destroyed or else catastrophically downsized, if America's cities are eerily empty or reduced to smoking ruins, while the interstates are bumper-to-bumper with stalled vehicles and ragged columns of human remnants trudging vacant-eyed along freeways to nowhere, we know that what seemed inevitable—was. Instead, these shows turn their attention to survival, and their characters, having lowered their sights considerably, don't aspire to prevail but merely to endure. Whereas once we had *The Fugitive* (1963–67), now we are all fugitives.

The end of days has been just around the corner from the beginning of recorded history. Still, it seems that today, the professional doomsayers are working overtime. The dire warnings that come at us at every moment from every quarter have become a staple of global culture. Not a minute goes by without a new alert. Billy Graham, who popularized evangelicalism in the postwar era, prophesized the apocalypse way back in 1950, saying, "We may have another year, maybe two years." But then, he added, "It's all going to be over." More recently, according to astrologer Jeane Dixon, the end will come between 2020 and 2037; World Bible Society president F. Kenton Beshore expects the Second Coming in 2020 at the earliest, 2028 at the latest; in his book *The Cassandra Prophecy*, Ian Gurney favors 2023, while 2033 is supposed to be the two thousandth anniversary of the Crucifixion, during which something or other of an unpleasant nature is supposed to occur, even though the Raelians, who worship UFOs, beg to differ, anticipating extinction in 2035 and pinning their hopes on an alien invasion to make it a reality.

There's no question that apocalypse fever has hit epidemic propor-
tions. The "imagination of disaster" (to borrow Susan Sontag's term) has
historically accompanied periods of uncertainty and transformation, from
the fall of the Roman Empire to the present, but now it is fueled by the
unprecedented acceleration of change. Moreover, in 2001, 9/11's twin towering infernos gave Americans a taste of what the end of the world might be
like. With exemplary British understatement, Paul Greengrass, director of
*United 93* (2006), explained, "After the dramatic fears of 9/11 ... I think all
these stories are speaking to a sense of a future that is less assured." According to Robert Kirkman, auteur of the comic that serves as the basis for *The
Walking Dead* (2010– ), "Apocalyptic storytelling is appealing when people
have apocalyptic thoughts. With the global economic problems and everything else, a lot of people feel we're heading into dark times."

Putting aside the migrant crisis, growing poverty, and famine with all
its ancillary consequences, such as drug-resistant plagues, just when we
thought the curtain had dropped on the Cold War, the bomb, which was
the odds-on favorite to end life as we know it during the 1950s, has made
a comeback in the guise of dirty bombs fashioned from enriched uranium
purloined from the great powers, not to mention the spread of nuclear weapons technology to Israel, India, Pakistan, Iran, and now North Korea. The
*Bulletin of the Atomic Scientists*' Doomsday Clock is ticking louder than
ever. In fact, the hands were moved ahead in early 2015 to three minutes to
midnight, coupled with the warning, "The probability of global catastrophe
is very high." In 2017, after the presidential election, the hands were moved
ahead another 30 seconds, to two and a half minutes to midnight, and then
again in early 2018 to two minutes before midnight, the closest it's been to
the apocalyptic hour since the height of the Cold War in 1953.

Climate change provides us with something even more intractable than
terrorism or the likelihood of nuclear war to worry about, with climatologists, not kooks, predicting a "new Dark Age." After 2017's and 2018's serial
hurricanes, furious forest fires followed by mudslides in Southern California, a total eclipse of the sun, and the bellicose exchanges between Trump
and Kim Jong-un, even the late, lamented Christopher Hitchens might be
excused for consulting the Gospel of Luke, wherein it is written: "And there
will be signs in the sun and moon and stars, and on earth distress of nations
in perplexity ...

Almost by definition, science-fiction, fantasy, and horror narratives
anticipate the possible, no matter how unlikely. The blizzard of apocalyptic

shows gives us a glimpse of what the end might be like—thought experiments that provoke us to think about the unthinkable, dress rehearsals for a show we hope will never open.

Although the danger of a world-ending event is real enough, more often than not, the apocalypse is in the eye of the beholder. Speaking of the 2016 presidential election, both candidates appropriated the language of the end times. To Hillary Clinton, the apocalypse was manifest in the person of Donald Trump. She told her supporters, "I'm the last thing standing between you and the apocalypse." To Trump, the apocalypse had already happened, namely, the two-term Obama presidency, enabled by then secretary of state Clinton. He called his Democratic opponent, "the devil," adding, all Hillary Clinton had brought to the world was "death, destruction, terrorism and weakness." And it wasn't so long ago that former House majority leader (and "moderate") John Boehner referred to Obamacare as "Armageddon." In other words, each of the ideological tendencies mentioned earlier bends the apocalypse to its own purposes; it is inflected center, left, and right.

The ideology of the bipartisan coalition that comprised the postwar mainstream was called "pluralism." In an influential book called *The Vital Center* (1949), historian Arthur M. Schlesinger Jr. theorized a "third force" composed of "democratic socialists" and "liberal capitalists" intended to navigate a middle way between democracy's two enemies, communism and fascism, thus avoiding the bloodbath that engulfed Europe and ensuring America's leadership of the "free world." Schlesinger was prescribing a foreign policy, not endorsing an approach to postwar domestic governance, and he went out of his way to ridicule centrism, but he helped organize Americans for Democratic Action, which lobbied for just that at home, and his description of the third force perfectly described the coalition of Cold War Democrats and East Coast Republicans that ran postwar America.

Liberal intellectuals like Schlesinger, Daniel Bell, Seymour Martin Lipset, and others agreed that American society was a democratic, "open society" made up of people of many colors, ethnicities, and religions. It was a melting pot in which cultural differences disappeared in a soup of assimilation.

None of these groups could get the upper hand, because power was dispersed among them. Robert A. Dahl, the so-called dean of American political scientists, described pluralism as a "polyarchy," meaning that power is distributed among many competing centers of authority, and therefore no one group is strong enough to dominate the others. Contending factions are forced to compromise with one another. In other words, if everyone is powerful, no one is powerful, and power, in effect, doesn't exist at all in America, only in its totalitarian enemies.

In the world according to pluralism, consensus is based on abstract values shared by all. These were the principles that emerged from the Enlightenment, when the *philosophes* pitted them against primitive, parochial loyalties to clan or place. "By including fraternity, or the 'brotherhood of man,' among their ideals along with liberty and equality," writes philosopher Peter Singer, "the leaders of the French Revolution neatly conveyed the Enlightenment idea of extending to all mankind the concern that we ordinarily feel only for our kin."

Later, Darwinists provided an evolutionary basis for the same morality. Natural selection strongly suggested that humans prevailed over other life-forms because they evolved beyond the dog-eat-dog competitiveness that characterized the state of nature. Cooperation, or sociability, not self-interest is the key to survival of the species. Or rather, sociability is in the self-interest of the human species. The relatively new discipline of evolutionary ethics was christened by Edward O. Wilson in his landmark 1975 study *Sociobiology*, the goal of which was to remove morality from the purview of theologians and philosophers, and claim it for biology.

Contra Republicans' confidence that Adam Smith's invisible hand would ensure prosperity for all, liberal Democrats feared that it would pick the pockets of the poor and deliver wealth into the pockets of the rich. Capitalism was a given, but it had to be managed. Therefore, in pluralist poker, the public interest, which is identified with abstract moral principles, supersedes private interest, which is merely selfish. Those who put their own private interests ahead of the public interest are punished for it. They are bound by the imperatives dictated by social groups of escalating generality. The rights of the individual are trumped by the claims of kinship, that is, the blood ties that bind the nuclear family. These in turn give way to the extended family, then the tribe or ethnic clan, then the region, and then the nation. Beyond the nation, as the ripples spread outward, we have gender, the species, and even the universe.

Citizens of the vital center were expected to play by the rules of pluralism, which favored pragmatism, compromise, tolerance, democratic decision making, and the rule of law. The East Coast Republicans and Cold

War Democrats agreed that the bigger, more capacious and inclusive the tent, the more stable the consensus and the fewer the number of crazies lobbing grenades from beyond the perimeter. Tolerance, therefore, was not only a virtue in itself, it was a strategy that ensured stability, and more, survival.

Pluralists worshipped at the altar of progress, and science was the tip of its spear. After all, science had just given us the A-bomb that ended World War II, followed by the H-bomb that seemed to guarantee America's security for the foreseeable future, then the Salk vaccine that erased the terrifying scourge of polio, and finally the double helix that unlocked the secrets of the genetic code—all in quick succession. Meanwhile, a revolutionary pesticide, DDT, kept the little buggers at bay, enabling us and countries like us to become breadbaskets to the world.

Science's dominion over nature reduced it to fodder for our culture, our civilization. Nature tamed meant mountains leveled for their coal, rivers harnessed for electric power, forests cut for their lumber. Ever since the Industrial Revolution, nature has been the enemy of culture; it gets in the way of new homes, malls, golf courses, and interstate highways. Nature is no more than development waiting to happen. In the mainstream, therefore, disasters—earthquakes, floods, hurricanes, and other catastrophes—are often rendered as nature's revenge against culture, nature run amok.

Science and technology were the engines of progress. We were assured that the future was going to be better than the present, just as the present was better than the past. The postwar faith in progress was symbolized by the 1964 World's Fair, a futuristic extravaganza that beguiled visitors with sugarplums of endless improvement, like the space program that electrified the imagination as well as promising, on a more mundane level, victory over the Soviets in the space race.

George R.R. Martin, who wrote *A Song of Ice and Fire*, the series of books on which *Game of Thrones* is based, remembers, "When I was a kid in the 50's, and even into the 60's, everyone thought life was getting better and better. You'd visit the Carousel of Progress at the World's Fair, and you could see all the amazing things the future had in store for us: robots and flying cars, and so on. Life would be great."

The Fair pops up with surprising regularity in today's shows, a totem of sorts for the technological utopia that never happened. *Iron Man 2* (2010), contains a scene in which Tony Stark's father, launching a Stark Industries expo modeled on the 1964 Fair, extols progress: "Technology holds infinite possibilities for mankind and will one day rid society of all its ills." In Brad Bird's *Tomorrowland* (2015), we actually visit the Fair, and are dazzled by its wonders.

In the wake of the Fair, Albert Einstein became the posthumous poster boy for an era in which it seemed like science had all the answers. His likeness—twinkly eyes staring out from under wisps of white hair flying wildly in all directions—was blown up to poster size and took its place alongside Humphrey Bogart, Marilyn Monroe, and Marlon Brando on dorm room walls across America. The beloved mad scientists like Baron Victor von Frankenstein, who got us all in trouble by messing with God's works, discovered there were no longer jobs for them in mainstream shows and were relegated to the extremes, where they were still welcome.

Schlesinger was a great fan of Reinhold Niebuhr, the influential postwar theologian whose pessimistic Christianity (original sin, etc.) led him to step on the brake of the express train of progress. From his perspective, millennialism was a dangerous illusion, the province of totalitarians like Hitler and Stalin. Rather, tolerance of conflict, not the utopian promise of conflict resolved, was the key to a functioning democracy. Its momentum was so great, however, that most Americans ignored Schlesinger's misgivings. Cold War Democrats, standing on the graves of Soviet and Nazi messianism, assured us that utopianism was alive and well in the USA, and that our country was on its way to achieving the classless society that Marx had promised but the Soviet Union had so dramatically failed to deliver.

Capitalism with a friendly face, softened by those New Deal safety nets that the right ritually denounced as "socialist," had enabled us to reconcile the contradictions and transcend the divisions that had torn Europe to pieces. What we already had was more than we could hope for anywhere else. Americans could eat their cake and have it too. They lived in a both/and paradise that was realized in the here-and-now. Exuding the confidence of the home team, they were convinced that the grass could never be greener. Things were going their way. Contrary to Marx's dire predictions, capitalism was delivering the goods, so much so that left-liberal economist John Kenneth Galbraith could entitle a book *The Affluent Society*. Consumers were swamped by a torrent of cars, washing machines, air conditioners, and TV sets. Workers enjoyed a living wage that enabled them to step up to a brand-new Ford and a house in Levittown—that is, as movies like 2017's *Suburbicon* and *Mudbound* remind us, if they were white.

So confident were the Cold War intellectuals that in 1960, sociologist

Daniel Bell proclaimed "the end of ideology" in a book of the same title. Thirty years later, it looked like events had proved him right. Buoyed by the triumphalism that attended the fall of the Berlin Wall in 1989 and the end of the Soviet Union in 1991, Bell's intellectual heir, political scientist Francis Fukuyama, peering through rose-colored glasses, not only visualized the end of ideology but the "end of history." He wrote, "What we are witnessing is not just the . . . passing of a particular period of postwar history, but the end of history as such: that is, the end point of mankind's ideological evolution and the universalization of western liberal democracy as the final form of human government." Famous last words, as they say.

Prisoners of progress, of the American belief in improvement without end, in short, of postwar utopianism, mainstream shows have become fewer and farther between, but they have by no means disappeared. They are full of characters bursting with optimism, satisfied with the present, and filled with faith in the future. If they are fearful, it is the past that scares them, King Kong, not R2-D2.

Mainstream narratives still cling to the belief that the system works. They use national emergencies, a slightly milder version of the apocalypse feared by the extremes, to showcase the federal government flexing its muscles and saving the day. After all, big government was widely credited with rescuing the American economy after unbridled, unregulated capitalism had plunged the country into the Great Depression of the 1930s and then mobilizing the nation to defeat the Axis powers in World War II.

Even in a center-right film like *Independence Day*, soldiers and scientists work together, while the president informs the world, "We can't be consumed by our petty differences anymore. We will be united in our common interests." Indeed, the president of the United States forges a global coalition that includes, among others, the British, Japanese, Arabs, and Africans.

There is no apocalyptic event, as such, in *The Martian* (2015), but it too is a showcase for mainstream values. Matt Damon, a member of a Mars mission, is stranded on the red planet when his fellow astronauts, hastily departing to avoid a vicious storm, inadvertently leave him behind. He manages to survive until he's rescued by living on the potatoes he somehow cultivates in the meager Martian soil. In other words, the American pioneer spirit is very much alive and well, able to domesticate nature, no matter how inhospitable.

Here, the National Aeronautics and Space Administration (NASA) is a thriving government agency that launches regular voyages to Mars. The picture cuts back and forth among its far-flung facilities—Cape Canaveral in Florida, the Johnson Space Center in Houston, and the Jet Propulsion Laboratory in Pasadena. NASA has a vast reach—but maybe not quite so vast as it used to. In the old days of American hegemony, it would have scrambled to send another rocket to Mars to retrieve Damon, no big deal. But in the current atmosphere of cutbacks, NASA needs help, and which country should it turn to but China, which has coincidentally helped save the film business with its robust grosses. China rides to the rescue, sending a rocket "booster" to save Damon. The film extends the reach of pluralism to include the world, an expression of the globalism now derided by the extreme right. And like a good centrist show, *The Martian* reconciles opposites: Damon's individualism with big government's emphasis on cooperation. And note that the Martian of the title doesn't refer to a bug-eyed monster, but rather to an American—not Them, but Us.

In 2016's *Hidden Figures*, a drama that takes place at the height of the Cold War, the apocalypse is the prospect of a Soviet weapon in space, not so far-fetched in that Russia was the first nation to launch a satellite, and then to put a man into orbit. The national emergency is Russia's lead in the space race, along with the so-called (and illusory) missile gap, dramatically rendered in the film by the hysteria of NASA bigwigs, augmented by documentary footage of President John F. Kennedy soberly rallying Americans to catch up to the Soviets. NASA's efforts are in trouble, however, until its white male scientists learn that African Americans, who happen to be female, are not only people too, but scientists and mathematicians with skills that are equal if not superior to their own. As in *The Martian*, the mission succeeds by extending tolerance to those formerly considered Other, inhabitants of the badlands beyond the boundaries of the vital center. Racial and gender inequality is overcome, NASA is integrated, and an American astronaut successfully orbits the Earth.

If ever a country, or in this case a continent, could use a good dose of pluralism, it is Westeros and its Seven Kingdoms in *Game of Thrones*, which is rent by family feuds, endless dynastic wars that tear it apart. Westeros is dominated by over a half-dozen "houses." Most of these houses have at least one vendetta going, and some have two or three: the Lannisters against the Starks, the Targaryens against the Lannisters, the Tyrells against the Starks, and so on.

It's not until Season 7 that this system is tested, when a common enemy emerges—the White Walkers—representing an existential threat to all the houses. We know what pluralists think of blood ties and the parochial self-interest that motivates each of the clans, so it comes as no surprise when Jaime Lannister tries to convince his sister, ice queen Cersei, to rise above primitive tribalism by explaining what's at stake in the coming conflict with the wights. "This isn't about noble houses," he says. "This is about the living and the dead."

Jon Snow, King of the North, and ostensibly the bastard son of Ned Stark, the late patriarch of House Stark, gets it. He is the only ruler who has seen the wights in the flesh, so to speak, and he knows that no house can go up against them alone. As Sansa Stark says to her sister Arya, "When the snows fall, and the white winds blow, the lone wolf dies, but the pack survives."

Snow plunges into feverish coalition-building, defying the tribalism that is destroying the Seven Kingdoms. We've seen alliances made and unmade before, but this time he's trying to fashion the ultimate alliance against the ultimate enemy. Approaching the imperious Daenerys Targaryen, Snow declares, "I must put my trust in you. A stranger. Because I know it is the best chance for my people. For all our people." She gets it too, but when Snow then tries to make common cause with Cersei, he discovers that Cersei doesn't. She refuses to forgive and forget her feud with the Starks. Mocking him, she says, "So we should settle our differences and live together in harmony for the rest of our days?" Echoing the president in *Independence Day*, Snow explains, "This isn't about 'in harmony.' It's just about living." In other words, for all its forays into magic and fantasy, for all its dragons, witches, zombies, spells, priests, and priestesses, *Game of Thrones* by the end of Season 7, turns out to be about America, circa 2017. It's a mainstream show adhering to centrist values.

Despite its trust in science, the postwar center made room for faith, so long as it cleaved to the tenets of pluralism. There was an uptick of religion during the 1950s, characterized by an interdenominational spirit that mirrored the political consensus. According to student of religion Ross Douthat, a "convergence [was] taking place towards a kind of Christian center." Despite the claims of Catholics, Jews, Protestants, and what-have-you to exclusive access to God's ear, they coexisted peacefully. It didn't hurt that the spectacle of multifaith civil rights workers in the South praying,

singing, and swaying while being beaten senseless by white deputies wield-
ing clubs and cattle prods was beamed into American living rooms every
night on the news. It sent the same message that Jon Snow was trying to
deliver to Cersei: Sectarianism is passé, and therefore self-defeating.

Generally speaking, excepting the run of biblical spectacles in the 1950s,
religion was conspicuous by its absence from postwar movies. Even as late as
2014 the crop of high-profile biblical epics—both *Noah* and *Exodus: Gods
and Kings*—flopped. The Hollywood community is generally a godless
bunch, and indicative of the lowly place religion has traditionally occupied
in show business, as of that year, over the previous two decades, only seven
Oscar winners thanked God in their acceptance speeches, while thirty
credited their good fortune to Harvey Weinstein.

Today, that has changed; shows of the ecumenical center with interfaith
themes reflect conservative mainstream values, family, and religion, like
the ones that pervaded ABC's hit show *Lost* which first aired in September
2004. The show began with a bang, that is, a plane crash. Oceanic Airlines
Flight 815 bound for Los Angeles from Sydney breaks up high in the air over
the Pacific Ocean. The passengers, along with their ephemera—baggage,
coats, books, magazines, soda cans, thumb-size vodka bottles—are sucked
out of the plane like so many matchsticks and unceremoniously dumped
onto sand beaches blanched salt white by the blazing sun. The laws of gravity would have predicted that they all should have died, but *Lost* doesn't
have much use for the laws of gravity. Miraculously, tumbling 35,000 feet
to the ground doesn't so much as muss their hair.

*Lost* ended, six seasons and 121 episodes later, in 2010. The intervening shows are devoted to a post-apocalypse purgatory that consists of an
array of peekaboo glimpses of now-you-see-them-now-you-don't monsters, sudden violence, torture, and dizzying disruptions of time and space
until the survivors wind up in church to discover that they have been dead
all along—perhaps—and only now do these ghostly infrequent travelers, dressed in their Sunday best, qualify for a nonstop flight to heaven,
first-class, with no blackout dates.

Looking around this church in the show's finale, we can't help but
notice that although Christian iconography predominates, it is an ecumenical smorgasbord displaying the sacred totems of other religions as
well—Judaism, Islam, Buddhism, and so on. After all, this is the church of
network television.

The feel-good finale is so banal, it became a touchstone for how not to end a series provoking George R.R. Martin to an inspired bit of vituperation: "Even as early as the second season and certainly the third season, I started saying, how the hell are they going to pull all of this together?" He added, "And then when I reached the end . . . they hadn't pulled it altogether [*sic*], in fact, they left a big turd on my doorstep."

Inclusion and diversity were central to pluralism, but firm boundaries were still important because they marked the line between those who qualified for membership in the center and those who did not and were thus excluded. Although such ideological cleansing seemed to fly in the face of pluralism, centrists found a friend in Karl Popper, who furnished them with a work-around in an influential book first published in 1945 called *The Open Society and Its Enemies*, in which he wrote, "If we extend unlimited tolerance even to those who are intolerant . . . then the tolerant will be destroyed, and tolerance with them."

To the center, Popper's "intolerant" were the "Geronimos" who turned their backs on the pluralist welcome wagon, thereby condemning themselves to the so-called lunatic fringe, a group for whom the world looked very different from the way it appeared to the center.

# 2
# Bleeding Hearts

*The left blames Us, not Them, for the apocalypse. Luddite shows like* Avatar *look to nature to save us from ourselves, while Dotcom shows like* The Imitation Game *look to machines.*

> I think everyone should be a tree hugger.
> —*James Cameron, writer-director,* Avatar

James Cameron's *Avatar* (2009) opens nearly a century and a half in the future. The year is 2154, and a spaceship is headed for Pandora, an obscure moon circling a gas giant in the Alpha Centauri system. The vehicle is called the *Venture Star*, a name that glitters with derring-do, teasing us with the promise of unimaginable exploits to come.

Space travel might once have been the domain of *Star Trek*'s benevolent United Federation of Planets, whose mandate is to bring civilization to the bad boy worlds of the universe, or even a federal government agency like NASA, as it is in *The Martian*. But the feds, instead of stepping up to become galactic players, seem to have faded away. Presumably, by this future date, the business-backed center-right Republicans and far-right ideologues have finally succeeded in starving the public sector to death so that the government confines itself to collecting garbage and clearing snow. NASA has apparently vanished.

Moreover, gone is the romance of exploring space. Earth has become one of those burned-out planets that needs to exploit other worlds to enrich its corporate rulers and, secondarily, to sustain itself. As in the first *Alien* (1979), where the *Nostromo* is no more than a tugboat towing 20 million tons of minerals to Earth, the *Venture Star* carries a complement of troops and scientists who have been tasked by a corporation with extracting ore (whimsically called "unobtanium") from Pandora.

This *Venture Star* is an ungainly thing, but some thought has evidently gone into its design, because it serves as an elaborate visual pun. Comprised of two sets of paired spheres that resemble oversize golf balls, one stacked upon the other, to which is appended a lengthy Eiffel Tower–like scaffolding, this intergalactic set of male genitalia tells us that Pandora is going to be royally fucked.

*Avatar* was not the first show to demonstrate the box office clout of sci-fi extremism, but it dramatically underlined the breakdown of the postwar consensus. The understanding between Republicans and Democrats on the fundamentals of domestic and foreign policy had become no more than roadkill beneath the wheels of the Tea Party bus, jeopardizing the American experiment with democracy.

After eight years of gridlock in Washington, with intransigent Republicans blocking Obama's agenda, one commentator described our vaunted system of government as "Weimar-lite democratic dysfunction." If frustrated citizens are any indication, democracy was indeed in trouble. One poll found that the percentage of Americans who were ready to abandon it in favor of military rule, which was rated as a "good" or "very good" thing, was on the rise, increasing from 1 in 16 in 1995 to 1 in 6 in 2014.

Schlesinger's vital center played its own part in making America safe for extremism. The mainstream's efforts to delegitimize dissent during the era of tweedle-dum, tweedle-dee bipartisanship were prosecuted with such vigor and were so successful that, shielded from internal opposition, it blinded itself to important truths and failed to evolve and adapt to changing times.

The leadership of both mainstream parties was oblivious to the fact that the service economy was wreaking havoc with their bases. The Republicans preached populism during the campaigns but practiced plutocracy when elected. Likewise, the Democrats, who courted labor and minorities when they ran, bent the knee to Wall Street when they won.

In a mea culpa published in the business section of the *New York Times* in 2012, writer Adam Davidson, wondering how establishment economists could have been so obtuse as to miss the run-up to the financial collapse of 2008, attributes it to the blinders imposed by consensus thinking. Establishment "experts" dismissed the canaries in the coal mine—that is, left- and right-wing economists—as "extremist" thinkers, mocking them as "prophets of doom." However, he writes, "the most accurate forecasts have come from the fringe."

Our prophets of doom are not outlier economists, but the directors and writers of extremist content. Although left- and right-wing shows share a good deal of common ground, both extending tolerance well beyond the magic circle of the vital center, they extend it in opposite directions. The far left reaches out to aliens, the Geronimos whom the center and far right would like to see dead, or if not dead, returned to wherever it is from whence they came. The far right reaches out to its own kind of extremists, the ones who had previously been beyond the pale: the so-called angry white males, a group that includes alt-right neo-Nazis, survivalists, militias, and America Firsters, all of which overlap. The gender fluidity welcomed by the left becomes gender instability, feared by the right. If the far left and the far right both locate their utopian, have-your-cake-and-eat-it-too happy endings in the there-and-then, that is, elsewhere, in another time, another place, rather than the here-and-now of present-day America, they also look to different eras, and do so for different reasons. To the left, the past can be painful, a time that incubated the problems that plague the present. To the right, the past is comfort food, a paradise lost, a free, white, Anglo-Saxon America. If the left embraces change, the right looks to restoration.

*Avatar* is an example of a Luddite-left film, in which the apocalypse is a world dominated by machines that has little use for organic life of any kind. In contrast to the center, in which technology is a tool for good, for the Luddite-left, technology causes nothing but harm. Ironically, according to two economists and a political scientist who have studied the habits of Italian voters, the same technological progress to which centrists pin their hopes for increased stability, causes dislocations that have sparked the rise of extremism: "robot shock increases support for nationalist and radical right parties."

Since the postwar center embraced science with a vengeance, the emergence of the Luddite-left may seem surprising, but America's infatuation with beakers and test tubes was marbled by a vein of distinct unease. There was the Bomb, of course, the very definition of a double-edged sword. It could easily have—and still could—destroy us all. Few Americans appreciated living on the lip of nuclear annihilation.

If there was a tipping point after which postwar optimism took a nosedive, it may well have been that World's Fair in 1964, the occasion for the last great outburst of American euphoria before the onset of the grinding disillusionment occasioned by the Vietnam War. The future didn't turn out exactly the way the corporate sponsors of the Fair anticipated.

The anxiety occasioned by the arms race just wouldn't go away. It was evident in the crop of pre- or postapocalyptic antinuke movies that were released in the late 1950s and early 1960s. Far and away the best of the bunch was Stanley Kubrick's *Dr. Strangelove or: How I Learned to Stop Worrying and Love the Bomb*, released the same year as the Fair. Kubrick always regarded technology as the devil's sport, and *Dr. Strangelove* features a so-called doomsday device set to respond automatically to an early warning of a Soviet first strike, so that humans are powerless to stop it even in the event of a false alarm. As Kubrick remarked at the time, "There is an almost total preoccupation with a technical solution to the problem of the bomb. Our theme is that there is no technical solution." In other words, we have abdicated responsibility for the survival of the race and ceded it to machines. The soldiers, scientists, and government officials, both American and Soviet, in *Dr. Strangelove* are either fools or knaves. Machines will not save us.

The year 1964 also marked the eve of the U.S. intervention in Vietnam. According to George R.R. Martin, "When the Vietnam War happened, we discovered that some of these technological things had nasty snaps at the end, like pollution and global warming and the hole in the ozone layer. People lost faith in progress."

The backlash against technology informed an array of low-, no-, and anti-tech shows in which machines were the bad guys. Kubrick followed up *Dr. Strangelove* four years later with *2001: A Space Odyssey*. The crew of *Discovery One*, on its way to Jupiter, has to contend with HAL 9000, the homicidal computer that runs the ship and thinks its IQ is higher than theirs. When Dave Bowman (Keir Dullea), floating outside the hull after an attempt to retrieve a fellow astronaut, asks HAL to let him back in, it replies, in an affectless robotic monotone, "I'm sorry, Dave. I can't do that," the battle cry of the mutinous computers to come. HAL claims to be "foolproof and incapable of error," insisting that mistakes are the result of "human error." In Luddite shows, however, mistakes are the result of "mechanical error."

The doomsday device is autonomous but not conscious. HAL, on the other hand, is both autonomous and conscious, and therefore represents a big step forward in the wrong direction, at least from the point of view of the Luddites, who question the docility of sentient machines. They regard computers and robots generally—along with their cousins, androids (robots that look like humans) and cyborgs (part organic, part inorganic)—with suspicion. As far as they are concerned, these devices are all HAL wannabes, just itching to tear out their kill switches and put their metal heads together to cook up ways to outwit their human masters.

*2001* was the template for science-unfriendly shows that followed. By the time it was released, the acrid smell of tear gas was hanging over American streets, and the Vietnam War had turned the country into a cauldron of hatred. If the civil rights movement had made visible the contradictions papered over by two decades of prosperity, the war tore America's illusions to shreds.

Shrinking from the atrocities perpetrated by their government in their name, the flower children embraced everything that ran counter to the mainstream. Adorned with bandanas, feathers, spangles, or nothing at all, painting their bodies and wearing their hair long, they distinguished themselves from the suits and uniforms who ran the straight world by proudly calling themselves "freaks." So it was that the military's marvels were the peace movement's barbarities.

As the conflict continued, the Luddites gained the upper hand. Demonstrating against the high-tech juggernaut devised by technocrats like Secretary of Defense Robert McNamara, who ran the war for Kennedy and gave us such wonders as the defoliant Agent Orange and the "electronic battlefield," the peace protesters took Kubrick's technophobia out of the theaters and into the streets. General Curtis LeMay may have threatened to bomb Vietnam into the "Stone Ages," but for the flower children, the Stone Age was the bucolic state of nature, a back-to-the-land commune in Vermont or Northern California. Stewart Brand's *Whole Earth Catalog* was to hippies what Mao's Little Red Book was to antiwar radicals, and the *Mother Earth News* became the *New York Times* of the ecology movement. The first Earth Day was held in 1970. In 1973, E.F. Schumacher presented his case for sustainable living in *Small Is Beautiful*.

Several decades later, PayPal cofounder, early Facebook investor, and Trump whisperer Peter Thiel, lamenting the "tech slowdown" in the pages of *National Review*, argued that it started in 1969, the year "the hippies took over the country, and when the true cultural war over Progress was lost." Thiel's point was vastly exaggerated, but there was more than a little truth to it. Hippies never took over the country, but you'd never know that from, say, watching Spielberg's *Close Encounters of the Third Kind* (1977) and *E.T. the Extra-Terrestrial* (1982), which expressed both the cynical, post-Watergate attitude toward mainstream authority on display in *Jaws* (1975) and the naïve confidence that aliens would be benign, particularly

*Close Encounters*, wherein Richard Dreyfuss confidently takes his place on line to enter the visitor's ship and experience the most fantastic voyage of his life.

The first *Alien*, directed by Ridley Scott, is a mess of contradictory phallic and vaginal signifiers, symbols, themes, memes, and what-have-you, all revolving around reproduction. Cameron's *Aliens*, released seven years later, resolves much of this confusion into a battle between the organic and the inorganic, that is, nature and culture. As Linda Hamilton, who played Sarah Connor in *The Terminator* (1984), and who later married Cameron, put it, "That man is definitely on the side of the machines." Characteristically, whereas an android is a bad guy in Scott's *Alien*, in Cameron's *Aliens*, it's been turned into a good guy. Moreover, the brightly lit interiors of the spaceship are defined by clean lines and metallic surfaces, while the alien queen is a primitive, reptilian creature with two sets of razor-sharp teeth dripping viscous saliva that scream *vagina dentata*. As each ovum in her dusky egg chamber gets ready to hatch, it extrudes four labial lips that ooze a glistening, mucus-like fluid in a male nightmare of carnivorous female fecundity. The film displays an almost visceral aversion to female bodily fluids. Of course, it's a woman—Ripley, played by Sigourney Weaver— who defeats the queen, but she's one of Us, or rather, one of the machines. Ripley employs a hydraulic power loader suit to square off against the alien ur-mother. Whereas the queen turns the male crew into wombs that nurture her eggs until they mature, Ripley is swallowed by the ponderous hydraulic suit she assumes, relinquishing the female body that was on full display in *Alien*, where, in a controversial scene, she stripped down to her panties.

In those days, Cameron's passion for the exo-rigs, robots, and cyborgs that populated his films was striking. When Sarah Connor agrees to lead the guerrillas against the machines in *The Terminator*, she puts herself through boot camp to turn her soft body hard, while suppressing the maternal instincts that she is convinced make her more feminine, human, and therefore vulnerable. In other words, like Ripley, she turns herself into a machine. In Cameron's machine porn, when metal meets flesh, metal wins.

By the time *Avatar* came around, Cameron had changed sides, turning his back on machines. He may have been late to the party, but he embraced nature with all the fervor of a new convert. Whereas the mainstream flogs nature with culture, extremists flog culture with nature. If nature is a jungle in mainstream shows, it's a garden in Luddite shows, albeit sometimes a wild garden.

Cameron didn't make any bones about his new eco-friendly, leftish politics. "I'm happy to piss those guys off," he said, referring to the mainstream and right-wing critics of *Avatar*. "I don't agree with their world view." He recalled that when Twentieth Century Fox executives read the screenplay, their reaction was, "We really like the story. It's great. But, well, is there a way to not have so much of this tree-hugging, 'Ferngully' stuff in it?" He replied, 'Not with me making it.'" He added, "I think everyone should be a tree hugger."

The enemy in *Avatar* is not so much U.S. imperialism, as it would have been during the Vietnam era, nor even globalization, the bugaboo of the new right, but old-fashioned corporate greed. The predatory company behind this mission is called the Resources Development Administration (RDA), a generic name standing for any of the unfettered multinationals that bleed poor countries dry of their natural resources while acknowledging neither homelands nor borders. It could just as well be the Weyland Corporation, the one that launched the expeditions featured in *Alien*, a company so corrupt that even though the eponymous creatures are decimating the crew of the *Nostromo*, rather than destroy Them and save Us, it protects Them in order to bring the creatures back to Earth so that its "weapons division" can figure out a way to monetize them.

In *Aliens*, Cameron reprises the same theme. When Ripley returns to Earth at the beginning of the film, she faces hostile questioning from Weyland, which strips her of her flight license and places her under psychiatric supervision. She gets reinstated, of course, and once aboard the ship dispatched to investigate the mystery of the *Nostromo*, lost in space, the company's man on the ship tells Ripley, referring to the creatures, "Those two specimens are worth millions to the bioweapons division." Not only does he try to protect them, he tries to kill Ripley.

Weyland is only one of a long list of fictional companies that the movies—left-wing movies in particular—have convinced us to regard as criminal. In *Westworld* (2017– ), it's Delos. In *Blade Runner*, it's the Tyrell Corporation, which manufactures replicants that are used as slaves on the off-worlds. In the *Resident Evil* series (2002–16), it's the Umbrella Corporation. The Detroit Police Department has been privatized in *RoboCop* (1987, 2014), in much the same way that the exploitation of space has been privatized in *Avatar*. The unscrupulous company there is called OmniCorp. Likewise, in the superhero series *Luke Cage* (2016– ), the violent prison that holds the eponymous hero has also been privatized.

OmniCorp and the Weyland, Tyrell, and Umbrella corporations could find real-world analogues in any one of a number of criminally negligent multinationals. Indeed, there is an embarrassment of riches: Exxon (the *Exxon Valdez* leak), Union Carbide (Bhopal), or BP (the *Deepwater Horizon* spill). In *Avatar*, RDA intends to sell the unobtanium it mines to the late great planet Earth.

Aboard the *Venture Star*, the traditional agents of government authority, our old friends the cops and docs, serve instead at the whim of the suits, in the person of Parker Selfridge (Giovanni Ribisi), the very image of the ugly American, an occasional visitor to postwar fiction who displays the mixture of arrogance and ignorance for which he was notorious. Unlike Robert Dahl's polyarchy, in this microcosm of America-to-come, business dominates the other centers of power, the soldiers and scientists, making a mockery of pluralism.

There is, however, a problem. Although the mission may be ho-hum and business-as-usual so far as the corporation is concerned, it's not going according to plan. Pandora is not a barren moon ripe for the picking. Rather, it is a beautiful world much like Earth used to be, covered with leafy jungles punctuated by mountain peaks that spike dramatically upward through gauzy curtains of mist. Moreover, it is inhabited by the Na'vi, a race of ten-foot-tall humanoids who live in a pretech utopia. They worship all living things, especially trees, one particularly large specimen thereof is sitting—where else?—on top of the rich deposit of unobtanium.

As we have seen, the center traditionally portrays aliens from outer space as just that—aliens. In far-left shows, on the other hand, aliens are benign, or even part of the team like *Star Trek*'s superstrong, mind-reading Spock, half-human and half-Vulcan.

If we look closely at the Na'vi, they begin to come into focus, even seem familiar. They are slender, graceful creatures, with Spock-like ears perched high on the sides of their heads. Their eyes are slightly slanted, their noses flattened, their hair plaited into long braids, and their muscular, Vishnu-blue bodies stippled with white polka dots and crisscrossed by pale stripes. They wear loincloths, ride equine-like animals, and hunt with bows and arrows. Which humans wore loincloths, rode horses, hunted with bows and arrows, and braided their hair? Right, Native Americans. Which humans are caricatured with broad noses? Right, African Americans. Which humans are supposed to have slanted eyes? Right, Asian Americans. Save for the tails, the Na'vi possess the stereotypical physical characteristics of historically marginalized Americans. They are a generic rainbow race, standing for all people of color. The most jarring element in this picture is that We aren't being attacked by Them; They are being attacked by Us. If black lives matter in *Luke Cage*, with its African American superhero, in *Avatar*, blue lives matter, and they're not the lives of cops. No longer are Others simply victims, as Native Americans were in postwar lefty westerns like *Broken Arrow* (1950); now, they are fully realized subjects, and the story is told at least partially (*Avatar*) or entirely (*Luke Cage*) from their point of view.

Even in the future, companies still need good PR. Selfridge knows he can't just drill and run, that is, make off with the unobtanium, leaving piles of dead Na'vi behind, so he tries the divide-and-conquer strategy favored by the center-left mainstream. He turns to Dr. Grace Augustine, played by Sigourney Weaver, heir to Ripley. Selfridge patronizes Dr. Grace the same way the Weyland investigators condescend to Ripley. Talking down to her as if to a child, he explains the facts of life. Clutching a chunk of unobtanium, he bellows, "This little gray rock sells for $20 million a kilo. That's what pays for your science." Elsewhere, he elaborates: "Killing the indigenous looks bad, but there's one thing that shareholders hate more than bad press, and that's a bad quarterly statement."

Dr. Grace's job is to mix human and Na'vi DNA, producing "avatars" that look just like the Na'vi but are run by human "drivers" lying in casket-like "linking beds." Through their avatars, the drivers gather intel and, more important, use the avatars to persuade the indigenous, or "hostiles" in imperialist-speak, to give up the unobtanium without a fight. In other words, she has been told to do what liberals do best: use the velvet glove, that is, manipulate instead of coerce. He tells her, "You're supposed to be winning the hearts and the minds of the natives!" Ah, "hearts and minds." This was the counterinsurgency strategy employed in Vietnam by the brainy wonks Kennedy recruited from Harvard to open his New Frontier. It was intended to lure the peasant Cochises away from their rice paddies into "strategic hamlets," leaving, it was hoped, no more than a handful of diehard Geronimos behind to join the Vietcong guerrillas. Of course, it failed.

Persuasion, however, takes time, and Selfridge is in a hurry. He complains, "Those savages are threatening our whole operation." Unfortunately for him, in this film, savages are noble. He cares about hearts and minds only because bloodshed will depress the price of the company's stock. A center-right conservative, he defends the self-interest of his stockholders, evidently in the belief that the invisible hand will magically turn their returns into the general good, but Dr. Grace knows that if personal gain and public interest have ever been wedded, they are no more. The company's tent is small. Like a good left-wing extremist, she, on the other hand, extends tolerance beyond card-carrying centrists to include the Na'vi, and she understands that satisfying the company's shareholders does not serve their interests.

Shouldering the white man's burden, Selfridge finishes with a plea and a threat: "Just find me a carrot that will get them to move, otherwise it's going to have to be all stick." "All stick" refers to a small army of extravagantly armed former marines on board the *Venture Star*, fielded by an unnamed security firm—Blackwater? It is commanded by Colonel Miles Quaritch, adroitly played by Stephen Lang. We know Quaritch is an old-school hard-ass because his biceps are pumped, his hair cropped short, and the right side of his head is decorated by three parallel battle scars. Like Trump's national security advisor, John Bolton, who said, some years later, "I don't do carrots," he favors the iron fist.

In traditional center-left postwar movies, a lab coat like Dr. Grace might have jockeyed with the uniforms, but she would have called the shots. At the very least, the soldiers and scientists would have found time for a congenial game of tri-dimensional chess, as they do in *Star Trek*, but now, the coalition of the center has broken down. The friendly fire exchanged by soldiers and scientists has escalated into open warfare. As Dr. Grace puts it, "They're just pissing on us without even the courtesy of calling it rain." As in *Man of Steel*, where General Zod, Krypton's fiercest soldier, squares off against its smartest scientist, Superman's father Jor-El, in *Avatar*, scientists and soldiers are at each other's throats.

The man in the middle is Jake Sully (Sam Worthington). He's also an ex-marine, but he's confined to a wheelchair. Nevertheless, Dr. Grace recruits him for her science project. Right from the start, we know that Jake is not only physically, but politically out of step with the robotic troops under the colonel's command. Sourly surveying Quaritch's army, Jake observes, "Back on Earth, these guys were marines, fighting for freedom. But out here, they're just hired guns. Taking the money, working for the company." The marines in *Avatar* have devolved into mercenaries.

Indeed, there's little glory in working for the company. Its site, an ugly gash on the face of Pandora, looks like a strip mine in West Virginia and then some. Earthmovers the size of locomotives churn up clouds of dust as they mow down trees like grass. Surrounded by barbed wire and guarded by watchtowers, the company's mine is a striking image of what sociologist Max Weber called "disenchantment," that is, a world stripped of spirit, of mystery, of the numinous, which for the Na'vi is the beating heart of every-day reality. The culprit here is capitalism at its most feral.

A measure of the distance we have traveled from the *Alien* franchise to *Avatar* is the difference between Ripley and Dr. Grace. In the former, Ripley fights the Other; in the latter, Dr. Grace fights the company, at the side of the Other. Observing the devastation Selfridge et al. have wreaked on Pandora, she angrily harangues him: "Those trees were sacred to the Na'vi in ways that you can't imagine." In other words, for the Na'vi, nature is not just fodder for their culture, as it is for humans, but a partner—more than a partner, the essence of who they are. But Selfridge doesn't get it. Echoing Reagan's secretary of the interior, the delightfully foot-in-mouth James G. Watt, several decades earlier, he sneers, "They're just goddamn trees."

The Luddites had their time in the sun, but as the fear of nuclear confla-gration receded, and the ICBMs snoozed in their silos, the love affair with science and technology was rekindled, thanks in part to the rise of Silicon Valley as the new, turbocharged engine of progress. But even in the 1950s, technophile Isaac Asimov dismissed the Kubricks of the world in his book, *I, Robot*, mocking the fear-mongering of those afflicted with what he called the "Frankenstein complex." Eventually, Steve Jobs would replace Albert Einstein, becoming one of the culture heroes of the twenty-first century.

Distinct from the Luddite-left in almost every respect, the Dotcom-left, along with its counterparts on the right, are disrupters par excellence. According to writer Noam Cohen, a student of Silicon Valley, its entre-preneurs are almost all libertarians. A sizable chunk of them, however, "liberal libertarians" like Amazon's Jeff Bezos, who owns the virulently anti-Trump *Washington Post*, and Apple CEO Tim Cook, who, among other things, denounced then Indiana governor Mike Pence's Religious Freedom Restoration Act of 2015, were in the Obama camp and subse-quently supported Hillary Clinton. If the Luddite-left distrusts machines, the Dotcom-left looks to artificial intelligence (AI) as the most likely way to achieve its utopian aspirations. Its wish list includes goals like saving the environment, world peace, and the extension of tolerance beyond the human to, say, sentient machines that it regards as benevolent.

The "singularity" refers to that stage in the development of AI when the IQ of machines surpasses that of humans and they become sentient and self-conscious. It has been popularized by the so-called artificial intelligentsia, among them futurologists like Ray Kurzweil, now Google's head of engineering. Singularians revere technology and disparage nature, like Selfridge in *Avatar*. For them, the apocalypse is nature run wild. In a Dotcom-left film, HAL would have been foolproof, and the culprit would indeed have been human, rather than mechanical error.

If, in their utopian musings, Luddites look to Jean-Jacques Rousseau and dream of re-creating an Edenic paradise before civilization messed things up, singularians dream of electric sheep, which is to say, instead of doubling down on the human, the way mainstream shows do, they long to free mortals from constraints imposed by nature, utilizing advances in nanotechnology, genetic engineering, robotics, and so on to improve upon or substitute for human biology. As Dr. Johnny Depp tells a black-tie audience in *Transcendence* (2014), an idea-driven thriller that provoked more thought than business, "A sentient machine will quickly overcome the limits of biology. In a short time, its analytical power will be greater than the collective intelligence of every person born in the history of the world." Singularians are given to making analogies between humans and computers, where the body is the hardware and the brain is the software. Rewriting the software rewires the hardware. Consciousness is code. Moreover, it is platform neutral, that is, consciousness can just as easily be an attribute of machines as humans. Those who prefer humans to machines and insist that the latter could never successfully imitate, not to mention surpass, the former are derided as "carbon-based chauvinists."

For the general public, AI remained the stuff of science fiction until 1997, when IBM's Deep Blue defeated world chess champion Garry Kasparov. Today, self-repairing, self-correcting intelligent machines that learn and continuously improve themselves without human intervention are no longer the stuff of science fiction, so how far off can sentient machines be? Kurzweil puts their ETA at 2045.

Alan Turing pioneered AI in the middle of the previous century. The story of this young, indecently gifted British mathematician is told in *The Imitation Game* (2014), a picture that has all the earmarks of a Dotcom-left movie, albeit devoid of the sci-fi trappings that are de rigueur for many shows like it.

In the early years of World War II, Turing, preternaturally channeled by Benedict Cumberbatch, went to work for the military at Bletchley Park, the top secret British code-breaking facility, trying to crack Enigma, the famously opaque German cipher. In the movie, Turing is unable to make small talk, understand jokes, and drink beer with his fellow code breakers after work at the local pub. In short, he is a nerd.

Nerds were once the butt of jokes for being poor at sports and awkward with girls. They had bad skin and paperclip posture, wore Coke-bottle glasses, and favored plastic pocket protectors. Once they came into their own in the 1970s, when the first wave of movie nerds—Spielberg, Lucas, Peter Bogdanovich, et al.—conquered Hollywood, it was their turn to laugh. Woody Allen in particular transformed the nebbish (the Jewish genus of nerd) into a culture hero. Two decades later, personal computing took the country by storm, transforming nerds into geeks, the darlings of Wall Street and the stars of Dotcom shows like *The Big Bang Theory* (2007– ), *Silicon Valley* (2014– ), *CSI: Cyber* (2015–16), and by far the best of them all, *Halt and Catch Fire* (2014–17). *Mr. Robot* (2015– ), featuring a nerdier-than-thou hero, picked up a basket of Golden Globes and Emmys in 2016. One year earlier, at Comic-Con, the nerds-on-parade conclave for fanboys and girls, Axel Alonso, then editor in chief of Marvel comics, reflected, "It used to be that cool people looked down on nerds." He continued, "Now I know a lot of cool people who pretend to be nerds." Even former President Obama lays claim to nerddom. "What's remarkable is the way 'nerd' is such a badge of honor now," he said. "I think America's a nerdier country than it was when I was a kid—and that's a good thing!"

At least in the beginning, before the utopian promise of the internet was monetized and then forgotten, nerd culture, especially in movies and TV, was to one degree or another oppositional, a subset of left-wing extremism, evident, say, in Judd Apatow's gross-out comedies like *The 40-Year-Old Virgin* (2005) or Todd Phillips's *Hangover* trilogy (2009, 2011, 2013) that reverberate with the anarchic energy of John Landis's 1978 landmark *Animal House*. Nerd culture heroizes outcasts whose antics insult and embarrass authority. As writer-director Harold Ramis once put it, "We represent the underdog as comedy usually speaks for the lower classes. We attack the winners."

In *The Imitation Game*, Turing is bullied for failing to be a team player.

"Team" may be a magic word for the center, but to Turing, it's an obscenity. Shows like this prefer the lone genius who bucks the system and disregards conventional wisdom. Turing is applauded for being different by his former fiancée, who speaks for the movie when she says, "The world needs people like you, Alan."

After months of frustration and failure, Turing concludes, "All this time we've been trying to beat the machine, but we should have been trying to beat the people who use the machine." Sounding very much like HAL, he continues, "Enigma is perfect. It's human beings who are flawed." In this movie he's right, and armed with this insight, he proceeds to crack the German code.

Turing's eureka moment occurs when he wonders whether machines can be made to think. "Most people believe that machines are inherently inferior to human beings," he muses. "Why are we so bloody narrow-minded about who we consider alive?"

Meanwhile, back in the Luddite world of *Avatar*, Jake Sully is trying his best to be a team player. He knows that the soldiers and scientists work for the same boss and strive for the same goal, albeit by different means, so for the moment he's prepared to play ball. As he settles into his linking bed and experiences a brief psychedelic interlude, he and his avatar boot up and embark on their fantastic voyage.

Deep within Pandora's jungles, avatar-Jake—an organism with Jake's consciousness in a Na'vi body—finds himself in a veritable botanical Disneyland filled with shimmering plants of every size, shape, and color, many of which undulate languidly as if they are being wafted by currents at the bottom of the sea. A particularly striking specimen resembles a compound toadstool, with glowing caps lapped over one another. It shrinks away from avatar-Jake's touch, folding in on itself until it almost vanishes, a vivid reminder of the vulnerability of the ecosystem to human intervention, no matter how mediated or gentle. Despite his blue Na'vi body, he's a fish-out-of-water, once a favorite Hollywood trope, rendered here as fauna-out-of-flora.

Avatar-Jake's idyll is abruptly interrupted by the arrival of Neytiri (Zoe Saldana), a Na'vi huntress. In the hallowed tradition of National Geographic, she is wearing little more than a few beads or a wisp of cloth no bigger than a cocktail napkin over her breasts. Neytiri is about to send Jake to join Cecil Rhodes in imperialist heaven when a swarm of luminescent, jellyfish-like spores descends lazily from above and alights upon his body, leaving her dumbstruck. They are the seeds of the sacred Hometree, the very tree sitting atop the coveted unobtanium deposit. Recognizing that the Hometree has given him its imprimatur, she takes him under her wing. According to the colonialist handbook, Jake should be civilizing Neytiri. But civilization counts for little here, and it is Neytiri who becomes the Henry Higgins of the film, instructing Jake in her values: the ways of the Na'vi.

Parenthetically, a lot can be learned about the ideology of a show by looking at who learns from whom, that is, which way values flow. Generally, although not always, if the teacher is a "manspert,"—that is male, expert, and centrist—expounding on the ways of the world (so-called mansplaining) to a woman, then we're looking at a mainstream show. When the reverse is true, as it is in *Avatar*, or *Arrival* (2016), where aliens teach linguist Amy Adams their language, we're looking at an extremist show.

Back on the mother ship, Jake confesses that his mission is a failure because the Na'vi are never going to go for the carrot and abandon the Hometree. "For what?" he asks, rhetorically. "Light beer? Blue jeans?" American civilization has devolved into little more than a flea market peddling trashy consumer goods that no civilization worth its name could possibly value, even one as apparently primitive as the Na'vi. Outside of pro basketball contracts, which Selfridge is not in a position to offer, Jake concludes, "there's nothing that we have that they want." The days when Peter Minuit could buy Manhattan from the Na'vi's spiritual forbearers for a handful of beads are long gone.

Staring glumly at his limbs, limp like string cheese, and increasingly confused, Jake realizes that with our civilization bankrupt, liberal social control has nothing to offer. He understands that, therefore, it will fail, and he'd better apply for Neytiri's Outward Bound program. By now, he's also figured out how the center Otherizes dissenters to justify destroying them. "When people are sitting on shit that you want, you make them the enemy," he says, angrily. "Then you're justified in taking it."

With the center-left's preferred method of social control off the table, the way is cleared for the center-right to fall back on force. Jake's red light is Quaritch's green light, freeing him to go "all stick."

When Selfridge finally lets Quaritch off his leash, it's the last straw for Dr. Grace. She jumps ship, taking her scientists, Jake included, out of the bipartisan coalition of the center. Quaritch sneers, "Hey, Sully, how's it feel to betray your own race?" But Jake doesn't see it that way. From his point of view, the extreme left stands for principle, and compromise is synonymous with fecklessness. Jake is just doing what's right, and if he has to leave the center for the extremes, so be it.

Dr. Grace et al. steal a pod that houses a couple of linking beds, escape from the mother ship, and set up shop among Pandora's legendary "floating mountains," which luckily for them lie within the "flux vortex," where the company's instrumentation cannot locate them. (Think spotty AT&T cell coverage.)

It's fitting that it is Dr. Grace who leads the defectors. In shows that lean left, and favor nature over culture, women are its avatars. They either enable their extremist heroes or become extremist heroes themselves.

It turns out, ironically, that it is neither nature nor culture that makes off with the unobtanium in *Avatar*. When the film premiered on December 16, 2009, reviewers were nothing short of ecstatic. Ticket buyers agreed. Released in 3,457 theaters in the United States, it quickly surpassed Cameron's own record-breaking *Titanic*, raking in $2.8 billion worldwide by 2018. It was nominated for nine Oscars, including Best Picture and Best Director, although it only won three. Despite its disappointing showing on Oscar night, it turned out that under the noses of Selfridge & Co., it was Cameron himself who made off with the unobtanium, which turned out to be *Avatar* itself, with its record-breaking grosses.

With the center suffering and the far left, in the guise of *Avatar*, grabbing all the party favors, was there anything left for the far right? As it turns out, there was plenty of swag left in the bag.

# 3
# Doing the Right Thing

*For the secular right, the apocalypse is democracy's assault on excellence and individualism, while the evangelical right welcomes the final days because they offer personal salvation.*

> We in our lifetimes potentially could see Jesus Christ return-
> ing to earth and the rapture of the church.
> —*Former Minnesota congresswoman Michele Bachmann*

As *Left Behind* (2014) opens, we find ourselves in the middle of New York City's bustling Kennedy Airport, with the characters debating that pesky problem of evil that Christianity has never been able to put to bed. As tall, good-looking celebrity journalist Buck Williams strides toward his gate, signing autographs along the way, he is accosted by a dark-haired woman wearing a lime-colored blouse, who says, "Can I ask you a question, Mr. Williams? Do you read the Bible?"

"I'm guessing not as often as you do."

"Well, Matthew 24, verse 7 says there's going to be famines, pestilence, and earthquakes in diverse places," she cheerfully responds, giving him a big smile as if she were telling him he's won the lottery. "All of these things, the disasters, the wars, are signs."

Chloe, a perky blonde who has just deplaned, overhears the exchange and butts in. "So God knew that all these things were going to happen?"

"Honey, God knows everything."

"Then why doesn't he do something? He's God, right? Couldn't he have stopped the flood if he wanted to, maybe send a little rain?"

"It's a fallen world. God created it perfect, and we destroyed it. With the first sin."

Speaking of sin, a cut takes us to the interior of a parked car. Peering into the rearview mirror, we see a bottle blonde applying bright red lipstick. Emerging from the vehicle, her long, shapely legs preceding her, is Hattie Durham, a flight attendant. She's wearing a white blouse at least one size too small. Cut to a close-up of a man removing his wedding ring. As he gets out of his car, we see that it is Nicolas Cage, at the head of a Z-list cast, wearing aviator shades and looking every inch the pilot Rayford Steele, who also happens to be Chloe's father. He catches up to Hattie, marching ahead of him in stiletto heels, and greets her warmly, perhaps too warmly. They enter the terminal together laughing. He spies Chloe, in town to give him a surprise birthday party that's not going to happen because he has to fly to London. Chloe is struck by his easy intimacy with Hattie and suspects that they're having an affair, but Rayford takes a moment to sit down and reassure her that his marriage to her mother is in good shape, even though the passion has leaked out since mom found Jesus. Rayford says, philosophically, "Hey, if she's gonna run off with another man, why not Jesus, huh?"

The concept of running off with Jesus takes a minute to digest, so we'll start off with the saner of the two right-wing tendencies, the secular right, before returning to Jesus and His affairs. From the secular right's point of view, the "swamp," as Donald Trump calls the center, is badly in need of draining, rife as it is with corruption, overrun with raping and pillaging immigrants, populated by America Lasters who wouldn't recognize God if He hit them over the head with a lightning bolt. Meanwhile, big government—a.k.a. the "administrative state"—stifles competition with overregulation, crushes initiative with an onerous tax structure, all the while punishing police for enforcing the law. As a result, delusional feminists noisily imagine men massaging their penises behind potted palms, militant blacks insist against all evidence that their lives matter, and sexual deviants who can't decide if they're male or female casually change genders like socks.

The secular right is a jumble of different tendencies from statist (Dick Cheney and his neocon friends) to populist (the Tea Party), but we will focus, for now, on the Dotcom-right, home to those Silicon Valley billionaires who are uncomfortable with their opposite numbers on the left and include the Übermensch-worshipping libertarians who fetishize genius and science. Some of them characterize themselves as "neoreactionaries." They chatter about the "Dark Enlightenment." Deriding democracy, they prefer a new techno-aristocracy based on IQ. Some of them would like to replace the president with a Silicon Valley CEO, preferably from a company like

Google, or if not that, any strongman will do. To the right-wing Silicon Valley technocrats, Kevin Spacey's Frank Underwood, the unscrupulous American president in the mainstream *House of Cards* (2013– )—who says things like "A lion does not ask permission before he eats a zebra" and "Democracy is so overrated"—would be a hero. He is right at home in the state of nature where might makes right. Like former Trump strategist and provocateur in chief Steve Bannon and the so-called kamikaze Republicans who court government shutdowns, or even Petyr Baelish in *Game of Thrones*, who says, "Chaos isn't a pit. Chaos is a ladder," Underwood is a chaos agent, explaining, at one point, "If you don't like how the table is set, turn over the table."

The fairy-godmother of the secular right is confirmed atheist Ayn Rand, who, going Adam Smith one better, espoused the virtue of selfishness and derided altruism. Long ignored as no more than the ravings of a crank, Rand's Objectivism has found a new lease on life in Silicon Valley.

*Atlas Shrugged*, Rand's thousand-page doorstop, portrays a dystopic America abandoned by industrialists and what are now called venture capitalists because they have been smothered by government regulation. The villains are the "moochers" and "looters," that is, the poor, who help themselves to the fruits of the labors of her entrepreneurial heroes.

It's not surprising that if Rand found favor among Dotcom billionaires, the Republican right wasn't far behind. In a 2005 speech, Paul Ryan said that he distributed copies of *Atlas Shrugged* to his staff, although he subsequently backed off, denouncing her as an atheist, perhaps to appease the evangelical right. Alan Greenspan, whom Reagan appointed chairman of the U.S. Federal Reserve, where he served for nineteen years, was also a disciple. He attended Rand's funeral in 1982. Trump's former secretary of state Rex Tillerson told *Scouting* magazine that *Atlas Shrugged* was his favorite book, and according to his successor, former CIA head, Mike Pompeo, it likewise "really had an impact on me." Then, of course, there is Rand Paul, although he denies he was named after the libertarian icon.

Out there on the edge is Anthony Levandowski, best known as Google's onetime developer of self-driving cars. Levandowski filed papers with the IRS naming himself "dean" of a church called Way of the Future. The church is dedicated to "the realization, acceptance, and worship of a Godhead based on Artificial Intelligence (AI) developed through computer hardware and software." If there's a Singularity University, why not an AI religion?

Peter Thiel is the poster child for the Dotcom-right. A fierce advocate of scientific research and the exploration of space, he participated in the Singularity Summit conferences in 2006 and 2011. Thiel is a veteran of the culture wars at Stanford, where as an undergraduate he founded the conservative *Stanford Review* in 1987, which resisted the call for diversity—the admission of more women and people of color—at the university. He has scratched his head over women's right to vote, and in 2009, he wrote an essay in a Cato Institute publication confessing that he no longer believed that "freedom and democracy are compatible." He has even derided competition and praised "creative monopolists," presumably like the "PayPal Mafia," of which he is a member in good standing. For this, he has been termed a "corporate Nietzschean." Like his PayPal friends, he is a passionate fan of science fiction. He once wrote that he "preferred the capitalist *Star Wars* to the communist *Star Trek*."

"Thielismus" animates the work of directors like Brad Bird and Christopher Nolan. *The Incredibles* (2004), is a clever animated fantasy given to us by Bird. It follows a family of superheroes consisting of Bob (Mr. Incredible), his wife Helen (Elastigirl), and their children. But like most superheroes, their fight against supervillains takes a heavy toll in collateral damage. They break windows, overturn cars, and demolish the occasional building.

In most superhero movies, the authorities confine themselves to complaining, but here, sick and tired of the lawsuits that follow in the wake of their superheroics, they actually ban Mr. Incredible, Elastigirl, and the rest of their super-ilk. The family is forced to hang up their suits, assume their secret identities, and join the Superhero Relocation Program. Mr. Incredible ends up as a clerk in a cubical, working for an insurance company.

The ostensible reason they are prevented from doing their job—rescuing kittens from trees and old men from muggers—is the mayhem they wreak, but their actual crime is that they are superheroes in a society where the lowest common denominator rules. The American government is devoted to stamping out distinction and enforcing mediocrity. The real supervillain in this picture is Uncle Sam, and the apocalypse is democracy.

In Bird's shows, America is in decline, the result of losing the "cultural war over Progress" in Thiel's words. Bird attributes the loss to a plague of defeatism that has mysteriously curdled the very pioneer spirit that saves Matt Damon in *The Martian*. Bird adds his voice to the chorus celebrating genius, American exceptionalism, and faith in progress. *Tomorrowland* (2015), which he directed and wrote, teamed with Damon Lindelof of *Lost* and *Leftovers* fame. It is a particularly preachy instance of a subset of Make America Great Again pictures.

The apocalypse hovers over *Tomorrowland* like a dark cloud. As George Clooney, playing a disillusioned inventor, puts it, "The future can be scary. Unstable governments, overpopulation, wars on every continent, famine, water shortages, environmental collapse . . . All true. The problem here is that nobody has the will to do anything about it."

The film opens with Clooney recalling that the last time he felt optimistic was when he visited—as a child—what else but the 1964 World's Fair. Cut to the Fair itself. It is the site of a futuristic city called Tomorrowland, whose soaring spires contrast dramatically with the devastated cities featured in the shows of the dystopian left. Tomorrowland is a sort of a futuristic Heritage Foundation for the best and the brightest, presumably providing them with tax-free condos that afford them the freedom to incubate great ideas. As someone asks, "Have you ever wondered what would happen if all the geniuses, the artists, the scientists, the smartest, most creative people in the world decided to actually change it?" (In a later scene, the characters get a chance to hang out with Thomas Edison, Nikola Tesla, and Jules Verne.)

By way of contrast, we are then transported from the past to the present, where we find ourselves in Cape Canaveral, the site of a NASA base. Reminding us that NASA is a no-show in *Avatar*, the base is being closed down, a victim of lack of vision, failure of nerve, and other maladies of the center. Poor teenage Casey encounters nothing but negativity wherever she turns. Force-fed dystopian classics like *Brave New World* and *Fahrenheit 451* in high school, battered by an endless drumbeat of doom and gloom, she raises her hand in class and asks, "Can we fix it?" The teacher just looks at her like she's crazy. *Tomorrowland* is a Randian nightmare.

*Gravity* (2013) is another survivor show like *The Martian*, but with a right-wing twist. This time it's Sandra Bullock lost in space when the satellite she's visiting is destroyed by Russian space junk. NASA is useless—all she gets is static when she tries to contact it, and although she does manage to make it to a Chinese satellite and get through to their space agency, they—guess what—speak Chinese. Too big for their britches, they haven't bothered to learn English! Unlike in *The Martian*, where the Chinese help rescue Matt Damon, in *Gravity*, they're no help at all. She's thrown back on her own resources, an accidental individualist forced to depend on good old American pluck. But not entirely. She's a novice at space travel, and initially she's paired with a veteran, George Clooney again, who shows her the ropes. He is killed in the course of their travails, but when she really gets in over her head and it looks like she too is going to expire in space, he comes to her in a dream, or hallucination, and tells her how to wriggle out of her predicament. Father knows best.

We get more—much more—of the same from *Interstellar* (2014), Christopher Nolan's visually arresting but banal riff on remarks like this one from Stephen Hawking: "Our only chance of long-term survival is not to remain inward-looking on planet Earth, but to spread out into space."

Set some years in the future, the film is a survivor story, planetary in scope. It begins with a bleak picture of the western United States, standing in for the entire world, a vast, sizzling frying pan overtaken by dust and sand, well on its way to the sixth extinction. Much of its population has starved to death thanks to a blight that has wiped out crops, and many of those who remain have died in food riots. This is not one of those left-wing shows that targets humans for hastening the end with their elephantine carbon footprints and other profligate habits. Far from attributing the blight to climate change, *Interstellar* actually goes out of its way not to. For example, the blight thrives on atmospheric nitrogen instead of carbon dioxide, which would be likely if Nolan were trying to target climate change. Moreover, the movie passes off the planetary dust bowl as a natural disaster: "Stuff," to quote Donald Rumsfeld, that just "happens." Once humans are off the hook, there's no point trying to convince them to burn less carbon; it's easier to explore distant galaxies.

Coop (Matthew McConaughey) is a former engineer and astronaut now turned farmer. NASA, instead of the thriving government agency it is in *The Martian*, has been defunded by the same myopic public presumably responsible for closing the base in *Tomorrowland*. His profession has ceased to exist. The absence of NASA is not a result of the unfortunate collapse of big government, as it would be in a mainstream show, but rather it is attributed to the decay of the American spirit and the shortsightedness of a public that no longer listens to the elites. Again, democracy is at fault.

Coop is another one of Rand's exceptional men disguised as a laid-back, down-home regular guy. He's forced into mundane labor by the stupidity of those garden-variety citizens who have refused to fund NASA. He utters nuggets of Randian wisdom like, "We used to look up at the sky and wonder at our place in the stars, now we just look down and worry about our place in the dirt." Vision-impaired Americans have turned their attention from outer space to feeding themselves. As a smug, know-it-all high school teacher remarks in one scene, "We need to teach our kids about this planet, not [distract them with] tales of leaving it."

NASA may have been defunded, but it hasn't disappeared as it has in *Avatar* or gone dark as it does in *Tomorrowland*; it has just gone underground, where it is financed off the books. Dropping by its headquarters, Coop encounters astrophysicist Michael Caine. He asks Dr. Caine, "What [is] your plan to save the world?" Contradicting the blinkered high school teacher, Caine replies with Hawking's jaw-dropper: "We're not meant to save the world. We're meant to leave it."

Dr. Caine recruits Coop to lead a mission in search of a habitable world. He goes on to explain that someone or something alien—They—has considerately placed a wormhole near Saturn that will enable our intrepid astronauts to exit the solar system, where none of the other planets can support life, and jump to the next galaxy without running out of gas. Coop agrees, and off flies our interstellar house hunter to find us the perfect home.

Sounding transparently obscurantist, if such a thing is possible, Nolan has been quoted as saying, "We try not to give any particular message or sense of things," but he gets it backward. *Interstellar*'s willful refusal to provide a "sense of things" is precisely its "particular message."

Moreover, Jonathan Nolan (Christopher's brother and co-writer of *Interstellar*) wonders why humans are so "obsessed" with Armageddon and "their own culpability." For the Nolans, it's as if climate change were a matter for social psychologists rather than climatologists. Christopher attributes it to the same "negativity" that dogs poor Casey in *Tomorrowland*. According to him, it is caused by "people trying to look in a more cynical way under the surface about motivations for why things happen." Thoughtfully providing a postwar primer for dummies, he says that "people aren't seeing the wood for the trees. We went to space because it was a cool thing to do. Kennedy sat there and said, 'Yeah. We should go to the moon.'" So much for the space race, or even, perhaps, the Cold War.

Nolan is skilled at decontextualizing, and dehistoricizing his subjects, all the easier to conform them to his own, lightly disguised political purposes. Or maybe he's not aware of what he is doing. Who knows? But imagine writing and directing *Dunkirk* and largely neglecting to name the enemy! If Nolan can't be bothered to pick up a history book, he should at least check out *Hidden Figures*.

Attributing the threats to life as we know it to left-wing pessimism, and pitting that against right-wing optimism, inevitably leads to the conclusion that, as in *Tomorrowland*, negativity and pessimism are un-American. The antidote to the apocalypse is chicken soup for the soul, the power, in other words, of positive thinking.

There are few aliens in any of these shows, but when they do pop up, the secular right has no more use for them than does the center, and of course none of the sympathy displayed by the left. By the mid-1990s, the center had edged right and regrouped under Bill Clinton, for whom "liberal" was a dirty word. *Independence Day*, reflecting the changed climate may, as we have seen, have been inclusive with regard to the world's humans, but so far as aliens are concerned—forget it. When Marine Corps captain Will Smith punches an alien in the jaw, he says, "Now that's what I call a close encounter." Take that, Mr. Spielberg.

Positive thinking is Sandra Bullock's *spécialité*, and turning to the religious right, we find her glowing up a storm in the 2009 hit *The Blind Side*, in which she plays a wealthy, obnoxious white evangelical. She packs a pistol, invokes the NRA, and wears a crucifix around her neck encrusted with jewels, but she has a heart of gold. She adopts Big Mike, a virtually mute, homeless black teenager who somehow attends the posh Wingate Christian School with her children. Bullock takes Big Mike under her wing and into her home, shepherding him through school and into the NFL, showing that not only can white people be blessed with earthly possessions, but they are rich in human kindness as well. Christian charity is the solution to racism, poverty, drug addiction, and so on. The sole function of Big Mike, a version of the so-called Magical Negro, is to bring out the best in Bullock, and the Academy of Motion Picture Arts and Sciences agreed, perversely giving her an Oscar for her performance.

*The Bible*, a dramatization of the Old and New Testaments, aired in 2013 and is said to have reached 100 million viewers. *The Bible*'s producers, actress Roma Downey (*Touched by an Angel*) and producer Mark Burnett (*The Apprentice*), explained that their "greatest hope" was that the series would "affect a new generation of viewers and draw them back to the Bible."

Christian grace notes abound in shows like USA's *Shooter* (2016– ), a crisply executed sniper thriller starring Ryan Phillippe that otherwise has little to do with religion. It features a former marine sniper nonpareil named Bob Lee Swagger. In between exceptionally difficult kill shots where he picks off targets at a thousand yards, Swagger conspicuously crosses himself, guaranteeing, apparently, that he hits his target. Afterward, sitting down to a hearty dinner with his perfect family, he won't take a bite without first saying grace.

Recently, there has been a resurgence of smaller, Christian-themed movies that have yielded extraordinary returns on tiny budgets. *God's Not Dead* (2014), which cost an estimated $2 million, scored an astounding $61 million at the domestic box office, while 2015's *War Room* took in $68 million, domestic, on a likewise infinitesimal budget, estimated at $3 million. *The Shack* (2017) raked in $97 million worldwide in 2017.

The studios and small-screen providers, looking at the bottom line, have decided they can ill afford to ignore the evangelicals and are using PR firms that specialize in religious-themed movies to reach this audience through an extensive network of pastors, who are even eager to flak shows that aren't overtly religious so long as they offer up "sermon starters." Sony has a faith-based unit innocuously called Affirm Films, and the other studios can be expected to follow suit. There are at least four Christian-themed movies slated for 2018.

The biggest box office hit has been generated by the evangelical right: Mel Gibson's *The Passion of the Christ* (2004), an amalgam of evangelicalism and conservative Catholic traditionalism that, needless to say, takes a dim view of Jews, blaming their descendants, friends, and nodding acquaintances for the Crucifixion, while caricaturing them with the requisite outsize noses, wild hair, and so on. When critics like Frank Rich, writing in the *New York Times*, took him to task, Gibson famously responded, "I want to kill him. I want his intestines on a stick. . . . I want to kill his dog." All of this seemed to strike a chord with moviegoers. *The Passion of the Christ* grossed $612 million worldwide, on a budget of $30 million.

The ecumenical center shows we have discussed like *Lost* are so vapid and anodyne in their efforts to be everything to everyone that it's almost enough to make one appreciate the bracing extremism of the evangelical right, which, instead of offering big-tent inclusiveness, raises the drawbridge. Religion, too, has signed up for an extreme makeover. "Yesteryear's supposed fringes are taking over American Protestantism's main square," wrote Kevin Phillips in his book *American Theocracy*, published way back in 2006.

Reflecting the changes that have winnowed America's white Christian majority—down 8 percent in 2014 from 2007—evangelicals have apparently decided that they have had enough of the melting pot and the mainstream Christian religions. Their views are particularly well suited to bottom-up, do-it-yourself populist Americans who privilege the heart over the head, and "enthusiasm" over reason. From their point of view, the primary role of the state is to legislate morality using the Bible as a guide. They attack secularism in all its guises, advocating theocracy and family values.

To the evangelical right, the apocalypse is God's way of saying that Adam shouldn't have bitten into that darn apple, and that sinners—the unhappy denizens of the center, left, and secular right—instead of wasting their time reading Darwin's *On the Origin of Species* should be studying the Book of Revelation.

The *Left Behind* novels, a series of sixteen pulpy, if prudish, checkout-lane fundamentalist thrillers, have spawned several unsuccessful movies, like Nicolas Cage's potboiler. The books, on the other hand, have sold north of 65 million copies worldwide to the tune of $1 billion and change and have spawned a veritable ecosystem of ancillary products, including a book series for kids, another for the military, an interactive game, CDs, mugs, T-shirts, comic books, trivia games, web discussion groups, screen savers, greeting cards, calendars, and so on. Said Moral Majority founder Jerry Falwell, "In terms of its impact on Christianity, it's probably greater than that of any other book in modern times, outside the Bible."

*Left Behind*, the first novel of the series, was published in 1995, roughly four years after the start of George H.W. Bush's Gulf War. The series showcases Tim LaHaye and Jerry B. Jenkins's literal, if fanciful, reading of Revelation, in which the Four Horsemen of the Apocalypse are coming to trample humanity. We're warned, "War is coming—famine, plagues, and death."

LaHaye and Jenkins purple prose ("Rayford Steele's mind was on a woman he had never touched. With his fully loaded 747 on autopilot . . . "), along with the names of two of their action figures, uh, characters, the aforementioned Rayford Steele and Buck Williams, might incline readers to mistake these books for Christian porn, but they'd be wrong, because the relations between men and women in this series are more *Boys' Life* than *Playboy*.

Somewhere over the ocean, in the course of Rayford's transatlantic flight, over one hundred passengers suddenly disappear from their seats, without so much as a wave good-bye. The disappearances are effected with surgical precision. Shirts, pants, blouses, dresses, shoes, eyeglasses, fillings, hearing aids, pacemakers, surgical pins, Band-Aids, corn plasters, and yes, Depends, are presumably left on their seats. The chosen are not allowed so much as carry-ons for their trip to wherever it is they are going. Where in heaven's name are they going?

We quickly learn that it's not only the passengers on Rayford's flight who have been victims of the divine, but people all over the world, in particular children, babies, even fetuses sucked out of the wombs of pregnant women while doctors watch flabbergasted as their swollen bellies deflate like so many punctured beach balls.

In the movie, the disappearances, signaled by a brief flash and a sound like thunder, occur immediately after Rayford exits the cockpit to share an intimate moment with Hattie in the galley. Thus, it seems like they are not only a reward for a life well-spent reading the Gospels, but a warning against impending adultery. Certainly, Rayford experiences it that way. When he finally returns home in the print version, he is stricken to find his wife and son, little Raymie, missing.

Strictly speaking, "apocalypse," a word most commonly taken to denote the end of the world, applies to a lengthy series of events that leads up to that unfortunate terminus, including seven years of torment called the Tribulation, during which catastrophe is piled upon catastrophe, as Christian soldiers battle the legions of Satan. Three-quarters of the human race are killed in the process. The Tribulation is followed by the Glorious Appearing, a.k.a. the Second Coming, in which Jesus touches down to gather his flock and lead them into the climactic battle at Armageddon, which is followed by the thousand-year reign of Christ, called the Millennium.

Mainstream Christianity, to the extent that it subscribes to any of this, has traditionally been postmillennial, or "post-mil," in church-speak, meaning that the Second Coming heralding Armageddon will occur after the Millennium, whereas evangelicals are "pre-mils," holding that the Glorious Appearing will precede Armageddon and the Millennium. The implications of this change in Jesus's ETA are plain: If His arrival were just around the corner, good works and long-term social change, that is, the progress promised by pluralism, becomes irrelevant. This-world utopianism would have to wait—for Jesus. Thus, evangelicals had no use for movements that promised progressive change. Rather, they emphasized personal salvation.

In the pre-mil *Left Behind*s, then, the King of Peace is MIA. LaHaye and Jenkins's Jesus doesn't return to Earth to distribute Hershey bars like the GI's who liberated Paris in 1944. Au contraire, in the battle of Armageddon, He lays waste—not only to the heathens but to everyone who isn't born-again. The Millennium follows. It's a pity there will be almost no one left on Earth to enjoy it. If this makes little sense, no matter; as Quaritch says in *Avatar*, "We're not in Kansas anymore." Driven by catastrophe theology, the books did much to establish the Book of Revelation as the GPS for the end days.

The Rapture Index, found on the Rapture Ready website, is the evangelical version of the *Bulletin of the Atomic Scientists'* Doomsday Clock. It rates 45 factors, from drug abuse and globalism to Satanism, that are said to contribute to pre-rapture conditions. Each factor is allotted a numerical rating, and if the sum total exceeds 160, the site advises, "Fasten your seat belts." As of February 2018, it stands at 185, well over the boiling point. Unlike the disaster heralded by the Doomsday Clock, however, the miracle promised by the Rapture Index is to be welcomed, because regardless of the cost in human life, the apocalypse is God's yellow brick road to salvation.

Were the *Left Behind* novels not so abysmally written, they might be as enjoyable as any other series of thrillers, say, Robert Ludlum's Jason Bourne saga. And then there's the discomfiting fact that a surprisingly vast number of Americans appear to think they are truly predictive. The notorious "Prophecy" issue of *Newsweek* that appeared in 1999 reported that 40 percent of Americans believed that the world would end with Jesus tussling with the Antichrist in the battle of Armageddon. Four years later, in 2003, undoubtedly jacked up by the 9/11 attacks, this figure rose to 59 percent, per a *Time*/CNN poll. Not much has changed since then. A 2010 Pew Research Center survey, found that close to 48 percent of American Christians were convinced that Christ would definitely (27 percent) or probably (20 percent) pay us another visit within the next forty years. Since he was born in a "terrorist state," however, he may have problems with extreme vetting.

In 2015, after the Obama administration's nuclear deal with Iran, former Minnesota congresswoman Michele Bachmann found herself pulled in two directions. She chastised the president for hastening the end times, "the midnight hour," as she called it, by putting nuclear weapons in the hands of the ayatollah. But virtually panting with anticipation, she exhorted Christians to "rejoice" at the prospect of an Iranian bomb, gushing, "These are wonderful times." The reason? Bachmann explained, "We in our lifetimes potentially could see Jesus Christ returning to earth and the rapture of the church."

The smiley face with which fundamentalists look forward to the end of the world is of more than academic interest. There has been considerable anxiety in some quarters that their influence has extended into the highest reaches of the American government. As Bill Moyers observed, "One of the biggest changes in politics in my lifetime is that the delusional is no longer marginal. It has come in from the fringe, to sit in the seat of power in the Oval Office and in Congress." Speaking of the United States, Phillips wrote in *American Theocracy*, "The world's leading economic and military power is also—no one can misread the data—the world's leading Bible-reading crusader state, immersed in an Old Testament of stern prophets and bloody Middle Eastern battlefields."

Jimmy Carter was our first born-again president, and Ronald Reagan was a fan of *The Late Great Planet Earth*, by former tugboat captain Hal Lindsey, and C.C. Carlson. It was a bestselling book in the 1970s. *True Blood* creator Alan Ball recalls the effect that Lindsey and Carlson's book had on him as a child: "My mom started reading those creepy end-of-the-world books, like *The Late Great Planet Earth*, and I would come home from school, the eighth grade, and she would say, 'Another prophecy has come true, and we're this much closer to the end times,' and I would say, 'That's great. I'm fourteen, thanks for pointing that out.'"

During Reagan's run for a second term in 1984, he was quoted by Ronnie Dugger in the *Washington Post* as telling a lobbyist for the powerful American Israel Public Affairs Committee, "You know, I turn back to your ancient prophets in the Old Testament and the signs foretelling Armageddon, and I find myself wondering if—if we're the generation that is going to see that come about." This unsettling remark from a president with his finger on the button created quite a stir at the time.

Reagan populated his administration with theocons like Attorney General Ed Meese, active in the creationist Discovery Foundation Institute, and Secretary of the Interior James G. Watt, whose credo was: "We will mine more, drill more, cut more timber." Watt was a self-confessed fundamentalist. As he put it, "The Holy Spirit moved on my life." Like Sarah Palin, he was (or is) a member of the Pentecostal Assemblies of God, who look forward to the Second Coming. Unfortunately for him, it didn't come quickly enough to keep him from being indicted on twenty-five counts of perjury, unlawful concealment, and obstruction of justice.

Right-wing evangelicals gained even more influence under George W. Bush, who during a televised primary debate with his rivals delighted religious viewers and startled secular ones by asserting that the thinker who had most influenced him was Jesus Christ. In 2004, evangelicals accounted for an estimated 40 percent of the Bush vote. Bush famously said in a 1999 Republican presidential debate, "When you accept Christ as the Savior, it changes your heart. It changes your life."

The influence of fundamentalists is not limited to the Republican Party. Harry Truman was a Southern Baptist. Lyndon Johnson belonged to the Disciples of Christ. Carter was a Southern Baptist as was Clinton. In 1996, midway into Clinton's presidency, the nation's highest officials, a cross section of Democrats and Republicans, including the president, vice president (Al Gore), Senate president pro tem (Strom Thurmond), and speaker of the House (Newt Gingrich) were all Southern Baptists.

After being virtually ignored by Obama, white evangelicals now have unprecedented access to the Trump administration, even exceeding their sway with Reagan and G.W. Bush, starting next door to the top with Vice President Mike Pence, who has described himself as a "born-again, evangelical Catholic." Subsequently, he joined the Grace Evangelical Church. He has also said he is "a Christian, a conservative and a Republican, in that order." He rejects evolution in favor of intelligent design, saying, "I embrace the view that God created the heavens and the earth, the seas and all that's in them." Prior to the 2016 election, he was perhaps best known for signing an Indiana law that required aborted or miscarried fetuses to be buried or cremated. Ben Carson is a Seventh-day Adventist, and Betsy DeVos a Calvinist. Attorney General Jeff Sessions has called into question the separation of church and state.

You don't need a weatherman to parse the politics of the *Left Behind* series; they're right there on the surface. In the novels, Nicolae Carpathia, an obscure member of the lower house of the Romanian legislature, hops from there to the post of United Nations secretary general, courtesy of a cabal of international financiers, stand-ins for the George Soroses of the world. Preternaturally poised, charming, well-spoken (in nine languages), and fashionably attired in suits by Ermenegildo Zegna, Carpathia instantly becomes a media darling. He is the best that civilization has to offer. Which is the problem. In these thrillers, civilization is godless.

Carpathia is a self-described pacifist and "antiwar activist" who campaigns for disarmament using phrases like the "new world order"—conspiracy-speak for totalitarian world government. He envisions "raising the level of Third World countries so that the entire globe is on equal footing." Rejecting Europe's extremist legacy of Us/Them ethnic cleansing, he plans to craft a true international community from the patchwork of fractious nations. Flying the flag of tolerance, he says, "We can only truly be a global community by accepting diversity and making it the law of the land." He adds, "I believe we are about to usher in an almost utopian global society!" Carpathia supports assisted suicide, and not only proposes legalizing abortion worldwide but wants the international community to foot the bill!

Nobody thinks Carpathia's lofty ideas have a prayer of being adopted, but when he opens his mouth and flicks his silver tongue, the diplomats stop their squabbling and swallow everything he says. A word cloud based on his speeches would yield "harmony," "brotherhood," "peace," "respect," "global," "diversity," "international," "disarmament," "community," and "cooperation." But these are dirty words in LaHaye and Jenkins's lexicon. Rayford warns, "Whoever [comes] forward with proclamations of peace and unity had to be suspect." That could be anybody from Martin Luther King Jr. to Pope Francis, but here it is Carpathia, and of course he turns out to be the Antichrist, just a sulfurous snort short of Satan himself. Parenthetically, Satan is the bête noire not only of evangelicals, but of conservative Catholics as well. In Rome, Albanian Cardinal Ernest Simoni gives an annual course in exorcism, now in its thirteenth year, to clerics and lay people. According to the *New York Times*, he conducts exorcisms by cell phone, and claims that "black magic can be transmitted through screens ('American films are also a problem')," and that "demons enter the body 'through the back of the brain.'"

Before long, Carpathia sheds the fig leaf of public service. Now the most powerful man in the world, he seizes power. Although the left, like the center, pretends to embrace democracy, from the evangelical right's point of view, their democracy is a tyranny. Carpathia creates a world government, called the Global Community, and a new global religion that he calls the One World Faith. It is non-dogmatic, relativistic, and anti-supernatural. But Carpathia appoints a former pope to run it, thus revealing its true nature: top-down, hierarchical Catholicism that mediates between—that is, stands in the way of—the faithful and their God. The evangelicals, on the other hand, with their belief in the authority of personal testimony, have no use for mediation. They are populists, and they lay claim to being the genuine democrats. From where they stand, it's not only leaders preaching peace who are dangerous, it's leaders per se. According to an evangelical pastor, "We may get to the point where every leader is suspect." When someone flatters Rayford, saying, "You're the chief," our hero snaps back, "There's no time for hierarchy anymore."

In the absence of leaders, the evangelicals rely on the Four Horsemen of the Apocalypse, who are poised to lay waste to the mad docs and bad cops who threaten the far right, but when all is said and done, their worries are for naught. It turns out that the authorities of the center are no more than paper tigers. When the going gets tough, the tough get . . . Well, they just fade away.

# PART II

# WHO'LL STOP THE RAIN?

# 4
# Gone Fishin'

*Faced with vampires and zombies, mainstream authorities are either missing in action, as in* True Blood, *or just collapse in the face of the Other, as in* The Walking Dead.

There's no government, no hospital, no police. It's all gone.
—*Rick Grimes,* The Walking Dead

On an otherwise uneventful night in Bon Temps, no more than a bump on the swampy backside of Louisiana, vampire Bill saunters into Sam Merlotte's roadhouse on the outskirts of town. He conspicuously orders a bottle of Tru Blood, "B negative." Many of the patrons, who have never seen a vampire before, gag on their po'boys. Worse, they can't help but notice that when Sookie Stackhouse, the belle of Bon Temps, waits on his table, it's love at first bite—almost. She and Bill are the star-crossed Romeo and Juliet of *True Blood*, HBO's kinky, taboo-busting vampire series that ran from 2008 to 2014.

Bill is Bill Compton (Stephen Moyer), a 140-something-year-old "vamper," in cracker-speak, indistinguishable from a human save for his chalk-white flesh that's cold to the touch and an alarming habit of "dropping fang," that is, releasing needle-sharp incisors that descend with an ominous click when he forgets his manners in moments of stress or sexual arousal.

Sookie (Anna Paquin) finds Bill not a little frightening, but captivating nonetheless, and altogether more interesting than the trailer trash lunks of Bon Temps. Pronounced with a short "oo" so it sounds like "took," Sookie is a pint-size, spunky blonde with a button nose, skimpy skirts, a stand-up character, and last but not least, the ability to hear people's thoughts, a gift she possesses because, although she doesn't know it yet, she's only half-human. The other half? Fairy! As conceived by Charlaine Harris, who wrote the book series on which the show is based, Sookie is a Nancy Drew in hell, that is, an amateur sleuth who parses the crimes and bizarre events that plague Bon Temps.

Bon Temps is the Roswell of Louisiana. It is not only infested with vampires who give "redneck" a whole new meaning, but all manner of telepaths, werewolves, fairies, witches, and shape-shifters, not to mention a parade of spirits that treat their human hosts like time-shares. They are collectively called "supes." There are so many of them in Bon Temps that Sookie complains, "Every time I get my head wrapped around one kind of supe, a new one comes along. I barely know any regular humans anymore."

Not every human, however, is as kindly disposed toward supes as Sookie is. The white trash Rattrays, already seated in a booth when Bill walks in, lure him outside into the woods, where they "silver" him, that is, subdue him with silver chains, silver being kryptonite to vampires. The Rattrays intend to drain Bill of his precious bodily fluid, that is, his blood, which is highly prized for its restorative, not to mention aphrodisiac, properties. Sookie impetuously rushes outside to save him, but she is badly mauled in the process. Not to worry, however. Bill graciously offers to open one of his veins, and after a few lusty gulps, she's restored to her habitual perkiness. Unbeknownst to her, however, the exchange of blood between the sucker and the sucked creates a series-long bond between them.

As we saw in *The Martian* and *Hidden Figures*, in traditional centrist shows, American institutions operate as they should. Ditto Steven Soderbergh's expertly executed 2011 film *Contagion*, in which the national emergency is a worldwide pandemic, but a government agency—the Centers for Disease Control and Prevention (CDC)—is more than up to the task of quelling it. Rather than the cumbersome bureaucracy it would be in an extremist show, the CDC's size, like NASA's, is an advantage, because only an organization with its global reach can track the epidemic to its source, identify the virus, come up with a cure, mediate the competing agendas of various players to deliver it to the infected, and, most important, do it quickly, in the time it takes for a feature film to unreel. Big is beautiful. Far from a sluggish and unresponsive bureaucracy, the CDC is flexible and resourceful. Its experts grasp the big picture, in contrast to a village of Chinese peasants blinded by shortsighted local interests, who can only see the little picture, and therefore kidnap one of the principal scientists, momentarily frustrating the international effort to contain the plague.

*World War Z* (2013), like *Contagion*, is a traditional centrist movie, in which Brad Pitt saves the world from the zombie apocalypse. Here, too, the institutions of authority work just fine. A viral plague has turned millions of people into zombies, called "zekes." The campaign against them is run by soldiers and scientists who, in contrast to those in *Avatar*, say, are alive, well, and cooperating with one another, working at a fever pitch on an aircraft carrier parked somewhere off the East Coast. Like the effort to rescue Matt Damon in *The Martian*, the struggle to contain the virus is not just an American undertaking—it's globalized. The carrier is part of the "UN Atlantic fleet," lending the effort an international flavor. Institutions—the navy, the UN, and a lab full of epidemiologists—do the right thing. The UN assistant secretary general dissuades Pitt, his former top investigator, from trading his career for his family, that is, the general good for private interest, which is made to seem parochial and small-minded. Rising to the occasion, Pitt puts his family on hold and resumes his work for the UN. He locates Patient Zero and comes up with a cure.

Soldiers and scientists, docs and cops have almost always taken charge in A-list movies like *Contagion*, *The Martian*, and *World War Z*, as well as their TV counterparts, the prime-time network shows that have historically been bastions of mainstream values. David Chase labored in broadcast television for years before he created and ran *The Sopranos* (1999–2007) on HBO. "One of the things that I find problematic about the network shows," he explains, "is that they're all about institutions: You have the courthouse, the schoolhouse, the precinct house, the White House. There is this desperate need to prove that people in authority in our country actually have our best interests at heart, that they're not incompetent, but rather, dedicated. Some of them drink a little too much, some of them are womanizers, but basically, they really give a shit."

Cable television and the streaming services changed all that. Led by HBO, whose slogan was "It's not TV. It's HBO," they arose in reaction to the mainstream networks and were not subject to the FCC regulations that governed NBC, CBS, and ABC, so their shows often indulged in graphic violence, raw language, and explicit, if tasteful, sex. Regardless, many cable and streaming shows remained within the center, but a significant number wandered beyond its borders into the no-man's-land of extremism. In *The Sopranos*, the institutions and the agents of authority are either nonexistent or corrupt, and the same can be said about the rest of today's cable content, like, say, *Ray Donovan* (2013– ), in which the cops and FBI are thoroughly compromised, or Season 7 of *Homeland* (2011– ), in which the enemy may be jihadist terrorists, but just as often it is the CIA itself. As opposed to the network shows, there are no Officer Amys trying to close the book on the Four Horsemen of the Apocalypse as there is in *Sleepy Hollow*; no honest FBI agents to reassure us, as there are in *The Blacklist* (2013– ), *Criminal Minds* (2005– ), and *Bones* (2005–17); no honest cops to bring criminals to justice as there are in the myriad of *Law & Orders* (1990–2010), *CSIs* (2000–15), *Blue Bloods* (2010– ), etc. While Frank Underwood's ruthless pursuit of power is all too easy to believe in *House of Cards* on Netflix, Kiefer Sutherland's American president on ABC's *Designated Survivor* (2016– ) is so virtuous he defies credibility.

Shows like *True Blood* took advantage of the new freedom allowed by cable, especially premium cable. Although it remains in the center, it is dark and pessimistic. Mainstream institutions are conspicuous by their absence. There are no schools; no churches; no functional, organized infrastructure of any kind to enforce order, uphold generally agreed-upon standards of behavior, and defend society against internal and external enemies.

Worse, there is no government whatsoever, no feds, no Renard Parish board of supervisors, no mayors, no town councils, not even sanitation workers to mop the blood off the sidewalks—there are no sidewalks. Says Sam Merlotte, "I don't think even Baton Rouge knows who's in charge. And don't talk to me about Washington, because they sure as shit don't seem to care what's happening down here." There's not even a TRUST GOVERNMENT sign hanging in Merlotte's, like the one on a wall of Ray's coffee bar in *Girls* (2012–17), however ironically meant. It's not until the very last season that the governor finally puts in an appearance, and he turns out to be a bad, bad guy.

Sookie almost dies assisting Bill, but she is lucky to get a mouthful of his blood, because there is no one else to help her. Where are the cops? They're off duty, presumably at Merlotte's enjoying a cold brew, allowing the supes to treat the town like their own sandbox. The two rocks-for-brains sheriffs who do finally make an appearance—Bud and his bumbling, if endearing, deputy, Andy—are helpless, flummoxed by the crazy occurrences in and around Bon Temps, and hardly up to the task of dealing with the supes. In one scene, Bud not only releases the prisoners from his jail, he follows them out the door. The phone rings, but there's no one to answer it, just a recording echoing hollowly throughout the empty building. Later, speaking of the supes run wild, Sookie's brother, Jason, asks deputy Andy, "Should we think about getting the law involved?" Even he has no faith in the cops, replying, "The sheriff's station was wide open and empty. They ain't gonna help." He complains, "This whole town's gone to shit. Nobody has any respect for authority no more."

Vampires in extremist shows like *The Strain* (2014–17) suck blood in blue-state cities like the Big Apple, polluted as it is, in Ted Cruz's words, "with New York values." But centrist shows like *True Blood* are more comfortable working in the vein of Southern Gothic, regarding small, backwater towns in red states as quagmires of bigotry and superstition. Indeed, Bon Temps is less Mayberry than Twin Peaks, and then some.

Nevertheless, the breakdown of authority is by no means unique to Bon Temps. In *The Strain*, one of the heroic band of resisters says, "We believed we no longer had any predators. We believed in the primacy of science and technology. But forty-one days was all it took [before] mankind stood on the precipice of destruction."

By 2016, a Gallup poll showed that Americans' average confidence in fourteen key institutions had fallen to 32 percent. The plunge was led by banks, organized religion, the news media, and Congress. According to the 2018 annual Edelman Trust Barometer survey, conducted by a marketing consulting film, "The collapse of trust in the U.S. is driven by a staggering lack of faith in government, which fell 14 points to 33 percent among the general population . . . at a time of prosperity, with the stock market and employment rates in the U.S. at record highs."

During his presidential campaign, Donald Trump was repeatedly accused of trying to delegitimize American institutions, when for example, he called the election rigged. He is both a cause and a product of the erosion of trust in government. The shows discussed above preceded Trump. Before fake news and the filtering of information by social media, throughout the postwar era, the feds weren't doing themselves any favors. They were behaving in such a way as to confirm the darkening image of authority. Demolishing the hard-won credibility the government had earned during the Depression and World War II, General Dwight D. Eisenhower, who emerged a hero from that war and won the presidency in 1952, was caught with his pants down in the middle of his second term when he lied about sending a U-2 spy plane over Russia. He was forced to come clean only when the Soviets produced the pilot, Francis Gary Powers, in 1960.

Meanwhile, Hollywood, as we have noted, generously contributed its cycle of Red scare movies, On the left, in films like Marlon Brando's *One-Eyed Jacks*, released in 1961, the authority figure, in this case the sheriff, is the bad guy, and the outlaw (Brando) is the good guy. Nevertheless, the new, youthful president, John F. Kennedy, was still able to inspire Americans to make sacrifices when, in his inaugural address, he famously declaimed, "Ask not what your country can do for you—ask what you can do for your country." One of the things Kennedy did for his country was to launch the CIA's failed Bay of Pigs invasion that same year, during which the president assured the world that "this was a struggle of Cuban patriots against a Cuban dictator." He added, "We [have] made it repeatedly clear that the armed forces of this country would not intervene in any way." This, after the CIA had leased a private island off Florida, where it paid and trained a brigade of fourteen hundred Cuban exiles, furnishing them with eight B-26 bombers tasked with destroying Cuban airfields. To add insult to injury, Kennedy sent Ambassador Adlai Stevenson, who was unaware that the United States was behind this adventure, to deny it to the UN.

The much-quoted takeaway from *The Man Who Shot Liberty Valance* is "When the legend becomes fact, print the legend." But if the media were printing the legend, how could we trust them? This was fake news five and a half decades before our fake president coined the phrase. Two years later, President Lyndon Johnson faked the Gulf of Tonkin incident that served as the pretext for dispatching ground troops to Vietnam. Later in that decade, when American intervention failed to produce the desired result, Johnson initiated the so-called Optimism Campaign, the goal of which was to mislead the American public with overly optimistic assessments of every aspect of the Vietnam War, including body counts.

By the early 1970s, after half a decade or more of light-at-the-end-of-the-tunnel assurances and tens of thousands of U.S. casualties, not to mention a million-plus Vietnamese, a big chunk of the public no longer found the American authorities credible.

In 1972, five operatives working in one capacity or another for the Nixon White House, broke into the office of the Democratic National Committee in the Watergate complex in Washington, DC, while the president was preaching law and order to his hard hat constituents. He subsequently resigned before he was impeached. It's no wonder that the so-called counterculture welcomed movies that would have been judged extremist by the standards of the preceding decade. *One-Eyed Jacks* was the canary in the coal mine, followed by films like *Bonnie and Clyde* and *The Graduate*, both in 1967, as well as *Easy Rider* and *Butch Cassidy and the Sundance Kid* in 1969, in which it was okay to rob banks, shoot sheriffs, deal dope, and sleep with your girlfriend's mother. Political messages that had hitherto been hiding behind genre conventions were suddenly visible for all to see. Into the new decade, *The Godfather* (1972) presented the mob as an inviting alternative—at least for a time—to an indifferent, callous government. *Chinatown* exposed the sleazy history of water politics in Los Angeles two years later, and both *The Parallax View* in 1974 and *Three Days of the Condor* in 1975 were informed by a conspiratorial view of American politics that gained currency in the aftermath of Kennedy's assassination in 1963.

With confidence in government at a low ebb, the studios released a series of pictures that featured corrupt authorities putting profit before principle. In *The Towering Inferno* (1974), it was greedy developers who frustrated attempts to avert disaster. A year later, *Jaws* showed local officials in a seaside resort bullying police chief Roy Scheider into covering up shark attacks because they were bad for business. Watergate underlined the lessons of Vietnam and taught us that all those extremist movies were right: the government was not to be trusted.

Watergate had barely disappeared from the headlines when the Church Committee investigation revealed that the CIA and FBI used the same dirty tricks they routinely employed against foreign enemies and domestic crooks to smother legitimate dissent. Both Democrats and Republicans had lied for so long about so many things that what was left of the government's moral authority evaporated.

What with a decade of bipartisan malfeasance, from Johnson's Gulf of Tonkin incident to Nixon's plumbers, the left regarded the American government as the number one lawbreaker; to the right, by virtue of coddling crooks, it was the number one enabler of lawbreakers. Either way, it was the enemy.

As the 1970s bled into the next decade, resurgent Republicans, smarting from the humiliating defeat at the hands of "gooks," rewrote the history of the Vietnam years, casting them in a more pleasing light. We didn't lose that war; we were stabbed in the back, betrayed by the politicians who refused to fully commit American power to the battlefield. When Ronald Reagan defeated Jimmy Carter by a landslide in 1980, the newly empowered hawks regarded those who hesitated to nuke Hanoi as next door to traitors.

As the counterculture (women's lib, civil rights, free love, power to the people) was absorbed by the center, the door was opened to a backlash from the new corporate counter-counterculture. Hand in hand, Reagan and Rambo were only too happy to walk through it. But Reagan led to

George H.W. Bush and the Gulf War, which eventually led to George W. Bush and the Iraq War. When no weapons of mass destruction turned up, it was Vietnam all over again, and confidence in the authorities crumbled. As the reconstruction of Iraq bogged down in guerrilla warfare, and Afghanistan increasingly appeared to be a forever war, handed down from president to president like the keys to the White House, the lying continued. Meanwhile, it seemed like foreign adventures sponsored by the worthless government were sucking the lifeblood out of America, eating its heart and soul. We had fallen prey to vampires and zombies.

In 1897, Bram Stoker published *Dracula* and launched modern bloodsuckers on their way to fame and fortune. But vampire fiction languished until it found its natural métier in film, starting with *Nosferatu*, directed by F.W. Murnau in 1922. Once Bela Lugosi brought the Transylvanian count to life in Tod Browning's *Dracula* (1931), there was no turning back. Something like 250 vampire films have been released in the United States alone.

It's easy to see the appeal of vampires over zombies. Homegrown aliens, they are for the most part charming, debonair salonistas, the aristocrats of supernatural society. Were they to consume human food, instead of human blood, they would make engaging dining companions, equally at home in the drawing rooms of *Downton Abbey* (2010–15) or at the baccarat tables of *Casino Royale* (2006). In Jim Jarmusch's *Only Lovers Left Alive* (2014), they're finicky eaters who wouldn't be caught dead—so to speak—biting the necks of sweaty humans, preferring instead to sip blood from crystal stemware. Vampires are endowed with an impressive array of cool powers. They have superhuman strength and move with quicksilver grace at startling speeds—no sooner here than there, making a whooshing sound, like email flying from a tablet.

Vampires are the centrists of the supe world. Convention holds that they hang back, waiting politely to be invited into our living rooms. They want us to want them, a favorite technique of therapeutic social control. Preferring seduction to coercion, they like to get inside our heads so that their commands are experienced as our wishes.

Among the zombies, on the other hand, we have wandered far from the enchanted fairy tale world of *True Blood*, where razor-sharp fangs flash silver in the light of the full moon. Zombies are extremists. They don't care what we want. They just crash the party. Marauding in mobs, they huff and puff until they blow the house down. If the iconic image of the vampire features incisors buried in a creamy female neck, the iconic image of the zombie is a mass of undead pressed up against a picture window like cluster flies.

On the face of it, zombies bring little to the party other than lusty appetites and poor table manners, drooling, eating with their fingers, chewing with their mouths open, and dropping bits of flesh on their shirt fronts, all the while making unappealing gagging noises. They are ragged, awkward, and altogether charmless, unwashed and unkempt, the homeless who sleep in public parks and dark alleys among the garbage cans. They stagger, shamble, and shuffle after their human meals like unstrung puppets.

Modern zombies first made their mark back in 1968, with George A. Romero's classic *Night of the Living Dead*, in which the director abandoned the haunted houses and moldering castles that brought down property values in so many horror films and moved from remote locations into our backyard, so that horror could intrude—and reflect upon—contemporary life. *Night of the Living Dead*, with its hero—played by a black actor, Duane Jones—who is killed by the sheriff during a zombie hunt, turned the genre into a vehicle for social commentary.

More readily than vampires, zombies lend themselves to metaphoric interpretation; they are an all-purpose Them, with their significance in the eye of the beholder. The *New York Times'* Maureen Dowd referred to "Tea Party zombies," far right know-nothings who march in lockstep to the commands of the likes of Ted Cruz. For the right, they are the mob, the ragged, disheveled welfare cheats, the Occupy Wall Street riffraff.

If zombies are no more than slobs and schleppers, bottom-feeders, what then has made them the darlings of pulp culture? Explains *The Walking Dead*'s Robert Kirkman, "A story about vampires or werewolves is a story about people going through that transformation. But zombie stories are about human beings doing relatable things: protecting your family, finding food, building shelter." In other words, with no inner lives, these stories are less about zombies than about people.

Moreover, vampires are somewhat deficient in the end-of-the-world department. They are lonely hunters, far more selective than their undead cousins. Taking down their victims one by one, it would take decades before they could drain the entirety of the human race. Zombies, on the other hand, can credibly threaten our extinction. A zombie plague is the apocalypse in slow motion.

Playful virologists and epidemiologists have modeled zombie outbreaks as if they were pandemics. Given that there are so many variables—bite rate, rot rate, response rate, etc.—predicting the trajectory of a zombie plague is a highly speculative business, but none of the scenarios hold out any hope for our species. According to one such model, it would take only one zombie to wipe out a city. The best survival strategy is not fight, but flight, preferably to the Rockies, but if you have a boat, an island will do (not Manhattan).

Two small-town deputy sheriffs, Rick Grimes (Andrew Lincoln) and his partner, Shane Walsh (Jon Bernthal), join a high-speed chase southwest of Atlanta, Georgia. Rick is a by-the-book, straight-arrow cop, but there's no book for what he's about to face. He's wounded and taken to a hospital. When he awakens from a coma, he discovers that the flowers by his bedside have wilted and the hospital is eerily devoid of the doctors, nurses, and orderlies who customarily bustle about the corridors, torturing patients with needless tests to milk Medicare. He can't help but notice a half-eaten corpse lying on the floor. The walls are pocked with bullet holes and spattered with blood. He makes it outside, only to discover neat rows of lifeless bodies laid out on the ground in the hospital parking lot, near some abandoned National Guard helicopters.

Stumbling through a park, Rick is menaced by a woman whose face has been stripped to the bone, clawing her way crablike over the grass while dragging the remnants of her body—ribbons of flesh and a ribcage trailing what appears to be a string of sausages. Closer inspection reveals that they are not sausages at all, but her own entrails. Moreover, she appears to be dead, although that doesn't seem to be unduly hampering her forward progress. Rick looks around at figures staggering about with a peculiar, herky-jerky gate, trampling the bodies in front of them as if they're not even there. It quickly becomes apparent that they, like the disemboweled woman hauling what's left of herself across the ground, are neither dead nor alive: they're you know what—zombies.

*The Walking Dead* (2010– ) is a survivor show in which the zombie apocalypse has already arrived. Like the zekes in *World War Z*, the "walkers" or "biters," as they are called here, are the product of a virus that reanimates the dead and sends them lurching after the living, attracted as they are to the sweet smell of life, perfume to these pungent creatures. Everyone has been infected; the living are zombies waiting to happen, and when they die, they are themselves reanimated.

*The Walking Dead* has managed to become the most successful cable series to date. Why? The show is marred by lame writing, like this specimen of painful psychobabble—"You needed your space, and I didn't give it to you"—delivered by one character to another in hushed whispers, "as if they were narrating televised golf," in the words of *New Yorker* reviewer Emily Nussbaum. But thanks in part to its appealing cast, wildly creative special effects, and inventive exploitation of its humdrum premise, surprisingly, *The Walking Dead* works.

Fleeing the zombies and searching for his family, Rick is quickly reunited with Shane; his wife, Lori (Sarah Wayne Callies); their son, little Carl (Chandler Riggs); and a handful of others, including T-Dog, an African American (IronE Singleton); Daryl (Norman Reedus), a white trash biker with a heart of gold; Andrea (Laurie Holden), a tough blonde; and Carol (Melissa McBride), a dishrag who morphs into a fearless fighter, along with her daughter, Sophia. In other words, the survivors are a model of pluralism at work, a mix of men and women, white and (one) black, married and single, adults and children.

Rick runs into a survivor who explains that the authorities have issued assurances that the military has things well in hand and that "the Center for Disease Control said they were working on how to solve this thing." But the survivors discover that they have been seduced and abandoned. Having seen the body bags full of dead soldiers on the ground outside the hospital, Rick knows that the army doesn't have anything under control. The vaunted military is reduced to a junk pile of sophisticated but useless weapons. Black Hawks are down all over the place.

It quickly becomes apparent that the feds' highly touted technology is useless against the walker tide. The internet is offline. Cell phones don't work. The power grid has failed. The Emergency Alert System is silent. In spite of the efforts of the best and the brightest, the government is helpless. The message is: Don't look to Washington for help. Don't look to Obamacare, Trumpcare, Medicare, or any other kind of care. The government is simply overmatched.

If the soldiers are ineffectual, so are the scientists. Rick leads the survivors' caravan of vehicles on a dangerous journey through walker-infested territory to CDC headquarters in the hopes that the government's top brains will have come up with a cure for the disease, only to be disappointed again. Arriving at the gleaming, high-tech tower, the survivors find it virtually deserted. Mopey Dr. Jenner, the last brain standing, can describe the virus, but he can't prescribe, and he is ready to go down with the ship, in this case, the building, which is set to blow up when the emergency generators run out of fuel. They do, and he does, perishing inside a spectacular fire-ball. In other words, it's not the fear that science will kill us all that agitates mainstream shows like *The Walking Dead*, but rather the fear that science, along with its daddy, big government, will fail us. As Rick puts it, "There's no government, no hospital, no police. It's all gone." Like the inhabitants of Bon Temps, Rick and Co. are on their own.

Civil authority may be a dead loss or a no-show, and science useless, but what about faith? Can God hold up his end of the center? Eventually, *The Walking Dead*'s survivors make their way to Hershel Greene's farm. Hershel (Scott Wilson) is a soft-spoken, elderly, silver-haired veterinarian, a man of science, and since the walkers are victims of a virus, to him, they're sick, not bad. He clings to the liberal ideology of therapy. The survivors insist that the biters are dangerous, but he isn't so sure. "Schizophrenics are danger-ous, but we don't shoot them," he observes. Like Sookie, he is reluctant to stigmatize the Other. Likening the zombie plague to the devastation caused by AIDS, he says, "It's nature correcting itself, restoring some balance."

Along with his bleeding heart, Hershel has a pious spirit. He is a "man of God," in Rick's words, a believer in the turn-the-other-cheek teachings of the New Testament. Alas, in this show, Christianity seems to offer little solace. The survivors occasionally console themselves with scripture, but to little effect. Their plight just worsens. In one scene, they hear church bells in the distance and make a beeline for the Lord's house. They are greeted by walkers rising from the pews. Rick addresses a plaster Jesus, and confesses that he's not a believer.

The faithful among the survivors are repeatedly disappointed. In one scene, Hershel's daughter Beth tells redneck Daryl, "It wouldn't kill you to have a little faith." Daryl responds, "Faith? Faith ain't done shit for us." When T-Dog, one of the band of survivors' original members, gets bitten on the shoulder, he says, piously, "This is God's plan. He'll take care 'a me." But T-Dog dies in a particularly grisly way; the walkers tear him to pieces. If this was God's plan, God is not good. If it wasn't God's plan, God is not omnipotent. Either way, God loses.

Midway through the series, a Catholic priest confesses that he chained the doors of his church closed, preventing his parishioners, who were being chased by walkers, from entering the sanctuary. In Season 8, an entire episode is wasted on this same priest's efforts to get Negan (Jeffrey Dean Morgan), the despot who rules Seasons 7 and 8, to take confession. Negan does, sort of, and the priest absolves him of his sins, but it's an exercise in futility.

Rick accompanies Hershel on a walk around his spread, pausing at one point to admire the bucolic vista of farmland, woods, and distant hills that unfolds before them. Hershel explains that he finds God in their beauty. Rick confesses that "the last time I asked God for a favor and stopped to admire a view, my son got shot. I try not to mix it up with the almighty anymore. God's got a strange sense of humor."

It is no accident that the zombie apocalypse in *The Walking Dead* is caused by a virus, like mumps or measles, making it a natural, not a supernatural phenomenon, but that doesn't make it any less dangerous. It's instructive to compare the treatment of nature here to the way nature is presented in an extremist show like *Avatar* where it is an ally. Throughout *The Walking Dead*, we are treated to picturesque shots of flowers, verdant bowers, and majestic forests, but at best the natural world is no more than a backdrop, neutral, a passive spectator, never lifting a leaf to meliorate the pageant of human pain unfolding before it. It's no wonder that Rick is unimpressed by the beauty of Hershel's farm. He remains an unhappy tourist among nature's splendors. Indeed, the more splendid they are, the more like mockery it feels. Watching *The Walking Dead*, it is hard not to feel that nature has betrayed humanity. Says showrunner Scott M. Gimple, "Sometimes it feels [like] the walker apocalypse is the revenge of planet Earth."

Unlike *The Walking Dead*'s attitude toward its zombies, *True Blood* is far from unsympathetic toward its vampires. It wastes no time in exploding species profiling and upending our expectations about who is a vampire and who is not, underlining the mainstream lesson that They are not so different from Us. In an early episode, the creepy goth clerk behind the counter of a convenience store who flashes a set of sharp incisors turns out to be no more than a playful human with a mouthful of Halloween fangs, while the beefy customer in camos with a buzz cut and a neck like a fireplug, buys a six pack of Tru Blood, the newly invented Diet Coke of the vampire diet, a synthetic blood substitute bottled like soda for sale at bars and convenience stores. So much for appearances. He's the real deal.

*True Blood*'s vampires have heretofore kept to themselves, preferring to pass among humans unobserved, like Philip and Elizabeth Jennings, the principals of *The Americans* (2013–18), a "realistic" variation on the same theme: aliens among us. They sleep during the day and do their blood-sucking at night when humans are counting sheep. The vampires have even created their own parallel institutions that are no more than variations on human ones, such as a magazine (*Fang*), a radio station (KDED), hotels, websites, and a club called Fangtasia in nearby Shreveport.

Tru Blood is so much like the real thing that it not only gives vampires the option of going cold turkey on humans, but of passing for living people, of "coming out of the coffin," as one of them puts it. They can enlist in the army or even marry. In short, they can become candidates for the vital center, for inclusion and eventual assimilation.

Following the centrist formula for a stable society, the majority of mainstream characters are happy to have them. They try to accommodate as many of Bon Temps's freaks as are willing to take shelter beneath the big, pluralist tent. (It is worth noting that Charlaine Harris is an Episcopalian, and once remarked that she admired that denomination because it is "an inclusive church.")

Speaking of "coming out," the plight of vampires, unable to express the hunger that dares not speak its name, is repeatedly compared to, nay, equated with the struggle of gays for acceptance in straight society. The analogy is underlined by a series of allusions and wordplays, like the flash cut in the credit montage to a sign that reads GOD HATES FANGS, evoking "God hates fags." Lafayette (Nelsan Ellis) is a short-order cook working at Merlotte's. He is a hip, dope-dealing flamer who swings the other way, occasionally wears lipstick, and is no more than a thong short of being a full-out cross-dresser, which doesn't go over so well in Bon Temps. Even his mother hates him. She pretends he's dead, explaining, "God killed him because he's a faggot."

When Alan Ball, who scripted *American Beauty* (1999) and developed the long-running series *Six Feet Under* (2001–05), pitched the idea for *True Blood* to HBO, he was asked, "What is it about?" Ball replied, "It's about 'the tragedy of being a freak, a mutant.'" He continued, "What it really means to be disenfranchised, to be feared, to be misunderstood."

For Ball, the "tragedy of being a freak, a mutant" was to be gay. Born in 1957, the youngest of four children, Ball grew up in a small town, Marietta, Georgia, before it was cannibalized by Atlanta. He was nurtured on the storybook values of rural America. But something wasn't right. "I knew at a very early age that I was different," he recalls. "I was attracted to men. There was some sort of power there that I didn't feel towards women. I was terrified of that. I didn't want to be different. I knew that it was something that I needed to keep hidden. Because it was wrong."

Despite the show's gay undertow, given the superior powers and louche theatrics of *True Blood*'s vampires, it's not surprising that there's an epidemic of interspecies sex in Bon Temps. Many of the town's bored, fang-banging females would rather donate blood to hungry vampire studs than drink beer and eat fried chicken out of cardboard pails while watching the New Orleans Saints on TV with their dreary human boyfriends. Our Sookie is no exception. It may not be that surprising that she risks her life for Bill, but what is surprising is that the distrust, paranoia, and cynicism that permeate extremist shows have leaked into the mainstream, where they show up, somewhat diluted to be sure, as skepticism toward mainstream values bred of loss of faith in its institutions.

Driven by an overwhelming sense of existential dread, wherein death presses heavily upon the remnants of the living, *The Walking Dead*'s unhappy wanderers are forced to relinquish family, home, and place, roaming instead like nomads in an eternal present where there is no past, no future, no before, no after, just endless repetition. Dusk is upon them, and night is falling fast.

Carol's daughter, Sophia, strays from the survivors and disappears. Rick repeatedly launches search parties to look for her, while Shane, his darker doppelganger, insists that he is wasting the group's resources. Shane is a right-wing extremist, ready, if necessary, to kill the living as well as the dead. He thinks Rick is too soft to lead and tells him, "Survival means making hard decisions." "Hard decisions" are the either/or choices forced on centrists by extreme circumstances.

Rick is indeed a moderate, the Obama of the group. For him, consensus is more important than principle. Far from a rogue cop, he's the captain of a team, an organization man, which makes sense. In mainstream shows, there's safety in numbers. Anticipating Hillary Clinton's slogan "Stronger together," and Kevin Costner's "We all get there together or we don't get there at all," in *Hidden Figures*, Rick says, "We survive this by pulling together, not apart."

Rick and Shane fall out, and their differences quickly escalate into a debate over values. *The Walking Dead* asks the question, Can pluralism survive under extreme circumstances? Luckily for Rick, in a centrist show like this one, the answer is "Yes." Still, when Shane disputes Rick's decisions, Rick wavers. Wracked by self-doubt, he runs to his wife, Lori. Lori is the good wife, the loyal spouse, cherished as Carl's mother and pregnant with a new member of the Grimes family. If women like Dr. Grace in extremist shows like *Avatar* are often feminists, in mainstream shows they keep the home fires burning.. They are custodians of culture, guardians of civilized, that is, pluralist values.

In the same way that the show asks us to choose between Rick and Shane, it asks us to choose between Lori and Andrea, who is headstrong, fierce, and defiant, in other words, this show's feminist. When she finds herself relegated to the kitchen, she complains, "I don't want to wash clothes anymore. I want to help keep the camp safe." Critical of Andrea for trying to step out of women's traditional role, for her desire to help Rick and Shane et al. fend off the walkers, Lori puts her in her place with a speech that nicely summarizes the role of women like her in shows like this one. "The men can handle this on their own," she says. "They don't need you. We are trying to create stability. We are trying to create a life worth living."

Consistent with his belief that walkers should be treated, not killed, Hershel, like the good, God-fearing Christian he is, holds out hope that some spark of the humans they once were lives on in the walkers, even though their bodies are dead, no more than inert flesh. Hershel is a Cartesian. René Descartes was famous for his body/soul dualism, that is, for taking the position that the body is one thing—material in nature, likened to a machine—and the soul is another—separate, immaterial, and immortal.

Consequently, Hershel houses walkers in his barn, feeding them chickens to keep their tummies full. When his secret is revealed, he explains to the outraged survivors, "My wife and stepson are in that barn."

When the survivors find out just what it is that Hershel is keeping in the barn, the tensions that are simmering just below the surface come to a boil. Shane, who's fed up with bleeding hearts, shouts, "These things aren't sick. They're not people. Enough living next to a barn full of things that are trying to kill us." He breaks the lock on the doors. As the undead clamber out, moaning and gagging, the survivors form a firing squad and pick them off, one by one.

The walker who used to be Hershel's wife, Annette, doesn't recognize him, and Daryl blows her face off with a charge from his shotgun. Hershel's daughter, Beth, tries to minister to her, but mom grabs at her with ill intent and Andrea has to split her head open with a pickaxe.

Just in time to punctuate this lesson with an exclamation point, who or what should come shuffling out of the barn, the last walker of the bunch, but Sophia, snarling and spitting like the vile creature she has become. It's too much, even for Rick, who has been hanging back with Lori and Carl, reluctant to take his turn in the shooting gallery because, like Hershel, he hoped that the old Sophia might still be in there, somehow, or that she might still be wandering in the woods. He draws his gun, steps up, and pops her in the face.

The therapeutic model of social control dies with Annette and Sophia. The distinction that hopeful liberals make between the ill and the criminal is simply erased, proving that force is the only way to deal with the walkers. "You told me there was no cure, these people were dead, not sick," Hershel confesses to Rick. "I didn't want to believe you. But when Daryl shot Annette in the face and she just kept coming, that's when I knew what an ass I'd been. That's when I knew there was no hope."

Hershel, a moderate, was comfortable with the messy world of the walking dead, the liminal space between life and death occupied by zombies. When he recognizes that he should have cleared out his barn long ago and fried up all that chicken for himself and his living family, he becomes an extremist. He dons the polarizing glasses through which Shane sees reality, accepts the Manichean division of the world into good and bad, black and white, that is gradually characterizing the point of view of the survivors at this point in the series.

Disillusioned, pious Hershel even turns against religion. Comforting himself with whiskey, he tells Rick, "Christ promised the resurrection of the dead; I just thought he had something a little different in mind."

# 5
# Coming Apart

*On the left, the authorities are not just derelict or inept, they're fools and knaves, turning on heroes and superheroes who are helping humans by seeking justice.*

I was thinking about what [it] would do to Captain America, if he really came to terms with the stark fact that America in practice is different from the ideals of America.
—*Steve Englehart, writer,* Captain America *comics*

The original *X-Men* movie (2000), opens in Poland, 1944. Shrouded in darkness, a huddle of frightened men and women clutching their threadbare garments about them against the rain are prodded, pushed, and beaten by German soldiers as they trudge through the mud toward the entrance of a death camp. An occasional yellow star furnishes the only dash of color, but it just serves to accentuate the bleakness of the scene. Parents are separated from children. The guards seize a couple and drag them through heavy iron gates, slamming them shut behind them. Their young son, from whom they have been brutally torn, cries out and flaps his hand in the general direction of the gates. Remarkably, they bend and twist toward him, as if drawn by a powerful but invisible force. They are. The boy, Erik Lehnsherr, who will grow up into Magneto, has a way with metal. In *X-Men: First Class*, we're again back in 1944 Poland as Erik watches, horrified, as Herr Doktor Klaus Schmidt, the Mengele of the series, orders the guards to execute his mother right in front of him.

Like many of Marvel's superheroes, the X-Men are mutants, possessed of extraordinary powers that humans can only dream about. They can read minds, bend steel bars with their thoughts, incinerate distant objects with rays beamed from their eyes, teleport themselves through time and space, control the weather, shape-shift, and so on. You name it, they can do it. Consequently, humans have suddenly found themselves thrust into the inferior position vis-à-vis these *Homo superiors*, the same one that chimps and bonobos, or at best, Neanderthals occupy relative to humans. Regular old run-of-the-mill *Homo sapiens*, no longer the dominant species, have suddenly found themselves playing catch-up, and they resent it. Once we get to the extremes, then, the clash with the center becomes more explosive. The gloves are off.

Blockbusters have gotten a bad rep, one that can be attributed in part to aesthetic snobbery, combined with the studios' fear of original material lacking a built-in audience, and finally to superhero fatigue. Fat and bloated, and beholden to overseas markets, many of these movies have simply fallen victim to their own more-is-more DNA.

The past few years have seen considerable hand-wringing over this state of affairs, not only on the part of the entertainment commentariat and thoughtful independents like Steven Soderbergh, but also, surprisingly, from the Drs. Frankenstein of the blockbuster era, George Lucas and Steven Spielberg, looking with dismay upon the monsters they have created. As Lucas complained, "Now, if you do anything that's not a sequel, or not a TV series, or doesn't look like one, they won't do it."

Blockbusters have also been attacked on political grounds, as well. In *Birdman or (The Unexpected Virtues of Ignorance)*, Alejandro González Iñárritu's 2014 Oscar winner about a recovering superhero actor, several characters denounce the genre in no uncertain terms, and Iñárritu himself has called the superhero movies "very right wing," "poison," and "cultural genocide."

Iñárritu was too hasty. If culture in general amplifies the cacophony of clashing ideologies, then pulp culture, in which the commercial impulse looms largest, is particularly susceptible to the winds of political fashion, and is especially canny at anticipating them. But comic book movies are no different from any other genre. Superheroes are the darlings of the secular right, in part because they are the perfect pulp culture incarnations of Ayn Rand's incredibles, and the franchises certainly include their share of hard-right shows, but goody-two-shoes Superman is quite comfortable in the center, fighting for "truth, justice, and the American way."

Historically, most of the Marvel superhero narratives have leaned left, despite the occasional feint to the center or right. If the crisis in authority is the hole in the doughnut, the vacuum at the center of mainstream society, it's not surprising that way back in the 1930s it seemed, as it does now, that regular old humans just weren't up to doing the job that was called for, and it was then that the earliest superheroes, like Superman, first stepped up. He first appeared in Action Comics #1 in 1938. Two years later, with Germany on the march in Europe, the United States was still officially neutral when, on December 20, 1940, almost a full year before Pearl Harbor, Captain America appeared on the cover of Timely Comics, which eventually evolved into Marvel, socking Hitler in the jaw. He represented writer Joe Simon's and artist Jack Kirby's contribution to the propaganda effort on behalf of America's entry into the war. The cover was so controversial that the two men required police protection against pro-Nazi German American Bundists.

Marvel never quite outgrew its antifascist antecedents. World War II has always served as something of a touchstone for its family of superheroes—and it is a family, thanks to the orgy of intertextuality that has them trading characters, themes, and even scenes—so much so that it seems that all roads lead back to the struggle against fascism.

Perhaps because pulp culture so often trades in extreme situations, it is haunted by the Holocaust. Robert Kirkman explains that when he began writing The Walking Dead, "I did a lot of research on World War II and the Holocaust, because that was the most modern equivalent to what it would be like to survive in an apocalyptic setting."

Bryan Singer, who directed four X-Men films, is Jewish. Thus, it is not too surprising that the heroes of this series are equated with Jews in Germany. "I was very obsessed with the Holocaust as a child," he has said. "My fear of intolerance . . . [was that] someone might want to cut my head off . . . for just being myself."

Singer was also an orphan, like Erik, and gay. As he explained, echoing Alan Ball speaking about True Blood, "X-Men has always appealed to people who felt like outcasts." In the comics, superheroes discover their powers in adolescence, a detail that Singer found significant. "A gay kid doesn't discover he or she is gay until around puberty," he observed. "They feel truly alone in the world and have to find, sometimes never find, a way to live." Singer once asked Stan Lee, former president and chairman of Marvel Comics, if the mutants are, in his words, "gay allegory." According to Singer, "He replied, 'Yeah, of course.'"

Like True Blood's supes, the mutants of the X-Men series are portrayed as pariahs who are refused admittance to the mainstream so it's no wonder that freeze-dried in gay pride spandex tights, they are persecuted by the suits, uniforms, and lab coats. Nor is it a surprise that the "yellow sign people" with their lemon-colored JESUS SAVES placards picket Comic-Con, displaying messages that read GOD HATES MARVEL.

Later in *X-Men*, we see Senator Robert Kelly, author of the Mutant Registration Act, trying to out the mutants, despite their efforts to stay under the radar, like the vampires of *True Blood*. He waves a sheaf of papers over his head, sounding very much like Joe McCarthy brandishing a list of two hundred ostensible "known communists" at the State Department making his infamous speech in Wheeling, West Virginia, in 1950. Addressing a Senate hearing, Kelly bellows, "I have here a list of names of identified mutants living right here in the United States, mutants so powerful they can enter our minds and control our thoughts."

As it so happens, mutants *can* enter our minds and control our thoughts. Still Jean Grey, herself a closeted mutant, gamely rebuts him, pointing out that "mutants who've come forward and revealed themselves publicly have been met with fear, hostility, even violence." Indeed, when she leaves the hearings, she is greeted by a noisy mob bearing signs that read, variously, SEND THE MUTANTS TO THE MOON and PROTECT OUR CHILDREN.

Thus it is that death camps and McCarthyism, which may seem at first blush to be anomalous intruders in the Marvel universe, make cameo appearances. Part of Marvel's mission has always been to serve its adolescent, nerd audience by embracing outsiders, the victims of capricious and ultimately illegitimate adult authority.

Animus against outsiders on the part of the authorities is by no means confined to the *X-Men* series. In *The Avengers* the costumed supergroup that includes Marvel's finest—Iron Man, Thor, Black Widow, Captain America, et al.—saves New York City from an invading army of aliens known as the Chitauri. Pouring through one of those ubiquitous portals like water through a broken main and finding themselves in Grand Central Station, the Chitauri proceed to treat it like their frat house, partying so hard they smash the magnificent windows of the main concourse. During the ensuing battle, midtown Manhattan is nearly leveled. Despite the heroics of our superheroes, one politician demands that they pay for the damage. They are peppered with headlines that read "Avenger Hoax," the same way Spider-Man is pilloried in the Daily Bugle as "the Spider-Man menace," when he first slings his web in the Big Apple.

It's not just the odd politician or newspaper that attacks the Avengers.

All the institutions of authority are arrayed against them—from the president of the United States on down to the cops on the beat. "The more I try to help the law," complains Spider-Man in one strip, "the more they hunt me . . . the more they hate me!" In *Luke Cage*, the white authorities—prison guards, cops, in fact, every white person in the series, including the doc whose experiment gives Luke (Mike Colter) his powers—exceptional strength and immunity to bullets, the superhero version of acquiring a thick skin—are racists who torment him.

If the principle of authority is perhaps the most fiercely contested issue dividing the center and the extremes, and the extremes from each other, it is understandable, since it is the institutions of authority that legislate reality, define our world for us, tell us what is real and what is not, what is seen and what is unseen, and after so doing, frame perception and set the terms of discourse about that reality.

In *Avatar*, authority rests in the hands of the company, represented by Selfridge, and he in turn relies on the authority of the military as well as science and technology. But here they fail. Mostly, the two men look at screens while we watch them watching simulations of the surface of Pandora displayed on large monitors or rendered as shimmering, freestanding holograms. Unlike a centrist movie such as *Lion* (2016), in which Dev Patel uses maps, courtesy of Google Earth, to track down his long-lost mother, in *Avatar*, images on screens are misleading. What the suits and uniforms don't understand is that for the Luddite-left, technology is not a window into the real world; on the contrary, it is a curtain that obscures the real world.

According to commentators like Oxford University neuroscientist Susan Greenfield, older technologies like the printed word were a means to the end of learning about reality. With regard to new technology, on the other hand, Greenfield argues, "Instead of complementing or supplementing or enriching life in three dimensions, an alternative life in just two dimensions. . . . seems to have become an end in and of itself." Instead of providing a map of reality, they substitute for reality

In *Avatar*, Jake understands the difference between simulations of reality and the "real" thing, even if Selfridge and Quaritch, who have unknowingly created their own reality, do not. Onboard the *Venture Star*, Jake observes, "Everything is backwards now," adding, "Out there is the true world. Back here is the dream." He recognizes that "sooner or later, though, you always have to wake up."

Cameron dramatizes the discrepancy between the virtual reality available to Selfridge and Quaritch and the reality on the ground, known to Jake through his avatar. As Jake moves toward extremism, he sees that "real" reality is the opposite of their reality, driven as it is by wish fulfillment and the profit motive. It is a false reality, one that the corporate and military elite substitute for actual reality, and hence they have as little luck with it as George W., et al. had in Iraq with theirs.

Cameron isn't satisfied critiquing technology; he goes on to discredit the act of watching itself, the stance of scientific objectivity. Ten years George Lucas's junior, the wars in Iraq and Afghanistan played the same role for him that the Vietnam War did for Lucas. "This movie reflects that we are living through war," he said, referring to Bush's invasion of Iraq. "There are boots on the ground, troops who I personally believe were sent there under false pretenses."

Lucas likes to think of himself as a product of his times, and to a certain extent he is. Looking back on *Star Wars*, he reflected, "My ambition then was to . . . cause trouble, because I grew up in the '60s, I'm a '60s kind of guy." Indeed, the original *Star Wars* trilogy dramatizes an asymmetrical struggle between a ragtag band of guerrillas and a galactic empire, and the guerrillas win. Lucas once referred to Emperor Palpatine as "Nixon," which would make the evil Empire the United States and the Care Bear–like Ewoks who attack the lumbering Imperial Walkers with slingshots in *Return of the Jedi* (1983) the Vietcong guerrillas. Lucas said as much in 2005: "It was really about the Vietnam War."

When Lucas started out, he wanted to make non-narrative experimental films. He disliked studio movies and was intrigued by the so-called New Hollywood directors of the 1970s, subversives like Stanley Kubrick, Arthur Penn, and Robert Altman who were deconstructing genre. These men created barriers between audiences and the shadows on the screen, utilizing unreliable narrators, self-conscious camera work, and framing devices of various sorts that destabilized the fiction by calling attention to themselves, thus taking viewers out of the pictures and forcing them to question the narrative, interrogate the image.

Historically, spectators, almost by definition, are passive, and passive spectators are uncritical spectators. Uncritical spectators don't disrupt the status quo, shake up the center, or abandon the mainstream. During the 1960s, when the Vietnam War polarized the nation, the bubble of security that enveloped spectators was increasingly regarded as unconscionable. Spectators were derided as little better than voyeurs.

Haskell Wexler's intermittently effective *Medium Cool*, released in 1969 and set against the tumultuous Democratic National Convention of the previous year, opens with an arrogant, hard-shelled cameraman working for a local Chicago news show casually filming a car wreck. We hear an injured woman moaning off-camera as the soundman fiddles with the dials on his Nagra, more concerned with his levels than her injuries. Later, at a cocktail party, the guests debate the ethics of looking versus acting. At the end, the cameraman loses control of his car, drives into a tree, and his companion dies as the vehicle bursts into flames. In the heavily ironic but nonetheless effective penultimate scene, help seems to be on the way as another car approaches. Instead of stopping, however, a man leans out of the window with a camera, snaps a picture, and drives on.

The *Hunger Games* franchise (2012–15), the cycle of four movies based on Suzanne Collins's YA novels, presents an entire society wherein spectating has become the primary method of social control. The apocalypse has already happened, as it has in *The Walking Dead*. Its nature and cause go unnamed in the movies, but in the print version, it appears to be something very much like climate change: "the droughts, the storms, the fires, the encroaching seas that swallowed up so much of the land, the brutal war for what little sustenance remained."

Collins has said, "It's crucial that young readers are considering scenarios about humanity's future. . . . About global warming, about our mistreatment of the environment, but also questions like: How do you feel about the fact that some people take their next meal for granted when so many other people are starving in the world?"

The capital of Panem, the country that has risen from the ashes of the nameless apocalyptic event, is home to the 1 percent, and tyrannizes over twelve vassal districts that accommodate the 99 percent, who subsist on a barter economy heavily dependent on hunting and gathering. It is their job to feed the seat of government. The inhabitants of the districts are treated like serfs, forced by their masters into an exploitative relationship with nature. Living off the land is far from the picnic it is in *Avatar*. Starvation is rampant. Nevertheless, they enjoy a kinship with nature that couldn't be more foreign to the artifice flaunted by the capital's decadent few. The capital sponsors a nationwide reality show meant to distract Panem's restless population by turning them into passive spectators.

Impugning the integrity of spectators, as Cameron, Collins, and the directors of the *Hunger Games* films do, is a bold move, because historically, their position has been unassailable, thanks to their affinity with movie audiences. Ever since the naïve patrons of the first silents dodged bullets that appeared to be fired directly at them and were relieved to discover that they weren't real, conventional cinema has depended upon a comfort zone created by just this safe remove. Enjoying the jolt that movies can provide depends on ping-ponging between naïve identification with the action on the screen and the knowledge that we ourselves are not being maimed and mutilated, making it possible for spectators to appreciate the aesthetics of disaster, thrill to the rush of danger dramatized but not directly experienced. Lucas and Spielberg preferred passive spectators comfortable with this illusion.

Perhaps it's too harsh to blame them for the avalanche of junk that followed in their footsteps, but the fact remains that today, we are still prisoners of the funhouse they built. As Joss Whedon, director of *The Avengers*, put it, "I regret the advent of Spielberg's worldview as much as the next person, even though I revere a lot of his work, because it took us to this nostalgic, fantastical place that ultimately led to the comic book era."

If the authorities regard the superheroes with suspicion, ridiculing Spider-Man and the Avengers, the superheroes return the favor. Needless to say, the American government is a fat target. In film after film, it is rife with rot, starting at the top. In *X-Men: Days of Future Past*, President Richard Nixon buys into the Sentinel program—an army of super-robots engineered to turn the mutants' powers against them—while in *Iron Man 3* (2013), the villain accuses POTUS of protecting oil company executives whose tanker, in an apparent allusion to the *Exxon Valdez* spill, dumped a million gallons of crude off the coast of Florida (instead of Alaska). Confronting the president, he charges, "Thanks to you, not one fat cat saw a day in court." POTUS never rebuts him. When the bad guy scores points off the president, there's a real problem. Worse, the vice president is in on a plot to kill his boss, hoping to succeed him in the Oval Office.

If the Executive Branch is riddled with corrupt and/or subversive officials, so is Congress. At one time or another, sundry superheroes are dragged before congressional committees to be grilled and bullied. Tony Stark, a.k.a. Iron Man, animated by Robert Downey Jr.'s droll performances, constantly clashes with the government. In the first installment, *Iron Man* (2008), the youthful owner of Stark Industries, inherited from his father, visits Afghanistan for the purpose of selling weapons and is captured by a brutal, Taliban-loving warlord. Tony builds an armored suit out of scrap metal—a crude prototype of Iron Man—that is serviceable enough to effect his escape from the goatherds armed with AK-47s who are guarding him.

Tony is an inveterate tinkerer, and back home in his multilevel Malibu Xanadu, he can't help but tweak that suit. Eventually, it molts into a burnished burgundy-and-bronze affair with slits for eyes that glow with a cold white light like halogen lamps, and it is tricked out with an assortment of accessories, including jet boots that enable him to fly and lethal repulsor rays that flash forth from the gauntlets that enclose his hands.

This is all well and good, but the feds are not amused. In the sequel, *Iron Man 2*, Tony tangles with a U.S. senator, played by Garry Shandling, chairman of the Senate Armed Services Committee. Red-faced and puffed up with patriotic fervor, Shandling announces, sententiously, "My priority is to get the Iron Man weapon turned over to the people of the United States of America."

There was a time, during the Cold War, when Tony would have clicked his heels, saluted the flag, and handed over the merchandise without a second thought. In one of the comics from that period, he says, "No one has the right to defy the wishes of his government! Not even Iron Man!" But no longer.

In the years that followed, Marvel charted a zigzag course, chasing the zeitgeist. During the Vietnam War, it was caught up in the falling-domino hysteria—if Vietnam went communist, there went Southeast Asia. Captain America, the Marvel character most closely identified with the American military, was doing his best to defeat the Vietcong. Stan Lee, who, along with Jack Kirby, became the principal creative force behind Marvel's most popular series, explained, "[We] genuinely felt that the conflict . . . was a simple matter of good versus evil." But as the war dragged on, he also understood that much of his soon-to-be-draft-age audience was turning against it. Marvel finally came to terms with the fact that it had a deeply polarized following and decided that neutral was the best gear for business.

Villains on the extreme right were balanced by villains on the extreme left, like Firebrand, a Weatherman-like character in the *Iron Man* strips who had an itch for violence. In 1968, Iron Man devoted himself to righting less controversial domestic evils like racism and poverty, while staying clear of Vietnam and other Cold War hot buttons that he used to find irresistible.

Still, in 1974, a year before the war's end, when Nixon's dirty tricks were revealed, Captain America discovers that the president, here called No. 1, but clearly Nixon (his aide is named "Harderman," after Nixon aide H.R. Haldeman), is the leader of the so-called Secret Empire, a cabal of Nazi plotters known as Hydra. "I was reacting to Watergate," said Captain America writer Steve Englehart. "There was no way Captain America could just keep fighting the Yellow Claw with that going on." At the shocking end of the series, Captain America tracks him down to his office in the White House, whereupon No. 1 commits suicide.

As the story concluded, continues Englehart, "I was thinking about what that would do to Captain America, if he really came to terms with the stark fact that America in practice is different from the ideals of America." The result was that Steve Rogers, Cap's not-so-secret identity, is so disillusioned that he repudiates Captain America in favor of a new superhero unaffiliated with America, called Nomad. Eventually, of course, he returns to Captain America, with the proviso that although he fights for America's ideals, he doesn't necessarily support its government.

During the George W. Bush years, Cap broke his vow. In 2005, along with Spider-Man, he put in an appearance with Donald Rumsfeld at the Pentagon to flack a comic book aimed at the troops in Iraq.

At the end the first decade of the new century, Marvel again veered left. "The readers—the young readers—if there was one thing they hated it was war, it was the military, or, as Eisenhower called it, the military-industrial complex," explained Lee. Returned from Afghanistan, Tony can't shake the images of American GIs—forget the Afghanis—maimed or killed by weapons bearing the stenciled logo of Stark Industries that have fallen into the wrong hands. "The political climate . . . [was] mirroring . . . the 60's when [we were] on the cusp of Vietnam," recalled *Iron Man* director Jon Favreau. It was "unpopular to have an arms manufacturer as your hero." Favreau explained that his superhero "reflected the politics of the day." Therefore, Tony takes his company out of the weapons business, making a stand, in effect, against that very same military-industrial complex.

No longer an anticommunist, Iron Man had become something quite different. When *Iron Man 2* was released, facing down Senator Shandling in those Senate hearings, Tony refuses to turn his invention over to the feds. He snaps, "Forget it." He's so contemptuous of Congress that he calls Shandling an "ass clown."

As it turns out, Shandling is something far worse than an ass clown. His patriotic rhetoric is compromised by the fact that he is revealed to be an agent of Hydra. Indeed, the entire U.S. government is honeycombed with operatives of Hydra, which started out, prior to World War II, as a division of the Waffen-SS and has since evolved into a multitentacled global organization. Hydra permeates the Marvel universe, making an appearance in both *Avengers* films and driving the plots of three *Captain America* movies.

With Shandling at once a senator and a Hydra mole who hides his true allegiance under the cloak of patriotism, *Iron Man 2*, in effect, equates the two roles. Our government, in other words, is run by Nazis. Worse still, the Avengers take their orders from S.H.I.E.L.D., the series' version of the Department of Homeland Security, which in turn answers to the World Security Council and its president, Robert Redford, who is also a Hydra agent. When he crosses paths with Shandling, they greet each other, sotto voce, with "Hail Hydra," a none-too-subtle echo of "Heil Hitler" and a prescient forecast of the "Hail Trump" salute delivered by the alt-right.

In 2014, directors Anthony and Joe Russo updated Cap's apostasy in *Captain America: Winter Soldier*, wherein Redford is outed, and S.H.I.E.L.D. exposed as little more than a Hydra front organization. According to screenwriter Christopher Markus, the point was to show Captain America (Chris Evans) "losing faith in all the institutions that had made him." When S.H.I.E.L.D. proposes blanket surveillance of American citizens "to neutralize threats before they even happen," Cap, sounding like a spokesman for the American Civil Liberties Union, replies, "I thought the punishment came after the crime. [You're] holding a gun to the head of everyone on Earth, and calling it protection."

Later, in an attempt to reveal the dimensions of the threat Hydra represents, Natasha Romanoff, a.k.a. Black Widow (Scarlett Johansson), goes all Snowden, stealing and then dumping S.H.I.E.L.D.'s top secret Hydra files onto the internet. Predictably, she's hauled in front of one of those congressional committees for whom our superheroes are catnip. A high-ranking army officer threatens her, saying, "There are some people on this committee who think you belong in a penitentiary, not mouthing off on Capitol Hill." Trump might have called her "Leaking Natasha," but the film is on her side, not theirs or his.

Over at DC Comics, even Superman couldn't avoid political entanglements. In 2011, David S. Goyer, best known for the scripts to the *Dark Knight* series, created a scandal by writing a story for the nine hundredth edition of Action Comics in which Superman turns his back on America. The target of protests for joining a demonstration in Tehran against government repression, Superman says, "I'm tired of having my actions construed as instruments of U.S. policy. Truth, justice, and the American way—it's not enough anymore."

Reflecting the widespread disillusionment with Bush's wars, as well as the growing foreign market for DC's product—both movies and comics—Superman goes before the United Nations to renounce his citizenship so that he can represent the global community, not just the United States. Of course, flinching from brickbats thrown by outraged fans, DC walked the story back in less than a week. Nevertheless, in *Batman v Superman: Dawn of Justice* (2016), Superman is called to testify before yet another congressional committee to justify his behavior, but before the gavel comes down, an explosion kills everyone in the chamber. Only Superman is spared, making him again the target of suspicion.

Back in in the 1970s, Lucas and Spielberg quickly realized that attacking the authority of genre in a popular medium like movies, albeit fun while it lasted, was virtually suicidal. They tried the opposite tack. Reconstructing the deconstructionists, they proceeded to dump the first shovelful of dirt onto the coffin of the New Hollywood. They strived to create the impression that their movies were not authored, that they were just there, or better, weren't there at all, no more than windows on the world, that is, unvarnished reality. Lucas regarded any trace of self-consciousness as a blemish. When Harrison Ford told him, "You can type this shit, George, but you sure can't say it," Lucas insisted that dumb or not, he couldn't play it for camp humor.

Despite the antiwar thrust of the original *Star Wars* trilogy, Lucas was no crusader. Tired of the turmoil of the Vietnam era, he seemed to welcome President Jimmy Carter's program of reconciliation aimed at ending the decade-long estrangement of the flower children from their parents. Lucas and Spielberg were nostalgic for the black hat and white hat melodramas of the studios' golden age. They gentrified, if you will, the shopworn Saturday afternoon cliffhangers of the 1930s with an eye to countering the dark, unsettling films that characterized the New Hollywood. In *Star Wars*, Lucas set out to make "a kids film," explaining, "Everybody's forgetting to tell the kids, 'Hey, this is right and this is wrong.'" He intended his trilogy, in his words, to "introduce a kind of basic morality."

Predating Bush and Rumsfeld by a quarter of a century, and speaking of movies not war, Lucas anticipated viewers' delight in "shock and awe," or, in his words, "awe" and "wonder." A good deal more benign than his

Republican successors, he, along with Spielberg, nevertheless bombarded viewers into submission with spectacle, with sights and sounds in an effort to return them to the naïve state of silent film audiences, to restore them to the innocence of childhood. In effect, Lucas and Spielberg reestablished the authority of mainstream cinema.

Neither of the two directors had any interest in exploring the morality of spectating. Rather, Lucas in particular ignored the morality and exploited the spectating. At its heart, *Star Wars* doesn't seem to care much about the Vietnam War nor even in teaching kids right and wrong. It does care about the spectacular dogfights in deep space, where it matters little which fighters belong to what side—Rebel Alliance or Empire, Jedi or Sith—so long as they traverse the big screen at high speeds, flashing colorful lasers at targets moving swiftly against a pitch-black background.

By harnessing the aesthetics of disaster, Lucas, anticipating Christopher Nolan, foregrounds the pictorial, the image itself, shorn of context, be it ideological, historical, or social, thereby introducing a conservative strain into the *Star Wars* trilogy so powerful that it overwhelms its anti-imperialist message. It's as if his script is telling us one thing while his camera is telling us another. Although Lucas was unhappy when Reagan dubbed his anti-missile shield "Star Wars," there was a certain poetic justice to it.

Having been a teenager during the worst of the Vietnam conflict, as well as a Canadian, Cameron seems to have been unaffected by the quietism of the Carter years that lulled Lucas to sleep. The ideological project of extremists like Cameron was to challenge the mainstream by attacking the claims of science and technology to accurately portray reality. But they needed to go further. They had to turn centrists into extremists, persuade them to get off the fence and fight for the right (or in Cameron's case, left) cause. According to Michael Cieply, writing in the *New York Times*, the filmmaker "said he had deliberately designed 'Avatar' to move the masses with a kind of emotional appeal that documentaries like 'An Inconvenient Truth' and his own undersea adventure films could never deliver." Therefore, *Avatar* extends its critique to the act of spectating itself, that is, watching and seeing.

For Cameron, spectators are indeed little better than voyeurs, bystanders on the side of the road taking vicarious pleasure in gawking at a pileup of cars. But his activist agenda—"*Avatar* asks us all to be warriors for the earth"—is urgent and overt, driven by adversarial fervor. It requires that he alarm and persuade, alarm *to* persuade. In other words, he turns spectators into actors, and not only spectators watching the movie, but spectators within the movie as well; he forces the likes of Dr. Grace and Jake Sully to choose sides.

With *Avatar*, Cameron did his best to drag *Star Wars* into the world of adults, so to speak. It is his anti–*Star Wars*, his revision of the revisionists, a return, of sorts, to the concerns of those innovative New Hollywood directors. As Lucas put it, somewhat plaintively, "He's trying to challenge [me]."

Of course, Spielberg and Lucas, like Cameron, also convert spectators to actors; witness the aptly named Han Solo transformed, *Casablanca* style, from a cynical loner to a leader of the rebels in the original trilogy. But their characters grow down, not up. Adults in their films, like spectators, tend to support the status quo, the world as it is. Children are the rebels, the extremists, and their radical innocence contrasts dramatically with the corruption and cynicism of their elders.

In keeping with Spielberg's and Lucas's project, which is to infantilize the audience, they infantilize characters within their movies as well. In *Close Encounters*, Richard Dreyfuss is heroized for preferring to chase flying saucers rather than spending time with his own family. He shrugs off his domestic responsibilities to build a tower out of mashed potatoes that eventually leads him to the visitors from outer space, for whom he abandons his wife and children altogether.

In *Star Wars*, the adult is Darth Vader, pitted against his own son, Luke Skywalker. Lucas takes pains to make sure that Luke remains a child. He short-circuits the potential romantic triangle between Luke, Han, and Princess Leia by making him her brother, so that adult sexuality is denied him. His asexuality is underlined by having daddy Darth slice off his hand in the course of their light-sword duel, suggesting you know what. Nevertheless, Lucas can't resist orchestrating a reconciliation between generations, father and son, that would have made Jimmy Carter happy. In effect, they kiss and make up, leading his films back to the center.

Ultimately, *Star Wars* can't decide whether Luke is an innocent child or a guilty adult. Not only does the camera contradict the script, but the script contradicts itself. It's a perfect Carter-era film, poised between the antiwar movement of the 1960s and the right-wing reaction of the Reagan years. Lucas may consider himself "a '60s kind of guy," but he was a '70s going on '80s kind of guy as well.

By the time we get to *Avatar*, on the other hand, the confusions that cloud *Star Wars* are resolved. The conflicts between father and son in

*Avatar* are more profound, too profound to be settled with a hug and a kiss. Jake eventually succeeds in separating from the older man, achieves the ability to think for himself. Not only is there no reconciliation between the two, but the romance that is suggested between Jake and Neytiri seems ripe for fruition in the sequels. Jake grows up, not down. Adulthood, which is admirable in the mainstream, remains questionable in the extremes, but as we shall see Jake doesn't remain an adult very long.

# 6
# Draining the Swamp

*On the right, Jack Bauer, Batman, and evangelicals declare war on aliens and mainstream authorities—terrorists and atheists all—in the name of God, family, and country.*

> Jack Bauer saved Los Angeles. . . . He saved hundreds of thousands of lives. Are you going to convict Jack Bauer?
> —*Justice Antonin Scalia, U.S. Supreme Court*

We're watching a bustling street scene in which women wearing head scarves speaking an unfamiliar tongue are picking through the stalls in what could be a bazaar in the Casbah, but a title tells us it is East London. Three men are pushing through the crowd. They're not Muslim, and they're not shoppers. A fourth man, lying under a blanket, apparently homeless, emerges long enough to toss what looks like a small barbell under a partially raised garage door. It rolls across the floor.

*24: Live Another Day* (2014) is a so-called encore presentation, arriving four years after its mother ship, *24*, which occupied our screens from 2001 to 2010 on the Fox network, aired its not-so-final season. Like *Live Another Day*, *24* starred Kiefer Sutherland as rogue antiterrorist agent Jack Bauer.

Cut to a large, redbrick factory building that has been repurposed to serve as the CIA's London Station. The station chief, eyes glued to a monitor, asks no one in particular, "Are we on real-time tracking?" One of the no one's chirps back in surveillance-babble: "Backdooring off a satellite the Brits have overhead." The chief looks at an image of a vast indoor space, delivered by the remotely controlled barbell. What is he looking for? "We got a tip that a high value suspect is here in London," someone explains. Meanwhile, the three agents on the street, guns drawn, enter the space. A man wearing a black hoodie springs from the floor and clocks one of the agents, while another agent announces the obvious: "Target's on the run." The target effortlessly overcomes another handful of agents who appear out of nowhere. The station chief cranes his neck to see the face beneath the hood and exclaims, triumphantly: "It's him, Jack Bauer!" Indeed, Jack is back.

The secular right tends to be identified with small government Tea Party values when out of office, but once in office, it is by no means allergic to a robust state, if its powers are confined to strengthening the police and the military, protecting our global interests, and ensuring its own grip on power. Although Donald Trump's America First version of the secular right embraces isolationism and rejects the big stick overseas, in other respects it is comfortable with Republican orthodoxy and follows in the footsteps of George W. Bush's neocons—Vice President Dick Cheney, Secretary of Defense Donald Rumsfeld, and Deputy Secretary of Defense Paul Wolfowitz—currently out of favor for having bequeathed us the mess in the Middle East. All of them advocated enhancing police powers abroad and at home, including torture and blanket domestic surveillance at the expense of civil liberties. The secular right's portrayal of mainstream authority and its institutions is as harsh if not harsher than it is on the far left.

In the real world, the rise and fall of George W. is yet another illustration of the crisis in authority. Bush forged a new consensus around 9/11, made up in equal measures of the Killer Ps—piety and patriotism—but he undermined it nearly as fast as he built it. It took the Vietnam War and Watergate over a decade to shred confidence in the American government, but Bush managed to do it in less than half the time. According to a Gallup poll, the former president's personal approval rating peaked at an astonishing 90 percent after the attack on the towers. By the time he left office, in January 2009, it had slid to 33 percent, and confidence in Congress had plummeted to a microscopic 7 percent by 2014.

Jack Bauer was employed by the U.S. government's Counter Terrorist Unit (CTU) to neutralize America's enemies, a nasty bunch of Russians, Chinese, and Muslim terrorists. In the process, he became so popular that bumper stickers wondered, "What would Jack do?"

24 more or less spanned Bush's two terms. It was the show mostly closely associated with his policies, and it was considerably more successful than he was. In fact, it influenced his policies. Administration officials were infatuated with 24, appearing to mistake it for a documentary. According

to Dahlia Lithwick, writing for *Newsweek*, Michael Chertoff, the secretary of homeland security, on a panel devoted to *24* sponsored by the Heritage Foundation, said it "reflects real life." On another occasion, in an interview, Supreme Court Justice Antonin Scalia defending torture, went further: "Jack Bauer saved Los Angeles. . . . He saved hundreds of thousands of lives. Are you going to convict Jack Bauer?" After Osama bin Laden was killed, Jack trended in the Twittersphere as ranks of tweeters showered him with gratitude as if he'd been part of the operation himself. So often had like actions been portrayed on the show, he might as well have been.

*24* dramatized a different end times scenario every season, whether it be a planet-scrubbing bioterrorism attack, the nuking of Los Angeles, or a nefarious attempt on the life of the president. It used the war on terror as a pretext for the establishment of the surveillance state. The apocalyptic dangers the show so vividly staged served to justify a panoply of Bush policies. Were it not for Jack's aversion to bureaucracy, *24* would have rung every note in the neocon songbook.

During the four-year gap between the end of *24* and *Live Another Day*, CTU was disbanded, and the CIA had picked up the slack. Even when he was working for CTU, Jack habitually tangled with his bosses, who at best were a bowl of mixed nuts, incompetent and occasionally downright malevolent. As a consequence, he always had one foot out the door in a right-wing no-man's-land where anything goes. Jack never met a law he couldn't break, or rather, he acknowledged no law except his own. He operated on the far fringes of legality, crossing the line, coming back, and crossing the line again. The Bill of Rights was collateral damage in the war against terror; his mantra was "By any means necessary."

In the 2010 series finale of *24*, things went sideways in a big way. Carrying on a vendetta against the Russians, Jack orchestrated a bloodbath in the course of which he killed the foreign minister along with his bodyguards, and he plotted the execution of the Russian president, all in revenge for the murder of his partner, who happened to be his girlfriend as well. As someone puts it, he "went on a revenge spree, killing and mutilating with no regard for the law or conscience." Even for him, he went too far. A hunted man, he dropped off the map.

When Jack resurfaces in *Live Another Day*, he is still on the run, and has been branded a terrorist by the State Department. He looks like he's spent the intervening four years sleeping in doorways and back alleys. His face is pinched and drawn. The spring has left his step. We can't help wondering whether his distaste for a fixed address is going to make it impossible for the post office to deliver his monthly Social Security check. Still, even a diminished Jack is more than a match for the CIA.

The agency may stumble over its own feet, but it means well, right? Wrong. We expect terrorists to be terrorists, but the CIA? Here, the London station chief is selling American secrets to the Chinese. Worse, he frames one of his own agents for the leaks, and that agent subsequently commits suicide. The chief impedes efforts to track down the terrorists by blaming Bauer, and sidelining or misdirecting his best agents.

Jack becomes the CIA's number one target. As the encore series opens, he is captured, or rather, allows himself to be captured, because in this show, government agents are bumbling fools, hardly up to nabbing a pro like him. Naturally, he has his own agenda, which is to free nerdy Chloe O'Brian (Mary Lynn Rajskub), who loyally supported him throughout those eight seasons by sitting at her workstation frowning and chewing her lip while spitting out facial recognitions and schematics as if she had digital Tourette's.

Bitter about being tossed out on her butt after so many years of loyal government service, Chloe has thrown in with the likes of Julian Assange. Fitted out in full goth (the producers seem to have confused WikiLeaks with Columbine), complete with a hank of brand-new dark hair, tats, and a long black coat, she has turned into a "free information hacker," poking holes in government security and stealing confidential information. She has made ten thousand classified Department of Defense documents public. Even on the run from his own government, Jack remains a loyal American, railing against Chloe and stoutly defending official secrecy. Still, when she's captured and tortured by the CIA, he risks his life to save her.

In far-right shows like *24*, even as they pay their respects to the security state, as that state stumbles and bumbles, they venerate individualism. Fewer are better than more. Elite SWAT teams made up of highly trained, heavily armed black-clad killers were once touted as the authorities' most lethal crime-fighting units, especially when compared to the sluggish metro police departments, but they became victims of mission creep and grew in size until today, they have become symbols of a heavy-handed, out-of-touch, last-to-know bureaucracy. Time and time again, the CIA's elite antiterrorist units break down the wrong doors of the wrong homes, cuffing or killing the wrong people. In Season 2 of *Homeland* (2012– ), best described as the thinking man's *24*, not too surprising since several *24* alums developed that show, the CIA's SWAT team descends on a dry cleaners in suburban Maryland where a dangerous terrorist is supposed to be hiding, but by the time they arrive, all they find is clean clothes.

*Homeland*'s Carrie Mathison (Claire Danes) shares a libertarian streak with Jack. The arithmetic of pluralism means nothing to them. Neither is a team player. Although both are dedicated to protecting their country, Jack behaves as if he agrees with Margaret Thatcher, who voiced a right-wing credo when she famously said, "There's no such thing as society. There are individual men and women and there are families." Carrie even violates the family, surrendering her daughter to her sister. Today, SWAT teams have ceded pride of place not only to slimmed-down squads like the Navy SEALs, but to teams of one, such as Carrie, who is pitted, like Jack, not only against terrorists but against her own intelligence bureaucracy, and sometimes it's hard to tell which does more damage. More than a shadow of sexism creeps into the way the two are conceived. Jack's insubordination comes off as dedication and always proves itself, whereas Carrie's is attributed to bipolar disorder and always gets her into trouble.

The same disdain for the authority of government and its institutions crops up repeatedly throughout the entire gamut of right-wing shows. *24* lives again in *Shooter*. When the FBI agent who becomes Bob Lee Swagger's de facto partner in Season 1 suggests that he enlist the bureau to guard his family, he refuses. She pleads, "You should have more faith in the FBI," but he ignores her, and rightly so. The authorities in this show are implicated in the conspiracy to frame Swagger. And like Jack Bauer, he's on the run throughout the series.

In Christopher Nolan's *Dark Knight* trilogy, the authorities are again the enemy, as toxic as its freakish supervillains: the Joker, the Penguin, the Riddler, et al. Young Bruce Wayne, studying at Princeton, takes his junior year abroad in a Bhutan jail full of jumbo-size Asian thugs who beat him senseless. Ducard, a.k.a. Ra's Al Ghul (RAG), head of the notorious League of Shadows—a band of assassins, terrorists, and vigilantes—breaks him out and whips him into fighting shape. The league entertains a dark view of American society, not all that dissimilar to Trump's. The difference is that there's no draining the swamp; it's too late to make America great again. Instead, the league borrows a leaf from the Book of ISIS. It is dedicated to purging depravity by destroying our country, one city at a time.

Gotham, a cesspool of corruption, is the worst, and therefore first on his list. Voicing the animus of red state politicians toward urban centers that we've heard before, RAG declares, "Cities like Gotham are in their death throes—chaotic, grotesque. Beyond saving." He sounds like a mouthpiece for Ted Cruz, or better, Frank Miller, upon whose Reagan-era DC Comics' series these movies are loosely based. Miller made no bones about his contempt for the left, particularly the Occupy Wall Street demonstrators, scornfully characterizing them as "pond scum," and "nothing but a pack of louts, thieves, and rapists, an unruly mob, fed by Woodstock-era nostalgia and putrid false righteousness."

Back in Gotham, we see that RAG is right. It *is* a sewer of venality, so rich and rank that it taints almost everyone in authority, from the top to the bottom. Mob boss Carmine Falcone (Tom Wilkinson) seems to have all the judges and politicians in the city on his payroll, while the police have ceded the streets to the thugs. The cops and docs, instead of competing for the right to run the centrist show, are allies in crime. Doc Crane (Cillian Murphy), whisks Falcone out of prison to safe haven in Arkham, the notorious insane asylum he runs. Ironically bending the center-left's faith in the therapeutic to his own purposes, he claims Falcone needs treatment, not punishment. Assistant DA Rachel Dawes (Katie Holmes), Bruce's childhood friend and grown-up flame, is wise to his tricks. She protests, angrily: "I put scum like Falcone behind bars, not in therapy." But no one pays her any heed.

Eventually, Crane returns his lunatics to the streets of Gotham, where they quickly join the army of goons working for Bane (Tom Hardy), the übervillain in *The Dark Knight Rises* (2012), the final film of the trilogy. Whether criminals are bad guys or patients is irrelevant. Extreme circumstances render the disputes between liberals and conservatives moot. Neither the law nor therapy does the trick. The mob, the working police, and the poor, demonized as menacing shadows lurking in the gloomy streets of Gotham, are all locked in the embrace of corruption.

In *Live Another Day*, jihadists have kidnapped an American drone and are threatening to turn it against civilian London. In this series, drones are not flying Tinkertoys struggling to deliver packages for Amazon Prime on time, but rather, massive black wedges that wheel and glide across the skies with demonic grace. Packing devastating firepower thanks to their robust complement of Hellfire missiles, they virtually reek of death. The president's chief of staff gives a passionate defense of drones, describing them as the most effective, precise, and therefore humane method of fighting terrorism. He's a bad guy, but, echoing the argument of the pro-gun lobby, the series maintains that drones themselves are blameless; the problem lies with those who control them.

Ever since Obama doubled down on drones, they have become a flashpoint in the war between right and left. In the USA network's space invader show *Colony* (2016– ), it's the aliens, along with their collaborators, the human occupying authorities with their Nazi iconography, who use drones. Left-wing shows like *RoboCop* are generally critical of drone warfare. In the reboot, released in 2014, we're meant to wince when the Rush Limbaugh soundalike played by Samuel L. Jackson, defends drones in an appeal to his TV audience: "Some of you believe that the use of these drones overseas makes us the same kind of bullying imperialists that our forefathers were trying to escape. To you, I say, Stop whining. America is now and always will be the greatest county on the face of the earth!"

In *Avatar*, James Cameron makes us aware that there is something distasteful about Dr. Grace's avatar project, which is analogous to the use of remotely operated drones in Afghanistan and Pakistan. Drivers like Jake Sully resemble drone pilots enjoying a Coors somewhere in Colorado, say, thousands of miles from Kandahar Province. If a drone is shot down, the pilot will not find herself parachuting into enemy-controlled territory. Likewise, if an avatar is killed, there will be no taps for the driver, who is insulated from the fortunes or misfortunes of his avatar, just as moviegoers are insulated from the spectacle they're watching on their screens. Killing at a distance, like George Lucas's aestheticizing of combat, sanitizes warfare by shielding the killers from the killing. Yes, onlookers have to become doers, but doers have to do the right thing, and the disconnect between act and consequence makes it easy for them to do the wrong thing.

Contrary to *Avatar*, in which technology creates its own false reality—a "dream" opposed to the "true world out there," as Jake puts it, referring to Pandora—in *Live Another Day*, it's noisy, antidrone demonstrators who create a false reality. They show up on cue, unwashed and ill-clothed, jeering, chanting slogans, and otherwise making themselves unpleasant by waving crudely lettered signs expressing fatuous messages like DRONES DESTROY OUR HUMANITY. It's the 1960s all over again, lobotomized. With Jack, its rogue agent, and its admiration for drones, computers, and technology in general, *Live Another Day* was a show that the Dotcom-right acolytes of Ayn Rand could admire.

The jihadist terrorists have intentionally chosen an inconvenient moment for their mischief, because POTUS is in London trying to persuade Parliament to renew the lease on the American drone base. The jihadists are hoping to derail the agreement. Given the circumstances, it might have been prudent for the president to move the base elsewhere, but no, he chooses to play cat and mouse with the terrorists, gambling on the off chance that Jack can catch them before the clock ticks down to the zero hour. After all, drones are beautiful, even though the American base has turned Britain into a target.

In the absence of legitimate authority, the far right falls back on patriotism. It's America First, and therefore who cares if Hellfire missiles turn London into toast. Certainly not the president or the agents of the CIA, who all behave as if it were their playpen. Britain's law enforcement is brushed aside, and when its antiterrorist units do put in an appearance, they blunder into Jack's operation. Jack, on the other hand, disregards England's laws and institutions with impunity, but he gets the job done.

America First is the attitude that characterized the Tea Party–friendly *Falling Skies* as well, a dumber-than-dumb hit series that ran for five seasons on TNT from 2011 to 2015. It arrived with an impressive pedigree, namely Steven Spielberg, whose company produced, and writer-producer Robert Rodat, who wrote *Saving Private Ryan* (1998). But Rodat also wrote Mel Gibson's revenge-happy version of the American Revolution, *The Patriot* (2000), which provided a preview of *Falling Skies'* politics.

Mainstream shows like *Contagion* and *World War Z* at least pay lip service to the rest of the world, the existence of other countries, other peoples. Disasters are most often global, affecting everyone. In the far-right shows, the focus narrows. In *Falling Skies*, it's America that's at risk, and it's not until the final season, in what feels like an afterthought, that the rest of the world gets a nod. Anticipating Trump, the show recasts this country, the world's only remaining superpower, as a victim, crushed by overgrown robots called Mechs, controlled by small, spidery creatures known as Skitters, which in turn may or may not be run by the Overlords, who are themselves subject to an all-powerful Queen.

In many far-right shows in which our army has been decimated, it is because it has been contaminated with the stink of big government. Therefore, in the aftermath of defeat, it's in need of a makeover, which takes the form of downsizing, freeing it from the bureaucracy that has famously hobbled it and its agencies. The army is reborn as a "militia," a people's fighting force full of survivors like you and me. "Soldiers" have become "fighters." The right has laid claim to militias at least since 1984, midway into the Reagan presidency, when they beat back a Soviet invasion in John Milius's *Red Dawn*, and a decade later patriotically nuked America's major cities in defiance of Nicolae Carpathia's ultra-liberal new world order in the *Left Behind* novels.

The other reason our military has been destroyed is that it was stabbed in the back by spineless civilian politicians, as we are informed by the tremulous faux-naïf voice of a child: "They said we're not going to attack them with nuclear bombs because they might want to be friends, but they didn't want to be friends." Once again, as in Vietnam, it is those trusting, credulous liberals and lefties who are to blame. The ugly truth, as Trump might put it, is that alien races just don't respect us anymore; they're laughing at us.

If American chauvinism dictates that *Falling Skies* sheds tears over what's left of the United States, in *Black Panther*, Marvel's 2018 blockbuster phenomenon, it's Wakanda that's in trouble. Wakanda is an African nation that has avoided colonization by passing itself off as a poor third-world country, whereas in reality, it is rich in vibranium, an ore that has fueled technologies way more advanced than those possessed by the nations of the first world. Wakanda is a wishful what-if or what-might-have-been nation had Africa never been pillaged by the colonial powers.

Initially, the film seems like it's coming from the left. It boasts of a nearly all-black cast, save for a few white characters who are either over-the-top villains, like Andy Serkis, or comic relief, like geeky CIA agent Martin Freeman, addressed as "Hey, colonizer!" He fills the bumbling sidekick role reserved for African Americans in the movies of the 1930s and 1940s, such as Charlie Chan's timid chauffeur, played by comedian Mantan Moreland.

In front of the camera, *Black Panther* features a small army of fierce women warriors, and behind the camera, almost all of the major slots, including cinematographer and production designer, are filled by women. Moreover, it offers a rich panoply of African culture, including architecture, costumes, pottery, and even hairstyles derived from Kenya, the Central Republic of the Congo, and other countries, all rendered in vibrant earth colors—browns, yellows, and gold.

Wakanda is ruled by T'Challa, a.k.a. Black Panther (Chadwick Boseman). T'Challa is an ambiguous figure. Although he is king, ruling by dint of dynastic right, he is loved by his people. Although he may be benevolent, he's still a strongman. Wakanda is less a democracy than an autocracy. His royal blood may ensure him the throne, but his rule is also based on physical strength, which he demonstrates in combat with his rivals. In Wakanda, might, in other words, makes right.

As a strongman, T'Challa bears some resemblance to Kwame Nkrumah, the leftist president of Ghana who was overthrown by a coup allegedly aided by the CIA in 1966. But there's little about T'Challa that would suggest he's a leftist, save for the fact that he rules over a country untouched by colonialism. If anything, he leans right. His beneficence does not extend beyond Wakanda's borders, sealed as they are against the poverty-stricken tribes on all sides by a ring of mountains. T'Challa believes that only by refusing to share its wealth and technology can his country protect its unique way of life. His Wakanda First isolationism flies in the face of Nkrumah's pan-Africanism, and even has a whiff of you-know-who about it. In fact, in this important way, he is more like Donald Trump than he is like Nkrumah.

Turning to the faith-based right, first up is ABC's *Lost*, which we've already discussed as an ecumenical epic from the Christian center. But many of these shows contain contradictory elements, and it can certainly be argued that *Lost* might best be described as *Left Behind*–lite, since it took six seasons to accomplish what the rapture did in the blink of an eye. Mild as *Lost* may seem, it is more comfortable with the Southern Baptist Convention than it is with the National Council of Churches for the simple reason that it is built around a relentless attack on the authority of science, and by implication, reason and fact, a conviction dear to the hearts of evangelicals for whom the inerrancy of the Bible supersedes empiricism, based on the evidence provided by the world around them.

Dr. Jack, the leader of the hardy band that survived the 35,000-foot fall to the island without the benefit of parachutes, believes in hard facts that he can see and touch. He repeatedly dismisses one or another of the otherworldly phenomena that are as common as coconuts on the island with the phrase, "This isn't real." But more than relegating this apparition or that prophecy to the realm of fancy, he's asserting his right, the right of science, to define reality. *Lost*, on the other hand, making room for all the faiths, affirms faith itself.

Dr. Jack is pitted against a character named John Locke, someone's idea of a joke, who, in the name of faith, believes lollypops grow on trees. Well, maybe not lollypops, but he is convinced, for example, that his sister's spirit, at loose ends after she was killed in an accident as a child, returned to inhabit her dog. He also believes in miracles, magic, and so on.

A tedious debate between facts and faith runs throughout the length of the seven-season series. Here's a typical exchange between Dr. Jack and Locke about the island on which they find themselves:

Faith (Locke): "You know that you're here for a reason."

Science (Dr. Jack): "It's [just] an island."

Faith (Locke): "It's not an island. . . . It's a place where miracles happen."

Science (Dr. Jack): "There's no such thing as miracles."

Muddled as *Lost* is in most respects, in this one it knows its own mind. Science is the loser. The island is a place where miracles do happen, again and again and again.

Like a dog with a bone, science versus faith is an issue that showrunner Damon Lindelof has gnawed in show after show. Post-*Lost*, he co-wrote *Prometheus* (2012), directed by Ridley Scott, which also slams the door on science. Originally conceived as a prequel to *Alien*, *Prometheus* features Noomi Rapace as an archaeologist with an overactive imagination. She sees a cave painting that she interprets as an invitation to look for the origins of our species in the stars. On the basis of this slenderest of reeds, she persuades Peter Weyland, naturally, to finance a billion-dollar expedition with a full complement of scientists. It's lucky that Weyland has lots of discretionary income at his disposal, since Rapace offers zero evidence to support her claim. But why should she? In a film touched by Lindelof, she doesn't need any. All she needs is faith. When challenged by leveler heads, she shrugs off the question, replying, simply, "That's what I choose to believe." This is apparently enough for Weyland and his scientists, who trade in evolution for creationism and hop aboard.

Lindelof would pursue his Sunday-school excursions into the mysteries of the universe yet again via HBO's *The Leftovers* (2014–17), a series based on a novel by Tom Perrotta in which millions of people abruptly vanish from the planet, à la the *Left Behinds*, but Perrotta's what-if story doesn't venture a metaphysical explanation. Inspired by the events of 9/11 instead of the Book of Revelation, it concerns itself with how those who remain deal with the grief and shock caused by the sudden departures. Lindelof, on the other hand, sees it as another opportunity to put faith through its paces. Observing that the book "lined up with the meta level of *Lost*," he went on to say that "whatever happened to them, it's a miraculous event and implies a higher power." He concluded, "You can't be an atheist anymore."

In Season 3, faith and science square off just as they did in *Lost*. Ex-cop Kevin Garvey (Justin Theroux) is haunted by Patti Levin (Ann Dowd), the former leader of the Guilty Remnant, a creepy, post-vanishing sect whose members chain-smoke cigarettes instead of speak. Kevin is faced with two alternative diagnoses. The first explanation is the medical one, presented by his ex-wife, a therapist, who argues that he's had a nervous breakdown and belongs in a psych ward. "There is no Patti, Kevin," she says. "There is only you." Alternately, there is the hocus-pocus explanation, ventured by a voodoo guru: Patti is real, a spirit, and Garvey has to observe the rules of the spirit world to get rid of her. In this case, he has to die and be reborn. He chooses the guru over the therapist, and of course, he's right.

Lindelof dismisses all this with a wave of the hand and a disclaimer: "It's going to sound like a cop-out, but I think . . . actual truthfulness is irrelevant to the emotional result of having a system of faith and belief, if it helps bring people together." Emotional truth subsumes factual truth. The heart over the head. Born-agains would agree.

The hard, evangelical right, however, will have none of this namby-pamby nonsense. There's a battle to be fought, and only one side can win. The same militancy that drives *Avatar* and leads Jake to join the Na'vi and take up arms not only against the company but against his own species fuels the zeal of the born-agains. As in *Avatar* on the left, spectating is suspect. On the right, *God's Not Dead* ends with a message that reads, "God's not dead. Text everyone you know." The film, in other words, urges its audience, that is, spectators, to get up off their butts and become actors. Turning to the *Left Behind* series, Rayford observes, speaking of flight attendant Hattie, "She was the epitome of a person who could know the truth without acting on it." Jews for Jesus head Tsion Ben-Judah, exhorts to his followers, "My challenge to you today is to choose up sides. Join a team. If one side is right, the other is wrong."

Evangelicals are unapologetic Manicheans, either/or polarizers. Lookie-loos and rubberneckers had better think twice. Both/ands had better become either/ors. For them, the light is green or red, never yellow. In *War Room*, a Christian sleeper at the box-office, Miss Clara, the spiritual anchor of the movie, grills a fence-sitter about her "prayer life," asking, "Is it hot or cold?"

"I'm not hot, I'm not cold. I'm somewhere in the middle."

Jesus "wants us either hot or cold."

Like *Lost*, LaHaye and Jenkins's series attacks the authority of science. When the rapture comes, the left behinds are flummoxed. Mars attack? A wrinkle in time? A hiccup of nature? Terrorism? There is no shortage of theories. Fundamentalists whisper the word "rapture" to one another in hushed tones, but they're dismissed as crackpots by the "experts" who cling to scientific explanations like drowning men. The scientists, like *Lost*'s Dr. Jack, so dear to the hearts of center-left Democrats, are misguided. Dr. Chaim Rosenzweig, the inventor of a synthetic fertilizer that has improbably transformed Israel's deserts into lush, high-yield gardens and turned that tiny nation into the world's breadbasket, is benign but naïve, and he is so besotted with Carpathia that it takes him five books—approximately 2,250 pages of my mass market paperbacks—to see through him, and even then he stubbornly refuses to come to Jesus.

Journalist Buck Williams interviews Carpathia about the mysterious disappearances. Carpathia's response is that he is "inclined to believe in the natural theory, that lightning reacted with some subatomic field . . ." Buck understands that's he's speaking gibberish, grasping at straws. As the narrator puts it, Buck "had come a long way from thinking that the religious angle was on the fringe."

The *Left Behind*s not only target science, facts, and reason, but schooling as well. Education edifies in mainstream movies, and also provides an avenue of opportunity to realize the American Dream, but the *Left Behind*s don't care about the American Dream. They regard Buck's schooling as indoctrination and hang it around his neck like an albatross. According to the narrator, it's his Ivy League education that retards his acceptance of divine revelation until, as in *Lost*, "the supernatural came crashing through his academic pretense." Harvard graduates flunk this series, while Bob Jones University alums get straight As.

Eventually, the supernatural does come crashing through Buck's academic pretense, so there's still hope for him. He is assigned a story on Rosenzweig and flies to Israel to interview him. One day, in the middle of Buck's visit, the sky suddenly goes dark with bombers and nuclear-tipped missiles. Russia, in decline for many years, has apparently harbored a grudge against Israel for refusing to share the secret of its Miracle-Gro formula and therefore has launched a sneak attack. But instead of being overwhelmed by Russian airpower, the Israelis emerge unscathed, with every yarmulke in place. The Russian Air Force, on the other hand, is consumed by a maelstrom of fire, hail, and rain. Buck is nonplussed. Indeed, he cannot help but detect the hand of God in the proceedings. Nevertheless, it is hard for him to shrug off a lifetime of skepticism, and like Dr. Jack in *Lost*, he continues to scoff at what he cannot see.

True Christians like Rayford's raptured wife, Irene—unencumbered by education or intelligence—who took the leap of faith before the Blessed Event are rewarded by going to heaven. God prefers these first responders to smarty-pants like Rayford and Buck who have to be convinced by evidence, thereby forcing Him to show as well as tell. As a consequence, while Irene is peeling grapes in heaven, they're living through the Tribulation, that is, hell on earth.

Evangelicals apparently regard America's major institutions of higher learning as hotbeds of militant atheists who bully well-meaning Christians. The plot of *God's Not Dead*, one of the best of a bad lot of evangelical films, unfolds on the campus of Hadleigh University, the kind of place where cars are covered with politically correct stickers reading AMERICAN HUMANIST, I LOVE EVOLUTION, and MEAT IS MURDER. Standing in front of a class of students eager to offer up their brains to be washed, philosophy professor Jeffrey Radisson (Kevin Sorbo) smugly points to his whiteboard, which is covered with names of famous thinkers like Bertrand Russell, Michel Foucault, Friedrich Nietzsche, and Noam Chomsky. He informs his rapt students that they're all atheists. Radisson insists that "science and reason have supplanted superstition," adding, "There is no God," in case the kids have missed the point. Not satisfied, he requires his students to write "God Is Dead" on a piece of paper, and sign their names to it under threat of a failing grade!

The film reflects the views of its director, Harold Cronk, who said, "I think we're seeing a level of intolerance of the Christian faith that we didn't have 20 years ago," notwithstanding the fact that recent polls show that the vast majority of Americans—70 percent—consider themselves acolytes of Jesus.

Professor Radisson is so blinkered that we know he's due for a divine wake-up call. It comes from the one staunch Christian in the class, who is compelled to defy his professor. Young Josh explains, "God wants someone to defend him." Toward that end, he debates Professor Radisson, and wins—hey, it's a movie! Convinced by Josh, the class rises, one by one, to assert that God is not dead.

Well, sorry, Josh! God may not be dead, but it looks like He's on holiday and has indeed turned the world, or at least America, over to Satan, who's having a blast. Americans used to learn to do the right thing from their elders. But with the Doomsday Clock ticking and the Rapture Index through the roof, Dad deported back to Mexico, Mom on her own raising kids with no money for food after paying her medical bills, teachers out of work or smoking dope in the lounge, and the priest from St. Whatever's reassigned to a village in Guatemala because the altar boys ratted him out for inappropriate touching, Americans are confused. Who is teaching them how to be in the world? How are they supposed to conduct themselves?

# PART III
# BREAKING BAD

# 7
# The Silence of the Lambs

*Despite extreme circumstances, centrists do their best to make their mothers proud, minding their manners and behaving in accordance with the dos and don'ts of mainstream morality.*

> I pledged to ride north. I intend to honor that pledge.
> —*Jaime Lannister,* Game of Thrones

*The Revenant* (2015) is set in the American Northwest, sometime in the 1820s during a brutal winter. A party of angry Powaqa tribesmen descend on a group of trappers camped in the snowy wilderness. Looking for their chief's daughter, who has been kidnapped, they nearly choke the life out of Leonardo DiCaprio, but he escapes with his son, Hawk, who is half Native American. Father and son take refuge in another settlement of trappers, but Hawk is baited by Tom Hardy, a man sorely lacking the milk of human kindness. DiCaprio vigorously defends his son but counsels him not to press the issue.

Clad in furs and skins, DiCaprio is subsequently attacked by a grizzly bear and badly mauled. After attending to him, the trappers prepare to move on. Hardy argues that taking the injured man with them will just slow them down and urges the others to leave him behind, but an army officer insists they bring him along, carried on an improvised stretcher. DiCaprio does hold them back, so Hardy takes things into his own hands. He attempts to finish the job the bear started, but Hawk intervenes, and Hardy stabs him. Helpless, DiCaprio can do no more than look on as Hardy lets his son bleed out and then buries DiCaprio alive, leaving him to die.

Of course, DiCaprio survives. He crawls out of the loosely packed earth and, half-dead, buffeted by fierce winds, and stung by frozen snow, he survives on roots and berries until finally, fortune smiles. He runs into a Native

American from a different tribe, who nurses him back to life. Trying to catch up to his party, he stumbles across the chief's daughter being raped by a French trapper, who shouts, as if to justify his actions, "We are all savages!" Instead of killing the man, DiCaprio holds him off at gunpoint, saves her, and resumes his journey. In other words, he's a good guy. Or was. Because now, consumed by vengeance, he is determined to kill Hardy.

DiCaprio spends the rest of the movie tracking his enemy. The army officer insists on joining him in the hunt. He is determined to bring Hardy back alive to face justice. However, Hardy shoots the officer, which just goes to show that doing it the right way and following the rules is a sure way to get yourself killed. Doing it the wrong way, DiCaprio bests Hardy in the movie's climactic fight, but just as he's about to administer the coup de grace, Hardy exclaims, "You came all this way just for your revenge, huh? 'Cause there ain't nuthin' gonna bring your boy back," words uttered so often in shows like this that they might as well be embroidered on a sampler. In centrist shows, they bring the hero to his senses, as they do here. In response, DiCaprio piously declares, "Revenge is in God's hands, not mine," and instead of crushing Hardy's head with a rock, as he's about to do, he pushes him into the raging waters of a river. The result is likely to be the same, but in case not, a war party of Powaqa that has been trailing them, accompanied by the chief's daughter, now recovered, gives Hardy his just deserts. The takeaway? By killing off the army officer who wants to do things by the book, the movie steps out of the center, doffing its hat to extreme circumstances, but by outsourcing revenge to the Powaqa, it steps back in again, as DiCaprio eschews extreme measures. By furnishing him with the fig leaf required by centrist heroes, he can have his cake and eat it too, enjoy the satisfaction of revenge, while dodging the stigma of having to perform the dastardly deed himself.

One of the effects of the rise of extremism is the acceptance of behavior that was once considered beyond the pale. Ever since 1930, when the guardians of virtue at the Production Code Administration stepped in to stamp out "immoral" behavior and establish standards of decency, children in American movies grew up to be adults who got married and had children themselves. They loved them and were loved by them in return. Adults worked hard in socially sanctioned occupations and obeyed the law. They didn't run off with their neighbors' wives or husbands, didn't lie, steal, or kill.

They were generous to those less fortunate than themselves. The ones who did behave badly were the exceptions, bad apples, black sheep, good-for-nothings who were duly punished for their transgressions.

The rule of law is one of the pillars of the social contract that is the foundation of pluralism, and therefore, flagrant violations like killing, stealing, raping, lying, and so on are strictly prohibited. Ditto revenge. The Motion Picture Production Code states, "Revenge in modern times shall not be justified." But revenge has always been a problem, because if avengers have indeed been grievously wronged, they have a strong emotional, if not ethical, investment in punishing the guilty party. The issue, though, is how guilt is to be determined and by whom, and who is going to exact the punishment.

Revenge—sanctioned by the state and rebranded as "justice"—has long been regarded as the prerogative of the authorities who operate within a framework of rules that are supposed to be applied equally, so that like grudges, feuds, vendettas, and whatnot, which are purely personal, revenge, is proscribed. Thus, *The Revenant*, clinging by its fingertips to the old consensus morality, wriggles and squirms to avoid it. If individuals—most often heroes and superheroes—are occasionally entrusted with the right to exercise force, they are supposed to have internalized the rules of the game. In the immortal words of Spider-Man, "With great power there must also come—great responsibility."

In 1983, George Lucas changed the name of the final installment of the original *Star Wars* trilogy from *Revenge of the Jedi* to *Return of the Jedi* because the former contradicted the wisdom of Yoda, who warned Luke Skywalker in his broken, English-as-a-second-language patois, "Beware. Anger, fear, aggression. The dark side are they." Revenge was for Siths, as in *Revenge of the Sith*, the third of the *Star Wars* prequel trilogy. In other words, what's right for the Sith is wrong for the Jedi, because they're good guys.

Released in 2005 in the midst of the George W. era, *Revenge of the Sith* was perhaps the most overtly political of the entire saga. Nixon was no longer the emperor. As Lucas explained, "George Bush is Darth Vader. Cheney is the emperor." Supreme Chancellor Palpatine manipulates fear to turn the Republic into the Empire. With eerie prescience, Lucas told the *Chicago Tribune*, "Democracies aren't overthrown; they're given away."

Today's mainstream shows still discourage revenge. *The Americans* draws a distinction between the methods of the FBI and those of the Soviet moles, who are considerably more ruthless. In one scene, FBI Agent Stan Beeman asks the widow of his former boss, who has been killed by the Russians, what she wants him to do. "Revenge," she says, emphatically. He responds, mildly, "It's not about revenge." In *Godless*, a 2017 Netflix western, fast draw Roy Goode instructs his surrogate son to be wary of it, saying, "If a person ain't careful, he can make a profession outta revenge." In *Captain America: Civil War* (2016), in which T'Challa makes his debut, he admonishers a revenged-crazed character, "Vengeance has consumed you. I am done letting it consume me." Thus, it comes as no surprise that in *Black Panther*, Erik Killmonger's quest to exact revenge for the crimes against his people is eventually repudiated, and mercy is rewarded.

In *X-Men: Apocalypse*, directed by Bryan Singer, Polish cops kill Erik/Magneto's wife and daughter early on, provoking the mutant to make one of his periodic trips to the dark side. He embraces revenge and throws in his lot with the bad guy Apocalypse (attended by the ubiquitous four horsemen) to wreak havoc on the world. Apocalypse is a chaos agent, a Nietzschean/Nazi/Randian figure who believes, in his words, that "the weak have taken the Earth." Echoing the millennialism of the kamikaze Republicans, and the Rapture Ready evangelicals, he tells Erik/Magneto, "Wipe clean this world, and we will lead those that survive into a better one." The much-aggrieved Erik/Magneto embraces revenge with enthusiasm: "They took everything away from me. Now we'll take everything away from them." Along the way, he makes an obligatory stop at Auschwitz, now a tourist attraction (Naziworld), and destroys it as well. But he is uncomfortable in the role of the avenger. He exclaims, "Is this who I am?" and eventually Raven/Mystique (Jennifer Lawrence), a shape-shifter and mainstay of the *X-Men* films, talks him down, persuading him to break with Apocalypse and turn from the path of revenge.

The mainstream frowns upon revenge not only because it undermines the rule of law, but because it is personal. Although trying to fulfill its utopian promise, making every effort to reconcile public and private, under pressure from the extremes, more and more often, it fails, and the general good is pitted against private interest, in which case, the latter, as we have seen, makes way for the former.

Still, the center worries that public servants will be held hostage by threats against private life that prevent them from doing their jobs. Family is a perennial vulnerability, giving bad guys leverage over good guys, like the

FBI director in *Designated Survivor* (2016– ) whose son is kidnapped by terrorists, forcing him to do their bidding.

NBC's *Crisis* (2014) was a mainstream thriller built around just this conflict between public and private. In Washington, DC, a vengeful former CIA agent hijacks a busload full of kids whose parents are powerful government officials and pits their love for their youngsters against their love for their country by threatening to kill the hostages if the parents don't commit acts of sabotage. He calls each parent, always with the same greeting: "How far would you go to save your child?" One by one, the parents make the wrong choice—from the center's point of view—jeopardizing their country for the sake of their children.

When the men and women who serve America's institutions can expect to lose their loved ones to a grab bag of ruthless killers, it becomes obvious that their country is far from the paradise it appeared to be in the era of postwar consensus. Reconciling opposites—in this case public and private—wasn't working.

Nonetheless, in mainstream shows, the public servants who are the targets of these kinds of threats generally get around to doing the right thing, or at least regretting doing the wrong thing, like that FBI director in *Designated Survivor*. Even though he obeys the kidnappers, they kill his son anyway, and he recognizes that he made a mistake by capitulating to their demands.

In *Game of Thrones*, family is a flash point as well. Cersei Lannister accuses her brother Tyrion of "the destruction of [their] family." For her, family is all, even to the point of taking her brother Jaime as a lover. Incest, in this instance, becomes a metaphor for the narrow, tribal obsession with blood ties that will be her undoing.

Tyrion has become the Hand—that is, the chief counselor—to Daenerys Targaryen, Cersei's sworn enemy. When Daenerys allies with the North against the White Walkers, Cersei pretends to join as well, and her brother Jaime, who leads her army, promises to take it into battle against them. When he discovers she's lying, plotting to betray Daenerys and Jon Snow, he reproves her. No surprise, she turns her back on the general good, confessing, "I don't care about checking my worst impulses, I don't care about making the world a better place. Hang the world."

Jaime, on the other hand, refuses to follow her down this particular rabbit hole, putting principle before family. "I pledged to ride north," he says. "I intend to honor that pledge." An extremist show in which the ends justify the means might well approve of Cersei's treachery, as well as her determination to revenge herself against Tyrion, but *Game of Thrones* frowns upon both. Besides, history is on the side of Daenerys, whose vision of a "modern" monarchy supersedes Cersei's medieval notion of private fiefdoms ruled by family dynasties. Cersei sees Jaime's pledge as a betrayal, but the Amazonian warrior Brienne of Tarth has the last word: "Oh, fuck loyalty." Well, not quite the last word. It matters to whom and what one is loyal. Jon Snow is loyal too, but his loyalty is to his species, not his family. When family collides with the general good, the general good prevails.

As the pillars of the mainstream's institutions of authority begin to crumble under the pressure of extreme circumstances, with the government, church, schools either absent, delegitimized, or broken and the private pitted against the public, the ideological glue that binds them together flakes and cracks. Citizens are thrown into a state of nature. Without a compass, what are they supposed to do? Mainstream shows struggle to answer the question posed by one of *The Walking Dead*'s executive producers, Gale Anne Hurd: "Is it okay to do anything to survive? Are there any limits?" *Game of Thrones* issues a resounding "Yes," there are limits, as Cersei learns to her sorrow, but in other shows, the answer isn't so clear.

In the face of the centrifugal forces ripping it apart, the mainstream has to struggle to maintain its integrity. In *True Blood*, the invention of a synthetic substitute for blood factionalizes the vampire world. The moderates retain their belief in assimilation, keeping the faith with the authority of the center, such as it is. They struggle for equality under the law—human law. Vampire Bill is an ardent believer in the mainstreaming agenda of the American Vampire League (AVL). Right off the bat, so to speak, at the beginning of the very first episode, the AVL spokeswoman is sparring with Bill Maher on his HBO show, making a convincing case for vampire rights, in the same way the synths lobby for their rights in AMC's *Humans* (2015– ) and the replicants rebel in their name in the two *Blade Runners*.

Meanwhile, the vampire extremists, the Geronimos of the vampire world, resist the blandishments of the center and prefer to pitch their camp outside of the big tent. Bill maligns them as "vicious, petty, vile creatures." They in turn scorn him as "Mr. Mainstream," a self-hating Cochise, an Uncle Vlad.

Likewise, vampire-hating humans refuse to put out the welcome mat for their fanged neighbors, because for them, the show's Gays "R" Us message doesn't go down so easily. Both nay-saying factions are guilty of what Peter Singer has called "speciesism," the conviction that one's own species is superior to others, and consequently, each has little respect for the moral codes or institutions of the other. Speaking for the vampire Geronimos, Eric Northman (Alexander Skarsgård), *True Blood*'s arrogant, bad boy vampire, says, "There is no right. Or wrong. These are human notions." He regards humans as a lower life-form, pets or property. At worst, mortals are no more than food: "blood sacks." As one bloodsucker complains, "If we can't kill people, what's the point of being a vampire?"

Pluralism rejects speciesism and teaches that if some vampires are bad, so are some humans. As in *Hostiles* (2017), a tediously portentous revisionist western starring Christian Bale, good humans have to learn that the real war isn't between the cavalry and Native Americans, or, in *True Blood*, between humans and vampires, but between good whites aligned with good Native Americans against bad whites and bad Native Americans, just as, in *True Blood*, the real struggle is between good humans allied with good vampires against the bad humans and bad vampires. In other words, neither species nor ethnic nor religious differences rules, but rather, morality, defined as willingness to live in peace under the big tent.

Spinning out of control, both *True Blood* and *The Walking Dead* are a long way from the upbeat fare of the postwar era, or even *World War Z*, *Contagion*, *Hidden Figures*, or *Game of Thrones*. With pluralism in disarray and civil authority asleep at the wheel or otherwise engaged, there's nothing and no one left in Bon Temps to stop the extremists from having their way with the center.

Like *True Blood*, *The Walking Dead* struggles against its extremist premise. It bumps up the hazard level so high that extreme measures and bad behavior seem the only alternative. According to one study, by Season 3, it was "the deadliest show on TV," with 308 dead bodies displayed over the course of the first eight episodes. In one scene in the first season, shot in this-will-make-you-barf close-up, Andrea, attempting to spay-neuter a walker, methodically hacks off its arms with a hatchet, places it face down on the crown of a rock, and stomps on the back of its skull, breaking its teeth and pulping its gums. Then, in case an incisor here or bicuspid there has escaped the demolition, she does it again. This scene affords a baseline, as it were, and things get worse from there.

Jumping to the Negan nightmare of Season 7, we watch him punishing truant followers with "face ironings" and bloody beatings with "Lucille," a baseball bat wrapped with barbed wire. "Gross" doesn't do this show justice; it violates every canon of taste. It's enough to make you nostalgic for the networks' Standards and Practices. The writers even debated whether to show the terrified victims wetting themselves. Still, regardless of the blood and brains spattered all over the place, extreme behavior is frowned upon.

Rick resists the temptation to "go all Darwin," as someone puts it, but after all, he's a deputy sheriff. Not everyone shares his respect for the law. In the series' opener, Daryl's brother, redneck Merle, wearing a wifebeater and crouched on the roof of a department store in Atlanta, amuses himself by taking target practice at the sea of walkers below. Merle is not a nice guy. He's a deplorable without a basket and directs a stream of sexist and racist epithets at the motley band of survivors huddled on the roof with him. He calls Andrea "sugar tits" and "rug muncher," and then shouts "nigger" and "spear chucker" at T-Dog while nearly bludgeoning him to death with the stock of his gun before brandishing it at the others. He bellows, "Talk about who's in charge? Democracy time, y'all. I vote me! All in favor?" Cowering before him, they meekly raise their hands.

It looks like Merle has made his point—power grows out of the barrel of a gun—until Rick shows up, slugs him with the butt of his weapon, and cuffs him to an iron pipe. Merle is a polarizer, but Rick announces, "Things have changed. There are no 'niggers' anymore. No dumbass shit inbred white trash fools either. There's us and the dead."

We have seen that Rick and Shane were at odds over searching for Carol's daughter, Sophia, the same way we have seen the characters in *The Revenant* argue over whether DiCaprio should be left for dead or brought with them, even though that makes them vulnerable to the Powaqa who are following them.

War films, which came into their own during World War II, were historically the genre that sorted out issues that divided moderates and extremists. They were our best laboratory for studying the effects of extreme circumstances. The genre conventions that codified mainstream values dictated that GIs never leave their wounded comrades behind. Audiences knew this, as surely as they knew American soldiers didn't kill or torture prisoners. If a foray to rescue a fallen comrade delayed an advance or retreat, so be it. On the other hand, the Germans, Japanese, along with the Chinese hordes that threatened South Korea, or later the Vietcong, invariably left their fallen to die on the battlefield. "The Oriental doesn't put the same high price on life as does a Westerner," General William Westmoreland infamously reflected in the Oscar-winning Vietnam War documentary *Hearts and Minds* (1974). "Life is cheap in the Orient," but not in America.

Steven Spielberg's *Saving Private Ryan* (1998) is the best recent example of this theme, and it highlights the contradiction between the mainstream's utilitarian ethic—the general good trumps the good of the few—and its insistence on the sanctity of human life, its inclination to double down on the human, not individualism, but the individual. Risking their lives to rescue the wounded distinguished Americans from the enemy, and by so doing, they transcend the contradiction between the individual and the group. By saving their fallen brothers, they are saving themselves as well, if not literally, then spiritually.

Moreover, wounded comrades are family. They are not kin, bound by blood ties, but members of an extended family, a bow in the direction of pluralism's faith in big-tent inclusiveness. The title of HBO's hit World War II series, *Band of Brothers* (2001), says it all. Wounded or not, a fellow soldier is a "brother," to be treated like an asset, not a liability.

In one early episode of *The Walking Dead*, Rick rescues Glenn, played by Asian actor Steven Yeun, who is being held hostage by a Latino gang. The gang leader asks Rick, "What's that dude to you anyway? You don't look related." Rick replies, "He's one of our group." In other words, Rick's survivors too are a band of brothers. And sisters. Sophia was not in fact Rick's blood relation, but he argued that she should be treated that way regardless, as if any kin of Carol's is kin of theirs. Everyone under the big tent is family.

In the face of Shane's objections, Rick persisted in searching for Sophia. When it turns out that she had been dead all along, it seems like Shane might have been right. Is he? Does this alter the show's ethical arithmetic?

Under extreme circumstances, mainstream series like *True Blood* and *The Walking Dead* flirt with extreme values, try them on for size, as it were. Rick's survivors, having demonstrated to Hershel that walkers are not sick but lethal, are halfway to extremism already. *The Walking Dead* even stoops to torture. In Season 2, Rick snatches a stranger named Randall from the jaws of the walkers and brings him back to Hershel's farm. So far so good, but such are the circumstances in which the survivors find themselves that good deeds don't necessarily lead to good results. Randall is a member of a group of survivors who are also scouring the land for food and shelter. Shane worries that if they let him go, he'll lead his group to the farm. The question is, What to do with Randall?

The first order of business is to find out if Randall's group is dangerous or not. He says "not," but Shane doesn't believe him. With the screw turning, Shane wants to force him to divulge the nature and whereabouts of his pals. Daryl gets physical and beats Randall senseless.

As a direct result of his beating, Randall confesses that he's running with a heavily armed gang of thirty marauding men who are looking for weapons to fire and women to rape. Torture may be morally repellent and illegal under the rule of law, but here there is no law, and moreover, it works. Under extreme circumstances, results are all that matter.

Shane wants to put him in the grave, and Randall's confession seems to seal his fate, but Dale (Jeffrey DeMunn), the most articulate spokesmen for pluralist values, speaks up, saying, "If we do this, the rule of law is dead." The survivors vote to execute Randall anyway, for no better reason than, as Glenn puts it, "he's not one of us." Dale stalks out of the meeting, but not before taking a parting shot: "This group is broken. . . . The people that we were, the world that we knew, is dead. . . . There is no civilization. How are we any better than those people that we're so afraid of?"

With dissension growing within the ranks of the survivors, the dispute between Rick and Shane, first over searching for Sophia and now about how to handle Randall, comes to a boil. Sensing that Shane intends to kill him too, Rick allows him to lead them deep into the forest. Shane pulls a gun. Rick tricks him into lowering it and plunges his knife into his heart.

In *True Blood*, when people behave badly, evil spirits feel free to disregard their boundaries and enter them at will. What is literally true there is metaphorically true in *The Walking Dead*. Rick may have disposed of Shane, but by acting like him, he allows his spirit to possess him. He becomes the new Shane. After all, when his late, erstwhile best bud said, "You can't just be the good guy and expect to live," Rick admitted, "I'm not the good guy anymore."

By the end of Season 2, Rick has lost his taste for consensus. When his band of survivors turns on him for killing Shane, he threatens to abandon them, but in the event that they choose to stay, he warns, "This isn't a democracy anymore." Not only has he become the new Shane, he has become the new Merle. With bad fast going to worse, and worst just around the corner, the liberal, pluralist values with which the show began seem to have been trampled underfoot. To the new, my-way-or-the-highway Rick, democracy is a luxury the survivors can ill afford. Welcome to the so-called Ricktatorship.

In *True Blood*, when the authorities abdicate their role in legislating what is real and what is not, the supes step into the vacuum. They play the same role that nature does in extremist shows, introducing another world with its own entities and rules antithetical to the mainstream world of reason, science, and technology. More recent shows like 2016's *Westworld, Stranger Things, Falling Water*, and *The OA*, as well as 2017's *Legion*, and 2018's *Counterpart*, go well beyond *True Blood* in positing no end of multiverses and alternative dimensions of which ours is just one. Of his *Ready Player One* (2018), Spielberg said, "Even with all the popcorn in a film like 'Ready Player One,' it does have social meaning." Americans escaping a future, dystopic Ohio, take refuge in the virtual reality created by a game called Oasis, to which they are addicted. When authority collapses, in other words, our heretofore shared notion of "reality" is bracketed by quotes and up for grabs, available to the center, left, and right.

In *True Blood*, Maryann Forrester (Michelle Forbes), first appears naked with the head of a bull standing in the middle of the road next to a pig—an eyepopper even in this Louisiana hellhole. Who, or what is Maryann? As Daphne, her acolyte, explains to Sam Merlotte, "People call her all kinds of things—Kali, Lilith, Isis, Gaia. But what she really is, is a maenad."

"What the fuck is that?"

What the fuck indeed. Maenads were devotees of Dionysus, the god of revelry known to us from Greek mythology. Following Dionysus, a.k.a. Bacchus to the Romans, they were wont to take to the forest, where they cavorted among the leaves and fronds. What did the frenzied followers of Dionysus do in the forest? They held orgies, of course. Daphne adds that the Greeks called Dionysus "Satan." "It's really just a kind of energy," she says, "wild energy, like lust, anger, excess, violence, basically, all the fun stuff."

Maryann proceeds to dissolve the social fabric of Bon Temps. She casts a spell over the not-so-good citizens of the town. Under her influence, they go berserk, making your everyday orgy look like a Baptist picnic. Maryann is the mistress of mobs. She represents the spirit of anarchy. Someone even uses the "t" word, wondering if they've been "attacked by terrorists."

In her book *Dancing in the Streets*, Barbara Ehrenreich calls Dionysus the "first rock star," which would make him the god of the 1960s, with both its anything-goes counterculture and its libidinous sexual revolution. The maenads, then, are the first groupies, and this subplot feels like an explicit takedown of that decade—down to one of its favorite slogans, "Fuck

Authority," scrawled on the wall of the police station, along with a capital *A* inscribed in a circle, for anarchy.

Maryann and her maenads attack the center from the left. The Fellowship of the Sun, on the other hand, part fundamentalist cult, part militia, and fully dedicated to the (ethnic) cleansing of vampires in the name of God, attacks it from the right.

While religion in *The Walking Dead* is merely useless, in *True Blood* it is the cloak for a hate group and an excuse for bad behavior. Sookie's brother, Jason (Ryan Kwanten), is a none-too-bright stud, squarer than a square peg. The Fellowship takes advantage of his good nature and recruits him, offering him a come-to-Jesus moment. As he puts it, "I was saved. For the first time in my life I feel like God has a purpose for me." He relocates to the Fellowship's boot camp in Dallas, where one of his new born-again friends echoes his teleological musings: "Everything happens for a reason." Explains *True Blood* creator Alan Ball, "It was fun to create an organization that uses religion as a tool of fear and power, because we know that happens on a daily basis."

Hoisting aloft the standard of values voters, the Fellowship's first family is a grinning Ken and Barbie couple called the Newlins (Steve and Sarah), who mix their Jesus talk with hate speech and kill instead of vote. They would be heroes in a far-right show, but not here, where they are just deranged. As one vampire tells Eric, the Fellowship is "overflowing with self-righteous extremists."

Smiling Steve sees the world in black and white. Using the either/or, apocalyptic language of the far right, and sounding very much like both the post-9/11 George W. Bush and Tsion Ben-Judah in the *Left Behind* series, he says, "What's going on out there is a war. We all have to choose sides. You're either on the side of darkness or the side of light."

In the postwar period, when pluralist ideology seemed to have all the answers, therapeutic social control was effective because American society had something to offer its discontents. As we saw in *Avatar*, Selfridge & Co. have nothing that the Na'vi might want. Likewise, in *True Blood*, with authority in crisis, the institutions and the ideology that inspire citizens to do the right thing no longer exist. There is no reason for the Cochises of the world to return to the reservation. They'd be better off with Geronimo, fighting for survival in a state of nature.

In the absence of civil and religious authority and/or the ideology that supports them, what motivates *True Blood*'s characters to do anything at all? To act in one way and not another? To get out of bed? It is the family that comes most readily to hand as a motivating principle and defensible unit. Indeed, *True Blood*'s characters cling to family and family values as civilization's last rampart against the barbarian hordes. When Sookie's best friend apologizes for her role in Maryann's carnival of lust, she says, "I got sucked in because she made me feel like I was part of a family."

Community, however, is hard to find, whether it be family, pack, or coven. Families may satisfy the demands of the heart, but not the head, and most families in Bon Temps are toxic. In mainstream shows, as we have seen, they are superseded by broader collections of people based on region, ethnicity, gender, and so on. But if the institutions that are supposed to represent broader and more inclusive communities of people are no-shows, restoring order is left to an ad hoc group of friends: Sookie, Jason, Sam, et al. As Jason puts it, "We have got to be the law."

*True Blood*'s slice of America is so bleak that it's clear that the center has lost its way. In this era of extremism, centrist shows continue to survive, but even the best ones most often seem a bit dotty, like ancient grandparents, lurching to the right and then to the left, trying, but never quite succeeding, to find their footing.

During the postwar period of bipartisanship, when the extremes were little more than clay pigeons for the center to knock down, they were reduced to defining themselves by negation. By the time *True Blood* arrived, some three and a half decades later, the mainstream was so demoralized that it was its turn to define itself by negation—negating both extremes. If vampire-slaying vigilantes like the Fellowship of the Sun fanatics are ridiculed as hate groups, so are the human-hunting vampire cults. If the authorities are either remote, inept, or malign, Maryann's crazies who scrawl "Fuck Authority" on the wall of the jail are no better. If one extreme is bad, so is the other.

*True Blood* is so dazed and confused that it doesn't even have the confidence of negation, and instead of rejecting the extremes, it just as often embraces them both, even if they are mutually exclusive. One character insists that "the truth will make you free," while another character insists with equal vehemence that ignorance is bliss. If one character is wrong to follow her heart, still another is wrong to follow his head. The show endorses both and neither. We are left on our own to guess the values that animate that which lies in the middle, between the extremes.

Weakened by the collapse of authority and battered by their enemies, the folks of Bon Temps still manage to thread the needle between the extremes, which is what the center is all about. Alluding to the Fellowship of the Sun and Maryann's maenad express, Ball articulates the classic mainstream strategy. "Repression and frenzy are two sides of the same coin," he explains. "If one can achieve a balance, and sometimes sway this way and sometimes that way, it's better than living in either extreme." Ultimately, when institutions fail, and family lets us down, centrist shows, as we have seen, double down on humans, fall back on the humanity of humans, who save the vampires from themselves.

Like *True Blood*, other mainstream shows such as *The Walking Dead* worry that, as Dale warned, their heroes, under the pressure of extreme circumstances, may devolve into the very extremists they are fighting. Adopting the methods of the enemy, they become like the enemy. In one memorable scene in the finale of Season 4, having fallen into the hands of a roving band of thugs who mean to kill Rick and rape young Carl, Rick mimics the questionable manners of the undead by leaping upon his captor and ripping a chunk out of his neck with his teeth. He doesn't actually eat his flesh, but it looks like he might. Even Carl himself frets that he feels like he is turning into a "monster," and he is, shooting a man who's trying to surrender, and then lying about it. So similar are the survivors to the biters, that the showrunner, Scott M. Gimple is said to have applied the show's title, *The Walking Dead*, to the survivors as well as the zombies.

Eventually, Rick and his band stumble on Woodbury, a seemingly idyllic sanctuary incongruously erected in the middle of walker territory and surrounded by a fortified wall from which a biter hangs by its feet. Its inhabitants enjoy relatively normal lives, thanks to its leader, known as "the Governor," who has in his home an aquarium filled with walker heads floating in formaldehyde, like a Damien Hirst installation. This does not bode well, and he turns out to be a bit of a psycho. Even more distressing, his head of security is Merle.

We last ran across redneck Merle in Season 1, cuffed to a pipe on the roof of a department store. When the survivors escaped the mob of walkers surrounding the building, they assumed that Merle had been eaten alive, but it seems that he cut off his hand with a rusty hacksaw blade and escaped. His close call has done nothing to improve his disposition. Since then, he has nourished a grudge against Rick and his friends. Like the bad guy he is, he seeks revenge. In Season 3, he gets his opportunity. He captures Glenn and his wife, Maggie and takes them to Woodbury, where the Governor orders him to force them to reveal the whereabouts of the prison where Rick & Co. are taking refuge.

When Merle gets the chance to torture Glenn and Maggie, he can barely believe his luck, but all good things must come to an end, and Rick, Daryl, et al. attack Woodbury and rescue their friends. Abhorrent though Merle may be, he is Daryl's brother, so they take him along as well. Needless to say, this doesn't sit well with Glenn and Maggie, who refuse to let Merle accompany them. "Merle's blood," Daryl objects. "Merle's your blood," retorts Glenn. "My blood, my family, is waiting for us back at the prison." Once again, two definitions of family—narrow and expansive—duke it out. The brothers go their own way and encounter an Hispanic family fighting for their lives against a herd of hungry walkers.

A similar situation arises in *World War Z*, where Brad Pitt stumbles across an Hispanic family hiding from the zekes in an apartment building. On the run with his wife and son, Pitt nevertheless offers to take the family with him, but the father refuses to abandon his home. Pitt volunteers to take his son to safety, and does so. By adding a total stranger he converts his kinship group into an extended family, thereby earning a pluralist merit badge.

In *The Walking Dead*, Daryl's inner Pitt eventually emerges. He springs to the side of the struggling Hispanics and lays waste to the walkers. Merle, on the other hand, who still clings to blood ties, refuses to lift a finger. "I ain't wastin' my bullets for strangers ain't never cooked me a meal," he drawls, sourly. It's too much Merle for Daryl. Stalking off, he says he's going "back where I belong," that is, with our survivors, his extended family.

Daryl returns to his extended family behind the walls of the prison, but things have changed. Rick, now hardened, and less a survivor than a survivalist, ignores the obligation to include, and instead turns away those who want to join his group, even expelling some when they become inconvenient. He is guilty of crimes against pluralism.

To avert a counterattack by Woodbury, he agrees to give the Governor a fiery fighter named Michonne, for whom the Governor entertains a particular animus. It's an unpopular decision, one that Rick has made without consulting the others. To make matters worse, Michonne is played by a black actress, Danai Gurira, although no one accuses him of racism. Of course, Rick can't bring himself to go through with it. Having stared into the abyss of extremism, he doesn't like what he's seen. He gathers the survivors, and reverses field, delivering his mea culpa: "I'm not your governor," he says. "We stick together. We vote."

Centrists, as we have noted, have made peace with the messy world in which they live and don't like to be put in the position of having to choose between A and B, preferring instead to have A and B. At the end of Season 4, Rick and his band end up at Terminus, run by cannibals. One of them explains to Carol that Terminus used to be a real sanctuary, until a gang of marauders attacked the people living there, raping and killing them. For those who survived, the takeaway was, "You're the butcher or you're the cattle." In other words, you have to become Them to defeat Them. It's exactly the kind of stark either/or choice that centrists try to avoid. In a replay of the debate over his search for Sophia, instead of pitting the individual against the group, Rick equates the welfare of the individual, in this case Michonne, with the welfare of the group. By protecting one, he protects the other. As he puts it, "I couldn't sacrifice one of us for the greater good because we are the greater good." A both/and kind of guy, he succeeds in reconciling polar opposites.

By including Michonne, Rick shuns the extremist inclination to go it alone, the path followed by the British in *Dunkirk* and *The Darkest Hour* (2017), T'Challa in *Black Panther*, and Trump's America Firsters. Instead, he commits to coalition building, which pays off in Season 8, during the struggle against Negan and his Saviors. Reverting to the mainstream mantra he expressed early in Season 1, he says, "We survive this by pulling together, not apart." Rick, meet Jon Snow, meet Hillary Clinton. When the new Rick—really a reversion to the old Rick—recommits to the pluralist principle of inclusion, he makes his way back to the human in himself. In fact, not only does Rick accept Michonne as part of his group, he hooks up with her, putting an interracial couple at the heart of the show.

Like *True Blood*, *The Walking Dead* attacks polar opposites: the Governor of Woodbury is too strong, while the leader of Alexandria, another walled community that has had the good fortune to be unmolested by walkers, is too weak. If Rick is wrong to waste the group's resources searching for Sophia because she's already dead, Shane is also wrong for refusing to search for Sophia because she might have been alive. At other times, instead of negating opposite extremes, it endorses them, seemingly unable to decide between them. Tyreese and Morgan, two of Rick's survivors, are right to try to preserve their humanity by declining to kill their enemies, but on the other hand, Rick and Michonne are also right to do the opposite, disposing of them to avoid being disposed of themselves. Carol is both right to kill and right not to kill, and wrong to kill and wrong not to kill. The implication is that the middle way, neither too strong nor too weak, is the best way, but no behavior seems right and proper, so *The Walking Dead* founders in the no-man's-land between the extremes, lurching one way and then the other.

Rick may return to the mainstream, once again walking the straight and narrow like the deputy sheriff he once was, but the road is no longer straight nor narrow. When the wholesale slaughter of as many ex-humans as possible is not only necessary but routine (and even fun), and torture, although reprehensible, shows results, and the 99 percent are so hungry that they dine on the living 1 percent, it is no longer your mom and pop's mainstream. Whereas the center and its shows were once dominated by center-left liberals, they have now ceded pride of place to center-right conservatives. Indeed, the show recalls the Vietnam-era bumper sticker that read EAT THE RICH, but it's on the other team. The bumper stickers displayed by Rick's fleet of banged up vehicles might well say KILL THE HUNGRY. As we leave the center, it seems that today's left-wing extremists are likely to be on the side of the zombies and vampires—and they are.

# 8
# Beauty in the Beast

*If the center frets because its heroes sometimes behave like beasts, the left doesn't care. It embraces Dr. Frankenstein and his monster, because the Romantics taught that savages are noble.*

> Was I then a monster, a blot upon the earth, from which all men fled, and whom all men disowned?
> —*Frankenstein's monster*

A team of workers rolls a large, grimy industrial canister scuffed and crusted with rust into the Occam Aerospace Research Center, a U.S. Army contractor. Following it is Colonel Michael Shannon, with a fixed frown on his face, dressed in a funereal black suit and tie, and holding a cattle prod at his side. The head of security, with a clipboard under one arm, and looking every inch the geek that he is, announces, "I don't wanna overstate the matter, but this may very well be the most sensitive asset ever to be housed in this facility." Whatever that asset is, it begins to thrash about, pummeling the tank's glass portholes from the inside, alarming its keepers.

Several cuts later, Shannon stumbles into a cavernous hall, bleeding profusely. An alarm blares. Sally Hawkins and Octavia Spencer, part of the lowly janitorial crew, carrying brushes and buckets, are summoned to clean up the bloody mess that covers the floor of a large, dimly lit laboratory. Hawkins plays an Hispanic waif who, like Jake Sully, is damaged. Three parallel scars on her neck that vaguely suggest gills indicate damage done to her larynx at some point in the past, preventing her from speaking, a clumsy metaphor, perhaps, that suggests the voicelessness of working women at the bottom of the economic heap.

In one corner of the lab, Hawkins can't help but notice a floor-to-ceiling glass cylinder filled with murky green water. Inside it, we barely make out the outlines of a large, vaguely humanoid biped floating upright. It has webbed hands and feet, fins, oddly expressive eyes, and iridescent green markings on either side of its head. For those who have seen Jack Arnold's 1954 classic, *Creature from the Black Lagoon*, it looks familiar, perhaps a friend or close relative of that movie's eponymous beast. There, the Creature, like most of Arnold's put-upon aliens, is abused by heedless scientists eager to discover what makes it tick. Guillermo del Toro, whose Oscar winning *The Shape of Water* we're watching, goes him one better. His creature, likewise unhappy, is released into the waters from which it came by sympathetic humans and takes one of them with it.

Unsurprisingly, attitudes toward behavior are inflected across the spectrum from left to right, which is to say, colored by the politics of the viewer. Helping the elderly cross the street may get you a pat on the back in the mainstream, but out here on the fringe, pushing them into the flow of traffic is more likely to be applauded. If the message of the center is about the strength of groups, the mantra of extremist shows is more likely to be "Everyone for his and herself."

Trump buried civility under a tonnage of tweets, but the movies were there first. It's instructive to take another excursion into the past, to revisit the golden age of the western, that quintessential American genre that was the most popular and therefore most effective vehicle for showcasing mainstream values from the silent era right on up to the mid-1960s.

Although sorely tempted, the western heroes of yesteryear never took the law into their own hands, never settled personal scores with a six-gun. Rather, they handed killers, rustlers, and bank robbers over to the sheriff for what audiences assumed would be a fair trial.

Over the course of half a century, the lean, weathered gunslingers who rode into the dusty towns with no names to set things right were held to a high standard. After all, they were bringing civilization to the lawless West, and revenge was just one item on a long list of the things they were forbidden to do. The Gary Coopers and John Waynes of yesteryear, despite their itchy trigger fingers and fast draws, never shot first; nor in the back; nor hit a man when he was down; nor killed women, children, or unarmed desperados, no matter how heinous their crimes. Cultural critic Robert Warshow, writing in 1954 about the westerns of the 1930s and 1940s, called the "Westerner" the "last gentleman." He adhered to the Code of the West.

Even on those occasions when the sheriffs turned out to be cowards, or were paid off by the cattle barons, the U.S. Marshals could be counted on to clean up the mess, because their authority was federal, not local. Indeed, the people's violence had no place in a democracy, and therefore it was criminalized. Individuals who took the law into their own hands were denigrated as "vigilantes." Collectively, they were the "mob." Craving justice or revenge—to them they were the same—they surrounded the jail and called for blood before the prisoner could come to trial.

The western eventually fell victim to changing times. The erosion of the Code of the West began in the early 1950s. In fact, the code was dying when Warshow wrote his essay. There was always a contradiction at its heart: For all that society liked to think that it had evolved beyond violence, it hadn't. Violence and vigilantes were necessary because the lawmen couldn't or wouldn't do what was necessary to bring righteousness to Tombstone. But no sooner did the gunslingers ride into town to restore order than they had to make a U-turn and ride out again, the way Shane does at the end of the 1953 film that bears his name, leaving little Brandon de Wilde calling, plaintively, "Come back, Shane! Come back, Shane!"

Get a grip, Brandon, because the town without pity is no home for a hero. Shane isn't coming back anytime soon. Ditto Wayne in John Ford's *The Searchers* (1956). There, he plays a former Confederate soldier turned vigilante by dint of refusing to pledge allegiance to the Texas Rangers—the only legitimate authority in shouting distance. He then embarks on a mission of revenge. Scar is the bad "Injun," who has kidnapped Wayne's niece Natalie Wood, slaughtered her family, and had his way with her. Wedded to vengeance as he is, he mimics the ways of the Comanches by gratuitously scalping Scar after he's killed him, indicating that he has more in common with the "savages" than he does with the "civilized" white man. For all that, he's returned Wood to a neighboring family at the end of the movie, but they shut the door to their home behind him in the famous closing shot, as he is exiled to the wilderness. He can't go home again.

Gunslingers may have been needed, but they weren't wanted. They were killers, extremists, far too dangerous to live next door on the other side of that white picket fence. Vestiges of the lawless past, they represented the repressed, and when they returned, they were repressed anew. Even Roy Goode, as upstanding a man as an outlaw is likely to be, can't settle down with Michelle Dockery at the end of *Godless*, and has to ride off.

As the years passed, however, the code was honored less in the letter than in the breach, so much so that eventually, the prohibitions against bad behavior not only deserted the western but other genres as well. On the left, there were so many voices going back so far preaching kill-or-be-killed violence—from the Jacobins to the Bolsheviks—that it was hard to choose, but in the 1960s it was Mao's Little Red Book that inspired the Weathermen: Power grows out of the barrel of a gun. The code was the casualty. If the Weathermen had taken time out to go to the movies, they might have enjoyed Sam Peckinpah's butchered 1973 masterpiece *Pat Garrett and Billy the Kid*, in which one of Garrett's deputies foolishly turns his back on Billy (Kris Kristofferson), saying, "You wouldn't shoot me in the back, Bill." Guess what? As soon as the man turns away, Billy does just that, shoots him in the back.

The New Hollywood may have gotten audiences used to antiheroes like Clyde Barrow and the Sundance Kid, but networks lagged behind. Jittery advertisers didn't want the cops and cowboys who sold their cars shooting lawmen, and it wasn't until cable shrugged off the dead hand of sponsored TV that Tony Soprano could beat, choke, and maim whomever he wanted—including (almost) his own mother—and no one changed channels. When the floodgates opened, bad good guys poured through. How bad could they break? Pretty bad. Dexter, a serial killer, had his own show, although his targets were confined to other serial killers.

Marvel played catch-up. When it challenged the Justice League, DC's gang of superheroes, with its own supergroup in 1963, they were called, simply, the Avengers. "Justice" had nothing to do with it. In *Luke Cage* a black female cop, defending the "system" to her white male partner, calls Luke a "vigilante" and rejects the practice of breaking the law to enforce the law. "There are rules and regulations to what we do," she says, primly. He responds, "Other than mopping up blood and arresting the same piece of shit over and over, there's not that much we can do as cops. This whole job is irrelevant." Luke agrees. "Forget the system," he says. "Arrests lead to indictments. And indictments lead to pleas. And boom, right back in business. I ain't going for that." Luke's girlfriend seconds him, chiming in, "Sometimes if you want justice, you have to get it yourself." These characters attack the authorities for being soft on crime, but they do so from the left, not the right.

Like many of the supes and semi-supes in *True Blood*, Luke says, "I don't know who I am." Experience has taught him to trust no one, but as a consequence, he's shut down, barely human, inhabiting a discomfort zone between human and superhuman. "I ain't no hero," he says. "I don't wanna be different than anybody else." He just wants to be normal. Eventually, like Raven, Luke finds himself when he accepts his superpowers, as well as his vocation, saying, "People needed someone who didn't require a warrant or a shield to get things done. Call it a vigilante, or a superhero, like or not, I finally accepted that that someone had to be me."

Whereas the center frowns on personal agendas, the left indulges them. In *X-Men: First Class*, Erik / Magneto, who has neither forgotten nor forgiven Herr Doktor Schmidt for killing his mother, proudly exacts his pound of flesh, disposing of him in a particularly gruesome fashion, and is never punished for it. When Tony Stark refuses to turn Iron Man over to the government, he pits his private interest against public interest. He invented it and it belongs to him. (He does eventually bow in the direction of the public interest by handing over a suit to his pal Colonel Don Cheadle so that the military can have its own Iron Man, called War Machine, to play with.)

Refusing to cooperate with Congress is not the first time Tony has revealed a personal agenda. He confesses to his assistant and sometime love interest Pepper Potts (Gwyneth Paltrow) that the reason he carried a World Security Council's nuke away from New York City at the end of *The Avengers* was not, as we might have imagined, to save millions of lives, but rather to save a single life. In his words, "I wanted to protect the one thing I can't live without . . . that's you."

In *Avengers: Age of Ultron* (2015), Thor decides to stay on Earth to help his pals defeat Ultron instead of hightailing it back to Asgard. Why? Because Earth "is his home for the moment," explained Chris Hemsworth, who plays Thor. "So the initial threat of attack from Ultron is personal."

The pursuit of personal interests by the likes of Iron Man and Thor et al. doesn't go unnoticed by mainstream authorities. In *Captain America: Civil War*, the Avengers are attacked for ignoring the collateral damage they inflict in the course of their heroics. Until *Civil War*, none of the superhero movies paid the slightest attention to collateral damage, save for corrupt politicians and ignorant newspaper editors. In fact, it has always been a fixture of comic book blockbusters, exploited as an opportunity for extravagant special effects. Perhaps it was the Iraq War, when critics charged George W. with invading Iraq for personal reasons—to finish what his father started—

and then turning his back while the country devolved into chaos that turned things around. In any event, only after the nation of Sokovia is destroyed in *Age of Ultron* does it become an issue too serious to ignore, even popping up in films like *Batman v Superman*.

Sokovia was the homeland of Zemo, the sympathetic villain of *Civil War*, who lost his family when it was destroyed in the battle between the Avengers and Ultron. For the first time, both Captain America and Tony Stark are brought up short by the consequences of their actions, forced to face the human cost of their victory over Ultron in damage to Sokovia.

The days of congressional hearings are over. Secretary of State, General Thaddeus "Thunderbolt" Ross, arrogant and abusive, ups the ante, using collateral damage as an excuse to bring the Avengers under his thumb. He uses the "v" word, calling Captain America a "vigilante," adding, "You've operated with unlimited power and no supervision. That's something the world can no longer tolerate." Ross adds that if the Avengers resist, they'll either have to agree to UN supervision or retire—shades of Brad Bird's *The Incredibles*. Regulation, oversight, supervision—these were the tools centrists traditionally used to bring the extremes under the control of mainstream bureaucracies, either national or, like here, international.

Collateral damage is dear to the hearts of the mainstream because it concerns the safety of noncombatants who are, after all, bystanders, spectators. There may be an ethical distinction between accidental spectators caught in the line of fire and intentional spectators who choose to stay out of the line of fire and watch others take the bullets, but the center protects both. With some exceptions, it doesn't care about turning them into actors, the way *Avatar* does on the left and the evangelical shows do on the right. Rather, it does the reverse, directing its ire at actors. In *Civil War*, those actors are the Avengers.

General Ross's threats divide the Avengers into two camps. Tony Stark and his followers accept supervision, whereas Cap rejects it. Although Tony's camp and Cap's faction both deplore collateral damage, the welfare of humans actually counts for little in their quarrel. Tony accepts supervision not because he agrees with the principle, but because he thinks it's unavoidable. Cap, on the other hand, rejects it because it's impractical. Indeed, whereas centrist Rick, unwilling to turn Michonne over to the Governor in *The Walking Dead*, refuses to sacrifice the one for the many, instead reconciling the one with the many, extremist Cap makes one of those hard choices that Rick resisted, by facing up to, nay, insisting on the inevitability of collateral damage. "We try to save as many people as we can," he explains. "Sometimes that doesn't mean everybody. But if we can't find a way to live with that, next time . . . maybe nobody gets saved."

Cap seeks advice from an old friend, who speaks with authority because her mother founded S.H.I.E.L.D. Her words give comfort to extremists: "Even if the whole world is telling you to move, it is your duty to plant yourself like a tree, look them in the eye, and say, 'No.'"

If indeed the answer is "No," to whom or what, then, if not the UN, are the superheroes responsible? With the mainstream authorities out to lunch or, worse, rife with corruption, superheroes have little choice but to fall back on themselves. Their private agendas do dictate their behavior. As Captain America, no team player, puts it, "I never really fit in anywhere, even in the army." "My faith's in . . . individuals," he confesses. To the center, this is merely selfishness, but to the left, it looks different. What appears to be selfish, even monstrous from the mainstream's point of view, is in reality the opposite. Cap knows that the personal and the public will never be reconciled within the here-and-now of the center, especially in an organization like the UN. We've repeatedly seen that mainstream institutions are not to be trusted. The World Security Council that previously supervised the Avengers was honeycombed with Hydra agents. Why should the UN be any different?

Collateral damage is not on the radar of our superheroes for another reason as well. There's simply nothing for just plain people to do in superhero movies; they are essentially useless. Samuel L. Jackson, who is, after all, a bigger star than most of the interchangeable ingénues of both sexes who wear those kitschy costumes, plays Nick Fury, and he could have been shoehorned into the story, but he has no more than a cameo. Speaking of *Age of Ultron*, Jackson observed, "It's another one of those 'people who have powers fighting people who have powers' [movies]. . . . There's not a lot I could do except shoot a gun." The same is true of *Civil War*. In *Captain America: The First Avenger* (2011), it's Herr Schmidt, the Nazi, who tells Cap, "I am proud to say that we have left humanity behind." But eventually, so do our superheroes.

Once *Avatar*'s argument against fence-sitting human spectators is undermined by their inability to provide actual help, they are no longer potential actors, recruits, soldiers-in-waiting in the war between good and evil; they become truly incidental to the battle the superheroes are waging, and therefore the bubble of security that formerly protected them can be pierced with impunity. Their role is limited to suffering collateral damage.

We recall that Rick's son Carl in *The Walking Dead* worries that he is turning into a "monster." If that show asks, "Is it OK to do anything to survive?" when centrist shows shout "No!" extremist shows shout "Yes!"

Violent behavior is forced upon centrist heroes who would rather be sitting by the fire reading Jane Austen than pick up the gun, but extremist heroes embrace it. They are blissfully untroubled by the prospect of behaving badly, because what is bad behavior in centrist shows is good behavior in extremist shows that therefore have no need for the dodges and ploys to which mainstream heroes resort to evade the taint of violence or revenge.

In *The Hunger Games* (2012), the capital's oligarchs force the "tributes," actually teenagers culled from each of the districts, to engage in a deadly game of hide-and-seek. Not unlike Rick and his band, the kids are dropped into a brutal state of nature. Survival requires them to kill their competitors, who are trying to kill them as well.

The Hunger Games are based on the premise that the winners are those with not only the best survival skills, but the fewest scruples. In the novels, Katniss Everdeen does manage to kill several of her rival contestants with a series of ingenious stratagems, but on the screen, she struggles against the logic of survivalism that pushes her peers toward extremism. The only casualties are the books, which are gutted for those PG-13 ratings, meaning she has to vanquish her competitors with a minimum of bloodshed. She only kills two tributes, one being a mercy killing, so that she has no trouble preserving her humanity. She gets through the second film, *The Hunger Games: Catching Fire* (2013), and another set of games, without killing anyone.

The winners of the games are expected to tour the country touting the benevolence and wisdom of the rulers. In *Catching Fire*, Katniss is escorted throughout the districts by storm troopers clad in white *Star Wars* body armor. She is appalled by the brutality of the "Peacekeepers," as they are called with heavy Orwellian irony, who behave like an occupying army, making their way through the rubble-strewn streets of squalid villages in their drab military vehicles, searching for dissidents, whom they shoot on sight or casually incinerate with flamethrowers.

The villain of the series, a white-bearded patriarch named Coriolanus Snow (Donald Sutherland) who rules the capital, worries that the

99 percent will rebel against the oligarchs. "What is to prevent an uprising that can lead to revolution?" he asks Katniss. What, indeed?

Led by President Alma Coin (Julianne Moore), the districts do in fact revolt. Katniss becomes the face of uprising, but at the end of the fourth and final film of the series, under the pressure of extreme circumstances, even she is finally forced to behave in an extreme fashion. She vows vengeance against Snow, whose army has bombed her district, killing nearly the entire population of ten thousand people. Eventually, however, she realizes that President Coin has betrayed the rebels and was behind her sister's death. She avenges her sister by killing Coin with an arrow. For this, she is exiled. Were *The Hunger Games* a mainstream picture, that would be that, but here, the exile is temporary. She is pardoned, revenge forgiven.

The X-Men, like the vampires in *True Blood*, are divided into two factions. One, led by Charles Xavier (Patrick Stewart), favors the low-profile path the mutants have always taken, coexisting with mortals as best they can. He's the moderate to Erik/Magneto's extremist, who is not only dedicated to avenging himself on Herr Doktor Schmidt, but also advocates war against humans.

Charles Xavier presides over the training of adolescent mutants at his School for Gifted Youngsters, but despite his opposition to Erik/Magneto's confrontational tactics, he encourages his youthful charges to bring out the monster inside them. In one of the films—they all run together—while racing nerdy Hank McCoy around the Mutant High track, he observes, "In each of us, two natures are at war." A quick study, and no stranger to the western canon, Hank fires back, "Robert Louis Stevenson, *Jekyll and Hyde*."

Hank is falling behind. Charles looks back at him and says, "If you want to beat me, you have to set the beast free." Instead of encouraging him to express his Dr. Jekyll, human nature at its best, Charles urges him to release his inner Hyde, human nature at its worst. This is inexplicable, until we realize that if people are torn between culture and nature, Jekyll and Hyde, it's appropriate that Charles, who has pushed through the looking glass into the topsy-turvy world of extremism, nurtures Mr. Hyde. Once again, in the world of the Luddite-left, the beast within, the feral child, is the noble savage, uncorrupted by civilization and therefore more human than humans. There's an exchange regarding Mike Tyson in *Luke Cage* that captures this nicely:

"Mike Tyson was a real nice guy."

"But he hit like a beast."

"There was beauty in that beast."

In the mainstream, savages are just savages. We recall that the French trapper caught with his pants down in *The Revenant* by Leonardo DiCaprio shouts, "We are all savages!" and in that film, it's true. There are more than enough to go around. Savages behave like animals, and we know what the center thinks of them. In David Lynch's *The Elephant Man* (1980), John Merrick, the eponymous hero famously cries, "I am not an animal," underlining the difference in kind between humans and animals that mainstream films insist upon. The CDC's Dr. Jenner in *The Walking Dead* showed us that the brain functions of walkers were reduced to the level of lower mammals at best, sub- or prehumans, that is, beasts. Nor does *World War Z* have much use for nature. Director Marc Forster makes the analogy between zombies and animals explicit. He based the behavior of his zekes on birds, fish, and swarming ants. As he spelled it out, "They're like this force of nature coming at you. I felt like the more I could base it in nature, viscerally, the more scary it [would] be."

For the alien-loving left, on the other hand, beasts are either victims or heroes. *Fantastic Beasts and Where to Find Them* (2016), written by J.K. Rowling, is the first of a five-film franchise that predates the *Harry Potter* series. It is a disappointing picture, with a plot too busy by far for its own good, yet for our purposes it is instructive. Set in 1926 on the eve of the Great Depression, and the rise of the Nazis in Germany, it is filled with foreboding, appropriate to what Rowling sees today as "nationalism . . . on the march across the Western world, feeding upon the terrors it seeks to inflame." More explicit, she continues, "'Make America Great Again!' cries a man who is fascist in all but name."

Newt Scamander (Eddie Redmayne) is a fantastic beast rescuer. After some of them escape, Newt explains, "We're trying to recapture my creatures before they get hurt." When he gets into trouble, as he does regularly, the fantastic beasts rescue him. In other words, in this film, They are just like Us, no different from centrists' image of themselves as vulnerable and benign.

Not so vulnerable and benign, as Charles Xavier knows, are superheroes who, with their secret identities, embody the dual nature of humans. The Bruce Waynes of the world are citizens of the center in whom the beast is cloaked by the apparel of civility. When they strip off their street clothes, like Batman in the Batcave, the beast is revealed. Thanks to the alchemy of extremism, however, he or she is a hero, not a villain. In *The Wolverine*

(2013) Logan, as his human doppelganger is called, gets off to a bad start in life. As a child, he kills his own father—by mistake, to be sure, but still . . . Eventually, he morphs into a powerful creature with a short fuse and long knife-like claws so sharp they perforate metal as if it were butter. Wolverine's personal agenda is straight-up revenge. To achieve it, he is told that he's going to have to stop "denying your true nature. . . . You're going to have to become the animal." Ratifying his transformation, he tosses aside the old dog tags from his army days that read LOGAN and insists that the fresh ones be stamped with WOLVERINE, more in keeping with the new him.

The Shape of Water, like Hidden Figures, is set at the height of the Cold War. It begins with a snatch of narration furnished by one of the characters, who describes the story to come as "a tale of love and loss, and the monster who tried to destroy it all." As it turns out, however, the monster he refers to is not the powerful amphibian brought back from a river in the Amazon, but a human, Colonel Shannon. More or less reprising his role in Boardwalk Empire (2010–2014) Shannon routinely jolts the Creature with electric shocks from his cattle prod, explaining, "It's an animal. Just keeping it tame."

Colonel Shannon just wants to kill the Creature, which would be a shame in a Luddite-left picture like this one, because this alien is benign, tortured by both soldiers and scientists, but particularly by the former, because here the soldiers, not the scientists, are in control, as they are in Avatar.

Charged with rooting out security risks, Colonel Shannon overlooks the janitorial staff so far beneath him as to be nearly invisible, so that Hawkins has ample opportunity to bond with the Creature by playing it music and feeding it hard-boiled eggs. It's up to her to save it, but she needs a little help from her friends, Spencer and Richard Jenkins, a gay commercial artist who is shunned because of his sexual orientation. They, however, drag their feet. Assuming the role of mere spectators, they don't want to get involved. Jenkins complains, "He's not even human," whereupon Hawkins snaps, "Do nothing, and neither are we." This alliance of outsiders—a poor Hispanic woman, a black woman, and a gay man—rescues the Creature.

Meanwhile, in Avatar, we recall that Jake's red light was Quaritch's green light. The colonel launches a full-out assault on the Na'vi. His army pits fire against foliage. The contrast between his deadly, if ungainly fleet of heavily armored gunships, bristling with spiky turrets and cannons carrying pendulous honeycombs gravid with missiles slung under their wings, and the delicate shapes and hues of Pandora's abundant flora says it all. When one of the rebels observes, "It's some kind of shock-and-awe campaign," we know Quaritch is using the George W. Bush playbook. He adds, "We will fight terror with terror." Amid a firestorm of flame and billowing black smoke, amplified by the deafening roar of explosions attendant on a nonstop rain of ordnance, he blasts the majestic Hometree into wood chips, turning the Na'vi's sacred ground into a blackened dead zone of ash, charred stumps, and scorched earth. But Selfridge and the colonel are unmoved. Casually sipping coffee, Quaritch remarks, "That's how you scatter the roaches."

The Hometree was the Na'vi's World Trade Center, only We—Americans—are the terrorists. (Cameron remarked that he was "surprised at how much it did look like September 11.") From the point of view of the Na'vi, the colonel's assault is genocide. Far more than just an attempt to drive them from the site of the unobtanium, the company intends to if not exterminate their species, to at least traumatize it profoundly. As the colonel explains before his second assault on the Na'vi, this one against the Tree of Souls, "The hostiles believe that this mountain stronghold of theirs is protected by their deity. When we destroy it, that will blast a crater in their racial memory so deep that they will never come within a thousand klicks of this place again."

The Na'vi can't defeat Quaritch's forces by themselves, but they get help, most dramatically from pterodactyl-like banshees so powerful they pluck choppers out of the sky and fling them like toys against Pandora's sheer cliffs. The beasts of the jungle join the big birds to wage war against the human invaders, making short work of the colonel's hardware, which is no match for the hammerheads—elephantine creatures with heads the shape of battering rams turned sideways. Selfridge and Quaritch can disparage the Na'vi all they want, call them "monkeys" and "roaches"—epithets drawn from nature—because in this picture, nature wins. As Cameron put it, "I think there's something amazingly satisfying when the hammerheads come out of the forest and start mowing down all the bad security enforcers. . . . Nature gets to fight back."

The victorious Na'vi escort their American prisoners to their ship, while human-Jake, making an entry in his videolog, sums it all up, reporting, "The aliens went back to their dying world." By "dying," he's underlining the fact that Earth has become one of those lifeless planets done in by its inhabitants. By "aliens," he means Us—Americans, Earthlings. If the show began from the point of view of the Americans, by the end, the point of view belongs solely to the Na'vi and those who have gone over to their side.

And from where they stand, the humans are indeed Other. The objects of study in, say, Chris Carter's *X-Files*—the aliens, freaks, and mad scientists who so piqued the curiosity of Agents Mulder and Scully from 1993 to 2002 on the Fox network—have evolved into subjects.

In the same way that savages are just savages in mainstream shows, so too are monsters just monsters. In the final season of *True Blood*, Sookie finds herself victim of one of the nastiest vampires of all, who says, as he's trying to rape her, "[I] just want to fuck you, and own you, and use you for your blood." She screams, simply, "Monster!" Likewise, *The Walking Dead*'s Andrea, referring to the biters in Hershel's barn, observes, "When they turn, they become monsters. That's all."

If beasts and savages get makeovers in left-wing shows, monsters can't be far behind. In *X-Men: First Class*, Erik/Magneto travels to Argentina looking for Herr Doktor Schmidt. When he finds himself in a rats' nest of Nazi émigrés and is asked his name, he replies, "Let's just say I'm Frankenstein's monster. And I'm looking for my creator."

References to Frankenstein's monster abound in these shows. It owes its life to the legendary summer idyll that famously brought Lord Byron together with Percy Bysshe Shelley; Mary Godwin, the future Mrs. Shelley; and Byron's physician, John Polidori, at the Villa Diodati on the shores of Lake Geneva in 1816. Unremitting rain kept them indoors, and they challenged one another to produce ghost stories for their diversion. Byron began a sketch for a story that he abandoned, which would metamorphose into "The Vampyre," written by his long-suffering physician-sidekick Polidori. But the most famous issue of that momentous sojourn was Mary Shelley's *Frankenstein*, the darkest and most profitable blossom of the Romantic movement. Imagine the blow to the bottom line of the monster business and the future careers of Boris Karloff, Bela Lugosi, Sarah Michelle Gellar, Anne Rice, and last but not least, Mel Brooks, had the four played charades instead.

Romantics like Byron and the Shelleys were inspired by a thirst for transcendence that prompted their acolytes to break the shackles of custom and tradition. In the words of Isaiah Berlin, they longed "violently to burst through old and cramping forms." They were barrier busters, and they favored monsters because monsters were often composed of a combination of human and animal crossovers, half one thing, half another. The symbol of the rebels in the *Hunger Games* series, for example, is the "mockingjay," a hybrid of two species of birds.

Moreover, traditionally, humans were thought to be composites as well, part soul and part body, an amalgam of the sacred and the profane. Monsters were human, too, and humans, monsters. It's no wonder that looking at those frightful faces, sympathizers discerned familiar features.

Reacting against the Industrial Revolution, the Romantics used nature in all its wild splendor to not only flog machine culture but classicism as well, for its sterile love of order, balance, and moderation. Instead, Romanticism flaunted decay, savagery, and ugliness. The writers of the Romantic left painted their pictures in the gloomy hues of the supernatural and extended their sympathies to the real and metaphoric victims of civilization, not only favoring Mr. Hyde over Dr. Jekyll, but the Beast over Beauty, and in Showtime's *Penny Dreadful* (2014–16), Dr. Frankenstein's tormented monster over Dr. Frankenstein himself. In left-wing shows, beasts and monsters are never really evil. They are, in fact, as Dr. Frankenstein's monster implies in his apostrophe, more human than humans. Praising said monster in *Penny Dreadful*, Eva Green says, "I think you are the most human man I have ever known."

While the Catholic right was busy with its exorcisms, the Romantics turned the bestiary of good and evil upside down, even dusting off and dressing up Old Nick. As Leo Braudy put it in *Haunted*, his study of the supernatural, "Instead of being the principle of evil, Satan assumes the role of the Great Rebel, challenging the standards of society, revolting against illegitimate authority of all sorts, from fathers to kings to God himself." In case professor Braudy's word isn't good enough, here's Gilfoyle on *Silicon Valley*: "There are very few things I will defend with true passion. Medical marijuana, the Biblical Satan as a metaphor for rebellion against tyranny, and motherfucking, goddamn crypto currency."

In *True Blood*, extremist Maryann the maenad has no trouble embracing her inner beast, explaining, "I slept outside last night and I communed with my animal nature." Like Maryann, Dr. Frankenstein's creature disputes the bad reputation that burdens him and his ilk. As the monster describes himself in Shelley's novella, "Was I then a monster, a blot upon the earth, from which all men fled, and whom all men disowned?" With some reason, he thinks he's better than humans. As he describes himself, "I was not even of the same nature as man. I was more agile than they, and could subsist upon a coarser diet; I bore the extremes of heat and cold with less injury to my frame; my stature far exceeded theirs." In effect, he was the first superhero.

The cry of pain with which he ends his speech could have been uttered by any one of the mutant X-Men. Like him, many supes are filled with self-loathing; they have internalized the center's disdain. We've seen Sookie try to repudiate her inner fairy and suppress her supernatural powers. So too, in *First Class*, does X-Men's Raven/Mystique, who hates what she is, worrying that she's different—ugly. When she shifts back to her true self, we understand the reason why. She looks like a monster. Yellow cat's eyes peer out from a turquoise face topping a body covered with scars and scales from head to foot, in all but color like Michael Gambon in the 1986 BBC miniseries *The Singing Detective*, disfigured by full-body psoriasis.

Even the other mutants find her repulsive. But Erik/Magneto is another story. Returning to his room one night, he finds her in his bed, looking, not surprisingly, like the comely Jennifer Lawrence. Nevertheless, he tells her, "I prefer the real Raven," prompting her to shed Jennifer and go all blue and scaly. "You're an exquisite creature," he continues, without missing a beat. "All your life the world has tried to tame you. It's time for you to be free."

Needless to say, Raven carries a heavy chip on her shoulder. She appropriates the gay slogan turned mutant mantra "Mutant and proud!" giving it a bitter edge. Muttering under her breath, she says, "Or is that only the pretty mutations. But if you're a freak, better hide!" She finds a soul mate in Hank, who is also finding it difficult to take Charles's advice and get in touch with his inner beast. He is mortified by his gnarly feet, hairy like a chimp's. Indignantly, she asks him, "Should we have to hide?"

"I don't wanna feel like a freak all the time. I just wanna look—"

"—normal," says Raven, finishing his sentence. "Normal" in the context that Raven and Hank use it means human.

Hank has developed a serum that he hopes will render his feet and her appearance normal. She refuses to take it, wisely, as it turns out, because it transforms him into Beast, who joins Thing and the Hulk in Marvel's menagerie of admirable monsters. "It didn't work," Hank complains, in despair. "Yes it did," Raven replies. "This is who you were meant to be. This is you. No more hiding." She continues, "We are different, and we shouldn't be trying to fit into society. Society should aspire to become more like us. Mutant and proud." Although society never does become like them, Raven finally embraces her true Otherness.

In mainstream shows, humans dehumanized by the inhuman world in which they find themselves eventually make their way back to the human within them, like Rick. In extremist shows, on the other hand, supes and superheroes like Raven become whole by accepting that they're not human. As we have seen, Luke Cage, after complaining that he doesn't know what he is, likewise finds himself by accepting the inhuman in himself.

In *True Blood*, Sookie, eventually accepts that she's half fairy. Vampire Bill too, has a lesson to learn. He is indeed a self-hater. The Geronimo vampires were right. "I have spent my entire life as a vampire apologizing, believing that I was inherently wrong, somehow, living in fear, fear that God had forsaken me, that I was damned." In the final season, however, like Hank and Raven, he comes to embrace his inner beast. He has, as he puts it, been granted "freedom from fear." But it's too late for Bill. In the same way that all those mainstream westerns expel the gunfighter at the end, *True Blood* doesn't tolerate true monsters. He kills himself.

In far-left shows, on the other hand, following Charles Xavier, Raven, Hank McCoy, et al., the mutants learn to freely refer to themselves as monsters, beasts, or just animals. The same is true for *The Imitation Game*, wherein Alan Turing becomes his own kind of monster, not only beyond his fellow mortals, but beyond God. Breaking the Enigma code, the British are able to anticipate the Germans' every move, but they must conceal their advantage from the enemy, which means refusing to warn an Allied ship targeted by a pack of U-boats. Appalled, a colleague challenges him, saying, "You're not God, Alan. You don't get to decide who lives and who dies."

"Yes, I do."

"Why? Why you?"

"Because no one else can. . . . Was I God? No. Because God didn't win the war. I did." Although he's not regarded as a mad scientist, due to the respect these shows have for science, his behavior, taking it upon himself to decide the destiny of humans, in another kind of film would be—monstrous.

# 9
# License to Kill

*Even harsher than the left, in the World According to Clint Eastwood and James Bond, it's an eye for an eye and a tooth for a tooth. Murder, torture, and revenge are all in a day's work.*

> You have to fight fire with fire. . . . We have to fight viciously. And violently.
>
> —*Donald Trump*

A man dressed in a low-rent Spider-Man outfit is riding in a cab, making small talk with the driver. Maybe he's on this way to a Halloween party, but after introducing himself as Deadpool, he peels away his Spider-Man mask and shouts, "Boo!" as well he might. He looks like a sideshow attraction, with a head that resembles a hunk of boiled meat. After he explains that he's "after someone on my naughty list to make him fix what he did to me," it becomes clear that he's on a mission of revenge.

The man he's after, who goes by the name of Ajax, is the swaggering villain of the piece, and it is he who subjected Wade Wilson, a.k.a. Deadpool, to a procedure that gave him mutant powers but also left him badly disfigured, for which "Mr. Pool" has never forgiven him. As he puts it, "Whatever they did to me made me totally indestructible . . . and completely unfuckable."

Chasing Ajax, Deadpool provokes a spectacular fight sequence on an expressway, in which he demonstrates considerable acrobatic skill nearly, but not quite, Spider-Man-class, as he runs, ducks, spins, leaps, and somersaults circles around Ajax's thugs, creating such mayhem that it makes the news, where Colossus, a metallic giant, sees it. Colossus has been trying to recruit Deadpool for the X-Men and is appalled by his antics. With Negasonic Teenage Warhead in tow, Colossus heads for the expressway. Meanwhile, Deadpool is having his fun, burning a hole between the eyes of one of Ajax's thugs with a red-hot cigarette lighter plucked from the dashboard of one of the cars splayed across the road. When Colossus arrives, he is not amused. Admonishing Deadpool, he says, "Wade, you're better than this. Use your powers for good. Be a superhero." Ignoring him, Deadpool impales another thug on his two katanas, hoists him aloft, and exclaims, "I may be super, but I'm no hero."

If the center shuns bad behavior while the left, following the radical Romantics, transforms it into good behavior, the right embraces violence, and revenge in particular, without tears. If breaking the law to enforce the law seems like a paradox, Ian Fleming's James Bond series found an elegant way out: MI6, the DMV of British intelligence, issued him a license to kill. In the very first film of the series, *Dr. No* (1962), there is a notorious preview of things to come, wherein self-defense shades into cold-blooded murder. Bond (Sean Connery) casually shoots a villainous geologist. Because he knows the man's gun is empty, it amounts to little more than an execution. He gets a pass because he is working for Her Majesty's Secret Service. Fifty-three years later, he finally comes clean. When asked for a job description in *Spectre* (2015), he replies simply, "I kill people."

Popeye Doyle shot a man in the back in *The French Connection*, and Clint Eastwood made his intentions clear in the original *Dirty Harry*, both released in 1971. Indeed, it was left to Eastwood to take a wrecking ball to the Code of the West. He is fond of telling a story about director Don Siegel, who asked John Wayne to plug a man in the back during the production of *The Shootist* (1976). Wayne snapped, "I don't shoot people in the back!" Siegel replied, "Clint Eastwood would." He was right. Eastwood would, and he did. The actor recalls, "In *Josey Wales* (1976), my editor said, 'Boy, you shot him in the back.' I said, 'Yeah, you do what you have to do to get the job done.' I think the era of standing there going 'You draw first' is over. You don't have much of a chance if you wait for the other guy to draw. . . . So, yeah, I used to shoot them in the back all the time."

Eastwood begat Reagan and Rambo, who came and went, but the culture continued its rightward drift, arriving at Steve Bannon, who famously said, "Darkness is good." He appears to embrace the idea of creative destruction, that is, redemption by means of violence, described in *The Fourth Turning*, by William Strauss and Neil Howe, said to be a book he is fond of. He is also said to have said, "I want to bring everything crashing down, and destroy all of today's establishment," and "Dick Cheney. Darth Vader.

Satan. That's power." Satan may have been Satan for the evangelical right, but for the secular right, like the far left, he is an inviting role model. In both varieties of right-wing shows, the heroes match the bad guys outrage for outrage. The worse they behave, the better.

In 1992, Eastwood played William Munny in *Unforgiven*, an artfully written revenge western that captures the essence of the iconic Eastwood gunslinger. In one climactic scene, Munny is confronted by Sheriff Little Bill Daggett (Gene Hackman), who incautiously killed Munny's pal Ned Logan (Morgan Freeman):

Daggett: "You'd be William Munny out of Missouri. Killer of women and children."

Munny: "That's right. I've killed women and children. I've killed just about everything that walks or crawled at one time or another. And I'm here to kill you, Little Bill, for what you did to Ned."

After Munny kills Daggett, he exits the saloon where the shooting has taken place, threatening, "Any sumbitch takes a shot at me, I'm not only gonna kill him, but I'm gonna kill his wife, all his friends, and burn his damn house down."

Unlike Wayne, Eastwood was comfortable with dialogue like this, because the law-abiding heroes Wayne played had been upstaged by the revenge heroes that Eastwood played. He knew his fans would swallow anything he did and like it. He made it possible for Trump to say, many years later, "I could stand in the middle of Fifth Avenue and shoot somebody, okay, and I wouldn't lose any voters, okay?"

Munny has plenty of company. "The world needs bad men," reflected Rust Cohle (Matthew McConaughey) in the first season of HBO's *True Detective* (2014). "We keep the other bad men from the door." Or, as Deadpool puts it, "I'm just a bad guy who gets paid to fuck up worse guys." In Eastwood's *American Sniper* (2014), Our sniper and Their sniper are on opposite sides, but they are both, after all, snipers, so instead of Us versus Them, it's more like Us as Them.

In the first season of *Shooter*, Ryan Phillippe's sniper, Bob Lee Swagger, gets the drop on a nastily insouciant psychopath who has kidnapped Swagger's wife and little girl, a crime against family, and therefore an incentive and excuse for revenge. Just as he's about to pull the trigger, his wife grabs the shotgun out of his hands. At another time, in another kind of show, she might have been expected to say, "Don't do it! Turn him over to the authorities," but instead, she demands, "Let me do it." Defiant to the end, the wiseass kidnapper says, "You'll never shoot. You're a housewife," but she gets the last word. Blowing his brains all over the ground, she proclaims proudly, "I'm a Swagger!"

AMC's *Justified* (2010–15), is a deliciously twisted six-season riff on a story by Elmore Leonard, set in hardscrabble Appalachian coal country—Harlan County, Kentucky. If it used to be poor manners to shoot bad guys in the back, now it's so common that U.S. Marshal Raylan Givens (Timothy Olyphant) uses it as the punch line of a joke. Toward the end of the final season, he shoots a fleeing killer. Surprised, the man exclaims, "You shot me in the back!" Rarely at a loss for words, Raylan drawls, "If you want to get hit in the front, you should'a run toward me." Eventually, in other words, nobody minds how the outlaws are killed, front or back, so long as they are laid to rest in an unmarked grave on Boot Hill. Fair play is for wusses.

In *Lone Survivor* (2014), a heavily armed SEAL team is "infilled" into the Hindu Kush on Afghanistan's inhospitable eastern border with Pakistan, where jagged peaks poke through the clouds like saw teeth. Their mission is to terminate a particularly noxious Taliban leader named Ahmad Shah.

*Lone Survivor* is virtually a recruiting film for the SEALs, except for one thing: the mission fails spectacularly, and they're all killed. The single exception is the star, Petty Officer Mark Wahlberg. The mission goes south when they accidentally run across a couple of goatherds. Very unfortunate. The alternatives are, kill them to prevent them from blabbing to the Taliban or let them go. "Shah killed twenty marines last week," says one SEAL. "We let him go, he'll kill twenty more next week. Our job is to stop Shah." Wahlberg responds, "The rules of engagement say we cannot touch them. They are unarmed noncombatants."

The center's rules of war dictate that spectators should be protected from collateral damage. Remember Sokovia! The SEALs do the right thing, freeing the goatherds, but it turns out to be the wrong thing here. The goatherds do give away their position to the Taliban. Wahlberg changes his mind: "Looks like I voted wrong." In other words, the rules of war don't apply—in war.

Snowflakes who weep over drowned kittens can't be expected to shed tears over the SEALs, but neither do Wahlberg, et al. get much help from the military brass. Whereas in *World War Z*, the UN officials give the principals every kind of support they can, in *Lone Survivor*, the commanding officers don't want to hear about a mission in trouble and kick the matter back down the line to the team at the forward operating base, where it seems that there is a shortage of Apache helicopters. None can be spared to rescue the embattled SEALs. As is often the case in these kinds of movies, the few brave men are stabbed in the back by both the army brass and the bureaucrats in Washington.

If goatherds are fair game, so are women, and to the far right, there's not much difference. In *Deadpool*, Colossus, the stodgy straight man to the potty-mouthed super, not-much-of-a-hero, is beating on a female mutant, but pummeling the fair sex makes him uncomfortable. He fastidiously explains, "I prefer not to hit a woman." Deadpool's reply? "Finish fucking her the fuck up."

Generally speaking, in the center, revenge is transformed into justice. As we move to the extremes, justice becomes revenge. The police are useless, and the victims, occasionally aided by friends, have to do it themselves. On the right, in *Ms .45* (1981), a cult classic, Abel Ferrara, whose previous film was *Driller Killer* (1979), about a mad artist who roams the streets at night killing the homeless with a power drill, turns vigilante justice into grand guignol. A woman raped twice goes on a killing spree against abusers, which gradually turns into a vendetta against all men, whom she shoots and dismembers.

Often, the victims in rape-revenge shows need the help of a man, putting patriarchy back in play. In Eastwood's *Sudden Impact* (1983), "Dirty" Harry puts his unique skills at the service of Sondra Locke and her sister, who are gang-raped at the beginning of the movie. Locke is itching to get even. Positively restrained by the standards of *Ms .45*, she shoots each of the rapists in the groin before killing him. When Harry discovers who is settling scores, he shields her from prosecution.

In Martin McDonagh's Oscar-nominated rape-murder-revenge dramedy *Three Billboards Outside Ebbing, Missouri* (2017), the cops are worse than useless to acid-tongued Frances McDormand, who hunts the men who defiled, killed, and burned her daughter. She taunts the cops for spending all their time harassing African Americans, leaving none to spare on solving crimes. When the chief of police dies of cancer, McDormand takes advantage of the vacuum at the center of authority to firebomb the police station—and gets away with it. A new African American police chief arrives in town, played by Clarke Peters, an actor who radiates intelligence.

With Peters in charge of the Ebbing PD, McDormand's problem would be solved—in a mainstream show. He and she would work together to solve the crime and bring the perpetrators to justice. Instead, she teams up with Sam Rockwell, the worst of the cops, now semi-reformed, who thinks he's identified one of the rapists, but the DNA evidence doesn't support his suspicions. No matter. Even though they know the guy they thought did it didn't, Rockwell is sure he raped somebody, so they decide to kill him anyway. Or not. In a car, heading off to find him at the end of the film, they decide to decide along the way. Guilty or not, the film wants him dead, and so do we. Forget due process. Revenge is all.

Christopher Nolan, rebranding Batman as the Dark Knight, brings out his shady side, turning him into a revenge hero as well. Tragedy comes early to young Master Bruce when, as a child, he witnesses—you got it—another crime against the family—the death of his parents at the hands of a mugger in a scene we have seen replayed so many times in so many shows—the *Dark Knight*s, Fox's Batman prequel *Gotham* (2014– ), and *Batman v Superman*—it feels like the Zapruder footage, indelibly inscribed in our memories as if it happened to us.

Bruce Wayne is another Steve Newlin, whose mom and dad were killed by vampires, motivating him to dedicate himself in *True Blood* to eradicating the toothy predators from the face of the earth. There, Newlin is just a jerk, but in the *Dark Knight* trilogy, he would have been a hero, like Bruce.

The Waynes are the wealthiest family in Gotham, and until they are murdered, the city's most generous benefactors. Wayne Tower is a virtual shrine to themselves, as someone describes it admiringly, "the unofficial heart of Gotham," the hub of an elevated monorail that comprises the futuristic transit system also funded by the Wayne family. Whereas liberals try to enlarge the public sector while shrinking the private, the *Dark Knight* movies applaud the privatization of what used to be called public works. It's also true that Bruce's training and self-discipline aside for the moment, his only real superpower is money, the dollars that pay for the toys that allow him to swing from Gotham's tallest buildings and run red lights in his Batmobile.

In *Batman Begins* (2005), the first and weakest of the three films (among its many eccentric casting choices, Tom Wilkinson bravely slings "dese" and "dats" trying to impersonate an Italian mob boss but just embarrasses himself), the Wayne slayer comes up for parole. Bruce (Christian Bale) attends the hearing, not with the expectation that justice will be served, as he would had he been raised on a diet of mainstream movies, but rather with the conviction that the soft-on-crime legal system will set him free—which it does. Prepared to administer his own brand of vigilante justice, Bruce has brought a gun, but he is frustrated by an assailant who shoots the killer first. In a centrist picture like *The Revenant*, this outcome might have been welcome. Bruce would have gotten his revenge without having to dirty his hands, but here, it just leaves him feeling hollow, disappointed, and unfulfilled.

Rachel Dawes, on the other hand, an assistant DA, is so appalled to learn he's carrying that she takes it upon herself to deliver a lecture about the difference between justice and revenge. "Justice is about harmony," she says. "Revenge is about you making yourself feel better. That's why we have an impartial system." This sounds right—she is part of the criminal justice system, after all, so principle, identified with the public interest, tops revenge. But the trouble is, extremist pictures like the *Dark Knight*s prefer the heart to the head, private to public, feelings to principles, so Rachel has a few lessons to learn.

Ra's Al Ghul (RAG), Bruce's mentor in the League of Shadows, had confessed to him that he joined the group to exact vengeance on the man who murdered his wife. During their training, he molds Bruce in his image. RAG sees that he is frustrated by his failure to even the score with his parents' killer. Apparently a lay therapist in his spare time, he diagnoses the source of Bruce's malaise, telling him, "You have . . . the strength of a man denied revenge."

If Rachel makes Bruce feel ashamed for trying to avenge himself on the man who killed his parents, Batman is less the sensitive flower. Acting out what Bruce would like to do but can't, he embraces the role of vigilante. There doesn't seem to be much controversy about that; he is freely referred to as such by friend and foe alike. And why not? On the far left and far right, it apparently takes extremists to defeat extremists, and therefore these shows disregard the stigma that centrists attach to those who take the law into their own hands.

Dirty Harry was the role model for Miller's Dark Knight, not too surprising, since Frank Miller wrote admiringly of Mr. Harry, calling him a "profoundly, consistently moral force, administering the 'Wrath of God' on murderers who society treats as victims." Miller added that Dirty Harry is "perfectly willing to pass judgment and administer punishment and make things right." According to Miller, "Clint Eastwood is more in touch with what we should do with superheroes than virtually anybody in comics."

In the *Dark Knights*, vigilantism is a growth industry. No less than Commissioner Gordon, one of the few honest cops in the city, defends it to his idealistic protégé, Detective Blake. Gordon says, "There's a point when the structures fail you, and the rules aren't weapons anymore, they're shackles letting the bad guy get ahead." Adds DA Harvey Dent, the other honest official, "Gotham's proud of an ordinary man standing up for what's right." Both Gordon and Dent agree that the rule of law has broken down, and only vigilante heroes, free from the legal dos and don'ts that hamstring ordinary folks, can set things right.

As the center diminishes in size and power, it has become increasingly irrelevant to the success of films like the *Dark Knights* and the *Hunger Games*, so that they shrewdly target both extremes—the new audience energized by today's polarization of opinion and taste.

*The Matrix* (1999) a brainy, cult blockbuster is a classic case of a left-wing picture that has become a talisman of the alt-right. Why left-wing? The multi-culti casting of the good guys is contrasted with the whitebread bad guys, all pale look-alikes with generic white-guy names (Agents Smith, Brown, and Jones).

The plot is constructed around the Luddite-left's distrust of machines, which in this picture have colonized humans. (The film even features a song by the band Rage Against the Machine.) As one character explains, "We gave birth to AI . . . a singular consciousness that spawned an entire race of machines." And another, "Your civilization? As soon as we began thinking for you, it became our civilization." Sounding like HAL, he quips, "Never send a human to do a machine's job." It seems that the machines farm humans as an energy source. People have been reduced to batteries—"coppertops."

Displacing human authorities, the machines are out to kill the plucky human rebels who form the Resistance. Laurence Fishburne plays Morpheus, whom the machines brand a "terrorist," while Keanu Reeves plays a computer nerd slash hacker named Neo, whom Morpheus thinks is "the One," who will inspire the humans to throw off the yoke of the machines.

Eventually, Neo develops superpowers (he moves so fast he can dodge bullets, he is way stronger than anyone sitting in front of a screen all day has any right to be, and he can bend spoons with his mind), but that can just as easily make him a Randian *Übermensch* of the right, as the left. The alt-right has keyed in on one scene in which Morpheus urges Neo to choose between a red pill and a blue pill. The red pill offers a secular substitute for being born again, that is, it will enable him to look at the world through new eyes. Neo will see that what he takes for reality is a sham, a computer-generated fake reality (the Matrix) created by the machines to convince us that we're free-range humans when in fact we're factory-farmed slaves. As such, we're constrained by rules and regulations imposed, according to the alt-right, by the enemy du jour, whether it be the "administrative state," "political correctness," or women, whom the MRAs (men's rights activists) have oddly equated with the machines. The real reality is a dystopic wasteland we've seen many times before in other shows, but here it is hidden from view by the Matrix. The blue pill, on the other hand, will allow Neo to continue living with his illusions in the fake world to which he is accustomed.

We've already seen that the proliferation of alternate universes in today's shows puts reality in flux, and therefore allows competing ideologies to lay claim to what is "real." To the alt-right, to be "redpilled" is to see through the fake reality imposed on us by the center and the left. Here, for example, is a redpilled Rush Limbaugh expounding on his "real" reality: "We live in two universes. One universe is a lie." This is the one run by government, academia, science, and the media, that together comprise what he calls the "Four Corners of Deceit." According to Limbaugh, "The other universe is where we are, and that's where reality reigns supreme and we deal with it. And seldom do these two universes ever overlap."

Neo, of course, chooses the red pill. The truth is revealed, and he joins the Resistance, which boasts of the unforgiving either/or, Us/Them Manicheanism we've come to expect from extremists. As the rebels put it, "If you are not one of us, you are one of them."

The *Hunger Games* franchise, although also coming from the left, throws a bone to the right, so that it too can assert ideological ownership over the series. Right-wing commentators have been quick to see that it can be interpreted as a libertarian Tea Party tract, in which the Capital is the much-despised Washington, DC, sucking the lifeblood out of the suffering states. "It's hard not to notice a nanny state which thinks its citizens should bow down and thank them for their very survival," wrote Christian Toto on *Breitbart*. Accordingly, Katniss is a pioneering frontierswoman like Sarah Palin, suckled by wolves. These shows are like figure-ground experiments in which each extreme sees the pattern it prefers.

Even *Avatar*'s politics did not limit its allure for the right. Indeed, when it was screened at U.S. bases in the Middle East, GI's loved it, ignoring its unflattering portrayal of the American military. And why not? After all, while applauding life among the fronds and ferns, *Avatar* is unable to entirely extricate itself from Lucas's aesthetic. It exploits images of warfare for their entertainment value. Then there's the lingering human chauvinism: when the Na'vi take on Quaritch's army, it's Jake's avatar, that is, a human, or partial human, who proves to be their bravest warrior.

*Star Wars*, too, as we recall, sent a double message, one carried by the script, another by the camera, allowing the right to come up with a plausible interpretation of the series totally at odds with Lucas's apparent intent, going so far as to champion the Empire in its war with the Galactic Republic. Read this way, the Empire is a "meritocratic force for order and stability led by a more-or-less benevolent dictatorship that seeks to maintain galactic unity, facilitate trade and head off a nasty intergalactic conflict before too many people can die. On the other [side], you have a band of religious terrorists whose leaders include a drug smuggler in the pocket of slavers." Empire apologists go so far as to justify the destruction of Alderaan, Princess Leia's home planet by the Death Star. Horrors!

If the politics of *Avatar*, as well as the *Hunger Games* and the *Star Wars* franchises are nevertheless ambiguous enough to please both the left and the right, so too can the right-wing *Dark Knight*s please the left and even the center. On the one hand, Batman has a code. He won't fire a gun, he won't kill the bad guys. Like the last gentlemen of the Old West, he deposits them on the steps of the police station, gift wrapped, bow and all, because, as Bruce confesses to Rachel, "You made me see that justice is about more than my own pain." But in another scene, Bruce turns around and admonishes her, "Your system of justice is broken." Repudiating revenge and embracing revenge—it's no wonder that the *Hollywood Reporter* asked, "Is Christopher Nolan's Batman Series Liberal or Conservative?" The answer is—both. Yes, justice is about more than his own pain and anger, but it's also true that the system of justice is broken.

Still, like most of Nolan's pictures, in the *Dark Knight*s, not only does right prevail, the right prevails. Batman may have acted the gentleman at one time, but his code no longer works. Given the degree of corruption in Gotham, if he expects the thugs he's caught to be punished by the courts, he's in for a rude surprise. And if he wants justice, he will have to try, convict, and punish the bad guys himself.

Indeed, mimicking the Marvel superheroes, he draws on his inner beast to avenge the murder of his parents by dedicating himself to punishing evildoers. In a key part of his backstory, he overcomes his fear of bats and reconfigures himself in their image. It is the opinion of Christian Bale, who plays Batman in Nolan's trilogy, that "he's got that killer within him."

Batman's code may inhibit him from killing, but it apparently doesn't stop him from savagely beating his enemies, most notably, the Joker, who describes himself as "an agent of chaos," making him an antecedent of Bannon and a frustrating enemy, because unlike Carmine Falcone and his gang, he doesn't care about money. In one scene, pulling a Jack Bauer, Batman jams a chair under the doorknob of the door to the interrogation room in which he's got the Joker cornered so that Commissioner Gordon, watching aghast through a window, is powerless to stop him from pounding, twisting, and throwing the grinning clown against the walls like a rag doll. The script directions provide a feel, however attenuated, for the violence of this scene: Batman "PICKS up the Joker and HURLS him into the two-way glass. . . . The Joker SMASHES into the wall—SLIDES to the floor. Batman stands over him, a man possessed."

Nor does his code prevent him from standing by while others kill his enemies. In *Batman Begins*, Commissioner Gordon blows up the tracks ahead of an out-of-control train carrying both RAG and Batman. Batman tells RAG, "I won't kill you, but I don't have to save you." That said, the Caped Crusader leaps to safety, while RAG plunges to his death. And since D.A. Harvey Dent has turned into a psychotic killer, it's okay for Batman to shove the demented DA off a ledge, breaking his neck. Even the Joker is impressed. At one point, Batman's nemesis comments, "You let five people die. Even to a guy like me, that's cold-blooded."

The final word on this subject is spoken by Detective Blake at the very end of the last film of the trilogy. Batman has been grooming him as his successor, the new Robin, or some such thing. When Commissioner Gordon once defended Batman's extralegal methods to Blake, then an idealistic, by-the-book rookie, the young cop didn't buy it. He admonished his boss, "Your hands look plenty filthy to me, Commissioner." Now, older and wiser, Blake has changed his tune. Gordon offers him a promotion, but the detective turns him down, saying, "You know what you said about structures becoming shackles? You were right." He prefers Batman to Gordon, breaking, rather than enforcing the law. We leave him, at the conclusion of the trilogy, exploring the Batcave to which he is heir.

Looking on the bright side, Bale said that although Batman has a killer inside him, "he's desperately not trying to let off his leash." Batman's ambivalence is commendable, and indeed, he doesn't kill wantonly, but when extreme circumstances require it, he rises, or better, sinks to the occasion. He may struggle against his inner beast, but eventually he gives it free rein. His descent calls to mind Dr. Jekyll's into Mr. Hyde or, closer to home, John Wayne's into Clint Eastwood. Perhaps the last word belongs to Batman himself. As he puts it in the animated TV series, "I am vengeance! I am the night! I am Batman!"

It took Batman a long time to shed his code and embrace the beast within. Not so the Punisher, Marvel's own dark superhero, whose family was also killed, gunned down by the mob. That sort of spoiled things for him. In the comics, he dons a T-shirt with a white skull splashed on the front that looks like it has bled in the wash until it resembles a mash-up of Edvard Munch's *The Scream* and Michael Myers's *Halloween* mask. The Punisher knows he should leave it to the cops, but he wants revenge, and he gets it, drawing quite the bloodbath as he makes short work of the mobsters who killed his family.

The Netflix series based on the comic (2017– ), opens with Jon Bernthal (Shane in *The Walking Dead*), playing the ex-marine, in a van chasing some bikers who are somehow implicated in the slaughter of his family. On the dashboard are pictures of his dead wife and two dead children. He races ahead of the bikers, blows them away, then turns around and runs over what's left of their bodies. Mission accomplished. But he's far from finished. Cut to a men's room in New York City's JFK Airport. The Punisher, wearing a black hoodie, barges into a stall, where a man is cowering. "You won," pleads the man, shaking so much he can barely speak. "An eye for an eye and all that. I got a family of my own." The Punisher replies, "I don't," whereupon the man repeats those tattered words that stopped Leonardo DiCaprio in his tracks in *The Revenant*: "For God's sake, man, killing mine is not going to bring yours back." Without so much as a pause, the Punisher strangles him anyway.

Like the Punisher, Deadpool doesn't bother to burnish his bad behavior with liberal pieties like the superheroes in so many Marvel shows. In fact, he wears his political incorrectness on his sleeve. He's one of those monsters, like Raven, mortified by his appearance. Deadpool complains, "I'm a monster inside and out. I belong in a fucking circus." He wears a mask to conceal his disfigurement. When he finally removes it, revealing his blistered face to his girlfriend, like Erik/Magneto who insists on sex with Raven as she is, blue and scaly, she isn't fazed in the least. She says, "Wow! It's a face I'd be happy to sit on."

Deadpool is so far beyond the pale that it would be fair to say that he's the first alt-right superhero. In one scene, beating on Ajax, who's no more than a bloody pulp, he quips, "This is taking unsportsmanlike conduct to a whole new level." At the end of the picture, there's another scene wherein Deadpool has again subdued Ajax after a violent struggle and is pressing the business end of his gun against his head. As he's about to pull the trigger, busybody Colossus tries to intervene, lecturing him in a lengthy speech, heavy with mainstream moralizing. "Four or five moments," he declares. "That's all it takes to be a hero. Moments when you're offered a choice. To make a sacrifice, conquer a flaw, save a friend, spare an enemy." In the middle of his recitation of the Boy Scout code of conduct, Deadpool, visibly impatient, pulls the trigger, killing Ajax once and for all. Colossus asks, "Why?" Deadpool, serious for once, replies, "If wearing superhero tights means sparing psychopaths, then maybe I wasn't meant to wear 'em."

Collateral damage may trouble centrists, but revenge heroes like Jack Bauer never shed a tear. In 2010, at the conclusion of the final season of *24*, he carried out that vendetta against the Russians for murdering his partner slash girlfriend, for which he was branded a terrorist by the State Department. So far as we knew, he never gave it a second thought. In *Live Another Day*, however, to the consternation of his fans, Jack appears to regret it. He confesses that revenge just never did it for him. Who knew? "Four years ago, my partner, my friend was killed," he explains. "I took as much revenge as any man could possibly take. Somehow I thought it would ease the pain, but it doesn't."

Fortunately for the show's ratings, following the next commercial break, all that talk about renouncing revenge is forgotten, as if the words never crossed his lips. POTUS's daughter, who happens to be the love of Jack's life, has been shot dead by one of his legion of archenemies, giving him the perfect excuse for running wild. Jack captures him after one of those heart-stopping chases that *24* raised to the level of a fine art. Instead of turning him over to the authorities, he simply slices off his head with a samurai sword, in the best jihadist tradition. So much for the rule of law. So much for not sinking to the level of the enemy.

At the end of the show, Jack gets the attention of jihadist queenpin by perforating her with bullets. When he notices that, despite his best efforts the drone-thief is still able to draw a breath or two, he throws her out of a window. Once again, no bringing the evildoer to justice for Jack. Fighting fair is a recipe for defeat, as Eastwood said of the Code of the West. Going toe-to-toe with terrorists requires swallowing whatever moral scruples heroes like Jack might have entertained in gentler times. He never does come in from the cold.

Nor did right-wing shows shrink from torture. In the mainstream, extreme circumstances may require extreme measures. In extremist shows, extreme circumstances are an excuse for extreme measures, despite the fact that torture requires that we abandon the moral high ground that we have occupied at least since World War II. This is not all that surprising in view of the fact that a survey of seventeen thousand people from sixteen countries conducted by the International Committee of the Red Cross in 2016 found that almost half of the Americans polled favored torturing enemy combatants to obtain information, in contravention of international law. Only 30 percent disapproved.

Discarding America's traditional role as a defender of human rights, no matter how selective and hypocritically self-serving it may have been, is business as usual for the far right. After all, Dick Cheney told TV journalist Tim Russert, "We also have to work, though, sort of the dark side, if you will." Torture was his tool, even at a time when photographs of Americans abusing Iraqi prisoners in Abu Ghraib were embarrassing an administration almost impossible to embarrass.

Trump has gone on the record in favor of waterboarding, Cheney's method of choice, and the president's eagerness to dog-paddle in the swamp of repression with Vladimir Putin by equating the United States with the Russian autocracy is well known.

*24*, which won an Emmy for Outstanding Drama Series in 2006, embraced torture, administered by Jack himself, which made the show a lightning rod for liberal and lefty ire. *24* used what's known as the "ticking time bomb" scenario to justify the rack, that is, it regularly manufactured emergencies so dire, crises so severe that extreme measures were not only reasonable but required.

Figuratively speaking, but capturing the can-do spirit that animated the show, when the president's life is threatened and Counter Terrorist Unit agents have an hour to find out the name of the would-be assassin, if tearing out a few fingernails or putting out an eye is the only way to get the information they need, so be it. According to the Parents Television Council, there are sixty-seven torture scenes in the first five seasons of *24*. Joel Surnow, who co-created the show, and mischievously referred to himself as a "right-wing nut job," explained to the *New Yorker*'s Jane Mayer, "There are not a lot of measures short of extreme measures that will get [the job] done."

Right-wing commentator Laura Ingraham once had Surnow on her show, telling him she watched *24* while she was being treated for breast cancer "It was soothing to see Jack Bauer torture these terrorists," she said. "I felt better."

Fox shows tortured best. The other networks played catch-up. NBC, albeit late to the party, got a piece of the action too. *The Blacklist* (2013– ) likewise ratchets the stakes up so high that the show's clean-cut, straight-arrow FBI agent says this to a Russian mobster he's interrogating: "I used to be a real Boy Scout. Followed all the rules. Then my fiancé gets murdered right in front of me. The guy who did it, the only way I could get him was to forget all the rules. The path I took, there wasn't any rules"—apparently including grammatical ones. He leaps out of his chair, grabs the suspect by the throat, and throttles him until he spills his guts.

Another Russian thug, just off the boat, croaks in heavily accented English, wantonly discarding indefinite articles, "This is America, yes? In USA I get lawyer." Wrong. "Let me tell you how it works in USA," the agent explains: either he talks or he gets turned over to people who are trying to kill him. James Spader, the show's master criminal–as–hero, perfectly encapsulates its me-first code: "Someone who is willing to burn the world down to protect the one person they care about," he says, "that's a man I understand."

In *Shooter*, the FBI is attacked for denying the sniper hero his rights. When he says, "I want to see my lawyer," the snotty FBI agent replies, "And I want two tickets to *Hamilton*." In *Patriots Day* (2016), Khandi Alexander, playing yet another FBI agent, is interrogating the widow of Boston Marathon bomber Tamerlan Tsarnaev. The widow says, "I want a lawyer. I have rights." Alexander replies, "You ain't got shit, sweetheart."

Then there's Season 2 of *Homeland*. CIA agent Saul Berenson (Mandy Patinkin) is trying to get a jailed female terrorist to ID a dangerous new face among the Al Qaeda operatives wilding in America's streets. She refuses. Instead of asking himself what would Jack do, he feels sorry for her, brings her wine and cheese, and returns her eyeglasses. Not only does she reward his trust by leading him astray, but no sooner is he out of the room than she breaks the lenses and slashes her wrists, depriving him of a source Jack would have squeezed dry. Postmorteming this intelligence failure, bleeding heart Saul admits, "I got emotional. It was sloppy."

In *Live Another Day*, it seems that the show's detractors may have made a dent, at least so far as torture is concerned. When Jack's former right hand Chloe is being held by the CIA's Special Activities Division for "enhanced interrogation"—the Cheney gang's Orwellian phrase for don't-call-it-torture—Jack refuses to cooperate with his captors. They plan to make sure he joins her. Someone observes, sympathetically, if ominously, "Those people will do God knows what to him. Once he's down that rabbit hole, he's gone."

Jack's captors are, however, naïvely unaware with whom they're dealing, and on his way down that rabbit hole, handcuffs notwithstanding, Jack disarms the two guards escorting him. Busting into the Special Activities section, he finds Chloe in an operating room, spread-eagle and strapped to a gurney, with a drip going into her wrist, while an agency tech fills a syringe the size of a thermos with some noxious chemical. Furious, Jack demands, "Did you do this to her?" The torture tech responds smugly, "It's nothing you haven't done." As the euphemisms fly, they throw his own fondness for the Iron Maiden in his face. But Jack is not to be deterred or denied. Amid wailing alarms, flashing red lights, and the *crack-crack-crack* of gunfire, he grabs Chloe and escapes.

It seems that Jack's enthusiasm for state-sponsored torture diminishes dramatically when Chloe is the victim, and worse, he finds his own thumb destined for the screw. Moreover, with Bush and his neocon familiars fading into history, torture had become oh so last year. Jack just moves along to drone warfare, which gets the tender loving care he once bestowed on waterboarding.

We have seen that from the point of view of the extremes, anything goes, a conclusion justified by their contempt for the mainstream authorities, who never manage to do anything right, even when they try, which isn't often. Whether cops or docs; soldiers or scientists; priests, reverends, or rabbis; teachers, journalists, or pundits, they're cowards all—bullies, turncoats, or liars, arrogant and corrupt. What's the matter with them? Did they all get dropped on their heads as babies?

# PART IV

# HEAVEN CAN'T WAIT

# 10
# What a Piece of Work Was Man

*The mainstream traditionally doubled down on humans, but as the clouds gather and the sky darkens, the extremes come to regard them as the problem, not the solution.*

> When the chips are down . . . these civilized people, they'll eat each other.
>
> —*The Joker,* The Dark Knight

An army of gorillas, chimps, and a potpourri of their primate relatives charge across San Francisco's Golden Gate Bridge toward a barrier of police cars parked bumper to bumper, blocking the Marin County side of the span. Cops crouch behind them, taking aim at the oncoming creatures with deadly looking military-grade weapons. The odds seem to be against the apes, but as we quickly learn, it is a mistake to underestimate them. They overturn a bus and use it to protect themselves against the fusillade of bullets as they push it toward the barricade. There's a momentary pause, as the police, recognizing that their weapons are useless, cease firing. Then, out of the mist emerges a figure on horseback, galloping toward them. It's not Clint Eastwood or John Wayne, but an ape. As it closes on them, it waves one arm in the air and lets out a battle cry. The simians attack, some swarming over and around the bus, others dropping from above, off the cables suspending the bridge. It's virtually raining gorillas. The cops don't have a chance as the hairy hominids pull them from their cars and fling them into the waters below. The survivors turn around and flee back to San Francisco. The apes head for the Muir Woods National Park—free at last.

We are, of course, watching a thrilling scene from Rupert Wyatt's reboot of the venerable *Planet of the Apes* franchise, called *Rise of the Planet of the Apes* (2011), which was so skillfully done that it successfully relaunched the moribund series.

*Planet of the Apes* (1968), the film that kicked it all off, was written by two lefties, blacklisted writer Michael Wilson and Rod Serling, of *Twilight Zone* fame. That movie begins aboard a spaceship heading away from Earth, toward a planet that is supposed to be orbiting a star in the constellation of Orion. Instead of HAL droning on about how smart it is, we hear the resonant voice of Charlton Heston, who plays the leader of a small crew of astronauts, wondering what he will find at the end of his journey. Due to the quirks of space travel, two thousand Earth years have elapsed during the span of two or so it has taken them to reach their destination.

When they crash-land on the strange planet, they discover that evolution, having bungled its attempt to make something out of the materials furnished on Earth, has rolled the dice again, this time promoting apes, not people, to the head of the class, only to have failed a second time. The apes merely replicate the worst characteristics of their human ancestors. They capture our space travelers and treat them with the casual cruelty with which people have customarily treated "lower" animals on Earth, that is, they hunt them down for sport, or capture them for the purpose of experimenting on them. In other words, the astronauts are victims of their new simian masters.

In the age of extremism, forty-three years after the original film was released, the reboot turns the original upside down. The film also reverses the terms of the master-slave relationship presented by its predecessor. The apes are victims of people, the vast majority of whom are vicious, corrupt, and entirely lacking in even the rudiments of morality, while the apes are principled, empathetic, and loyal.

In *Rise of the Planet of the Apes*, the docs and cops, scientists and soldiers are all bad news. The docs use the apes to test drugs for Big Pharma. The CEO of Gen-Sys Laboratories, the company sponsoring the tests, is cut from same the cloth as Selfridge in *Avatar*, while the keepers who tend the apes are a scurvy bunch who torment them with cattle prods and beatings, much the same way Colonel Shannon treats the Creature in *The Shape of Water*.

The drugs in question are intended to cure Alzheimer's, but they have the unintended side effect of raising the IQ of the apes to the level of their oppressors, and beyond. When Caesar (Andy Serkis), our hero, rebels and grabs one of the keepers, the man screams, "Take your stinking paws off me, you damn dirty ape!" It's an exact quote of a venomous line from the original *Planet of the Apes*, uttered by Heston when he's assaulted by an ape scientist intending to castrate him. There it's justified. In *Rise of the Planet of the Apes*, it's "speciesist," or whatever the term is that denotes prejudice against other species.

Caesar escapes and frees the primates in the lab, to whom he gives the drugs. Like Jon Snow in *Game of Thrones*, he is loyal to his species, not his family, in this case scientist James Franco, who raised him as he would his own child. Again borrowing a leaf from Snow, the Na'vi, and the other coalition builders we have encountered, Caesar transforms rival factions into allies, explaining, in words we've heard many, many times before in many different contexts: "Ape alone . . . weak. Apes together . . . strong."

The apes take over the Gen-Sys building. The only way the CEO can see to subdue them is to kill them. One of the few humane keepers implores him to back off, saying, "Lives are at stake. These are animals with personalities, attachments." Doing his best impression of Selfridge, the CEO replies, "I run a business, not a petting zoo. Find the most cost-effective way to put those apes down." That, of course, means calling the cops.

Later, after Caesar has taken to the redwoods, Franco pleads with him to stand down, warning him that the cops, his neighbors, and almost everyone else in his world will resort to violence. "This isn't the way," he pleads. "You know what they're capable of. Please come home." In a mainstream movie, Caesar would return to the fold, but here, referring to those redwoods, he whispers, "Caesar is home." He's more Geronimo than Cochise.

As the plot unfolds, we discover that the very same drug that raised the IQ of Caesar and his friends is fatal to people and, what's worse, the disease it causes is communicable. One of Franco's vicious neighbors accidentally inhales it in aerosol form. It so happens that he's an airline pilot. Flying to Europe, he becomes Patient Zero of a global pandemic. An animated sequence at the end that runs behind the tail credits looks like one of those airline ads displaying far-flung routes that cover the entire globe like spiderwebs, only this one isn't intended to sell vacation packages; it charts the extinction of the human race. In the famous ending of the original *Planet of the Apes*, this is a catastrophe. By the time we get to *Rise of the Planet of the Apes*, given the despicable way people have behaved toward the apes throughout the film, we have to conclude that maybe a world without people isn't such a bad thing after all.

We have seen more than a few people behaving badly before, but centrist shows never lose their faith in humankind. We have watched *The Walking Dead*'s Rick try extremism on for size, flirt with the zombie lifestyle, only to draw back and reject it. Like Rick, Tom Hardy, playing Mad Max in *Fury Road* (2015), is totally dehumanized after losing his wife and child in an extinction level event. "Hope is a mistake," he says. "My world is fire and blood . . . As the world fell, each of us in our own way was broken." Closed down, devoid of feelings, cold and uncaring, he is absorbed by trying to simply stay alive. As he puts it, "I exist in a wasteland, reduced to one instinct: survive." He and Imperator Furiosa (Charlize Theron), the ferocious feminist heroine of the movie, don't meet cute; they meet angry, as Max won't even tell her his name.

By the end of *Fury Road*, not quite as mad as he was, Max find his way back to his humanity. He volunteers his name, saves her life, and even acknowledges the possibility of hope and "redemption." Max manages to regain his humanity, but just barely.

In show after show, the agents of authority have dropped the ball, but the problem goes deeper. It's not just that we can no longer put our faith in the so-called experts; it's something else, something more general, more widespread, more fundamental.

We left Batman in a very dark place, embracing the role of the vigilante and abusing his enemies, but it wasn't always that way. Initially, we recall, he refused to go along with the League of Shadows' plans to destroy his hometown because he believed there were enough good people in Gotham to make it worth saving. Were there?

In *The Dark Knight Rises*, Bane empties Gotham's prisons and urges the convicts, the 99 percent, to rise up by inspiring them with class hatred. He declaims, "We take Gotham from the corrupt! The rich! The oppressors of generations who have kept you down with myths of opportunity, and we give it back to you . . . the people."

The mob spreads out over the city, hauling the prosperous burghers out of their beds, throwing their Armani Privé gowns and flat-screen TVs onto the street, and bringing them up before kangaroo courts, where they are likely as not sentenced to death. The cops may be on the take, and official justice bought and sold, but the peoples' justice is worse.

Is such venality, then, a class issue? It seems so. The corruption that gnaws at the moral fiber of Gotham is blamed on the riffraff, not the 1 percent. We have seen that the philanthropic Waynes are the saviors of Gotham. But it turns out that that their money doesn't buy them very much. The have-nots are such ingrates that they turn against the haves anyway, like the mugger who kills Mom and Dad Wayne.

Still, the 1 percent are not entirely free from blame. The film makes a gesture toward balancing the scales. "There's a storm coming," Catwoman (Anne Hathaway) warns Bruce. "When it hits, you're all gonna wonder how you ever thought you could live so large and leave so little for the rest of us."

Catwoman's jab at the rich is confined to one brief speech, whereas the angry mob ravaging the rich is starkly dramatized in a lengthy scene, so it's not hard to see where the picture's sympathies lie. Thus, *New York Times* critic A.O. Scott can register the film's "snarl of conservative anti-populism—respect the rich! Obey the police! Don't trust environmental do-gooders."

Still, it would be a mistake to ignore Catwoman. *The Dark Knight Rises* appears to blame the evil it anatomizes on the rich *and* the poor, the haves and the have-nots, the 1 percent and the 99 percent, in other words: everyone. It seems then that hatred, revenge, and violence do not begin and end with class.

X-Men's Erik/Magneto blames America and Americans for the misfortunes that have befallen him and his fellow mutants. Looking up at the Statue of Liberty, he recalls arriving at Ellis Island as a displaced person and the high hopes it inspired. "America was going to be the land of tolerance, peace," he says wistfully, but America has let him down.

Indeed, we have also seen that the American authorities in Marvel's universe are particularly odious, and that the character blemishes that disfigure them are not confined to a few bad apples, a bullying general here or a pettifogging senator there. The president, the Congress, the army, the CIA, state and local officials—they're all tarnished, or worse, leaving the secret Hydra agents among them to do what Nazis do.

If bad behavior is so widespread that it transcends class, is the source of the pollution to be found in one particular nationality? Is it then an American problem, as Erik/Magneto suggests? But even he concedes that it is not just America that has failed him. "There is no land of tolerance," he continues, bitterly. "There is no peace. Not here, or anywhere else." Indeed, there is little to distinguish the Americans from the North Vietnamese at the Paris Peace Accords in *X-Men: Days of Future Past*. Nor is there much to distinguish the Americans from the Russians *in X-Men: First Class* when somewhere on a sun-swept Caribbean beach in Marvel's version of the Cuban Missile Crisis, the X-Men face off against a flotilla of heavily armed American and Soviet warships.

After the first two decades of the twenty-first century, when terrorism and torture have become de rigueur, daily life is so dangerous for so many that even in the mainstream, people have begun to have their doubts about people. As Sam Merlotte puts it in *True Blood*, "People are scum." You'd think Rick and his friends would be worrying about biters rather than the handful of their fellow mortals who remain alive, but no. The walkers have become such easy targets that killing them is routine, like slapping mosquitoes. We almost feel sorry for them. As George Romero once put it, "In my work, [it's] usually the humans that are the worst. . . . I have a soft spot in my heart for zombies." Eventually, after the novelty of ambulatory corpses wears off, the walkers play second fiddle to live enemies, worse-than-walkers people like the Governor of Woodbury, the cannibals at Terminus, and Negan with his Saviors. As Glenn reminds us, echoing Sam Merlotte, "All this time running from walkers, you forget what people do."

Enter the Joker. In *The Dark Knight*, the grinning trickster, preternaturally channeled by Heath Ledger, devises an ingenious experiment intended to prove just how depraved people really are. As he tells Batman, "When the chips are down . . . these civilized people, they'll eat each other." He loads one ferry with convicts and another with law-abiding citizens. Both vessels are wired with explosives, but the detonator for each is on the other. If the convicts don't blow up the citizens (or vice versa) by midnight, the Joker threatens to obliterate both. As it turns out, neither the convicts nor the law-abiding citizens detonate their opposite numbers, forcing the Joker to reluctantly concede that Batman is right, people are basically good, and therefore Gotham is worth saving.

The Joker, however, makes for a poor oddsmaker, because he is too infatuated with his own cleverness and too busy tormenting his humorless, square-jawed opponent to do the numbers. The convicts, on message, indeed chose to blow up the law abiders. The surprise is that the law abiders voted two to one to sink the convicts. The leveler, as usual, is the pressure of extreme circumstances. Each group was only prevented from dispatching the other by chance. So no, the people of Gotham are not basically good. On the contrary, the Joker's experiment proves that there isn't much to distinguish the good citizens of Gotham from the bad convicts of Gotham's jails, because they all behave the same way—shamefully. They are as Ra's Al Ghul says they are, badly in need of stern correction.

If rich and poor, law abiders and law breakers, Americans and un-Americans are equally culpable for this pervasive malaise, on which color will the bouncing ball of blame land? Standing on that beach watching those warships in *X-Men: First Class*, Erik finally gets to the heart of the matter when he says, "I feel their guns targeting us, the Americans, Soviets—humans." He has seen the enemy, and it is Us. The misbehavers have one thing in common: they're all the same species.

Erik is by no means alone. Newt Scamander in *Fantastic Beasts* joins him, Glenn, Sam Merlotte, and the hominids of *Rise of the Planet of the Apes* in expressing his distaste for people. No longer, it seems, do they have to be saved from monsters and beasts; it's the other way around. Looking to rescue those exotic creatures that have escaped from his suitcase, Newt explains, "They're currently in alien terrain surrounded by millions of the most vicious creatures on the planet: humans."

*Avatar* too seems to be saying that humans, the species, like Jake, are hopelessly crippled, while random aliens inhabiting an obscure moon in a remote galaxy are both morally and physically superior. The worse humans look, the better the aliens appear. Critic John Podhoretz was right when he concluded in the *Weekly Standard* that *Avatar*'s message was that "to be human is just way uncool."

Set within the devastation of World War I, *Wonder Woman* (2017) is yet another movie that puts humankind on trial. Queen Hippolyta warns Diana Prince (Gal Gadot), as she bids farewell, "Be careful in the world of men, Diana. They do not deserve you." It quickly becomes clear that by "men," she means humans. Wonder Woman agrees: "I used to want to save the world. To end war and bring peace to mankind. But then, I glimpsed the darkness that lives within their light."

Once upon a time, humans were the be all and end all of creation. "What a piece of work is man!" Hamlet famously mused. "How noble in reason! How infinite in faculty!... In action how like an angel." Hamlet had his reservations, but he was only seconding the judgment of Genesis, which privileged people above all, asserting, "God created mankind in his own image." Humans are, however, a slippery lot, and parsing their nature is a tricky business at best. Noam Chomsky once observed that our attitudes on almost every issue imaginable presuppose assumptions about human nature.

René Descartes was, we recall, a body/soul dualist. With regard to knowledge, he supposed that God implants everything worth knowing in humans at birth. In other words, knowledge is innate, making Descartes an essentialist, at least in this respect, and to a degree, essentialism is self-evident. Humans are born with genes that guarantee that their embryos develop into *Homo sapiens*, and not, say, giraffes. But Descartes was overenthusiastic, intending his assertion to cover considerably more than DNA, provoking John Locke into contradiction.

Locke argued that knowledge is derived from experience. Humans are not born knowing, say, that elephants like peanuts, or that Trump is pre-disposed to erect tariffs, but rather as tabulae rasae, blank slates waiting to be inscribed by culture. Today we would say that they are socially con-structed. Society—civilization—makes humans "human," and since civili-zation has often been regarded as a record of human progress, enabling us, say, to emerge from the dark ages of theological fancy into the sunshine of reason, it follows that humans have the potential for infinite perfect-ibility, and thusly were they presented. As Sansa Stark puts it, "I'm a slow learner, but I learn," and indeed she does. If we compare the jejune teen-ager under Joffrey's thumb in the early seasons of *Game of Thrones* to the mature Lady of Winterfell at the end of Season 7, the difference is dramatic. Ditto Tyrion, who over the course of eight seasons is transformed from a self-loathing, drunken sybarite consumed by revenge, to the Hand of Daenerys Targaryen.

It was Locke again who argued against the Cartesian model in "An Essay Concerning Human Understanding," in which he substituted "mind" for "soul," a considerably less metaphysically loaded term. Locke's was a natu-ralistic approach to the mind/body problem. He held that thinking is a function of matter, thereby dispensing with the soul. During the Enlight-enment, the *philosophes* chipped away at the Christian God, severing moral-ity from religion and grounding it in the faculty of reason. Immanuel Kant, too, tried his hand at defrocking ethics and epistemology, freeing them from their traditional dependence on a deity. Twentieth-century material-ist philosophers like Gilbert Ryle mocked Descartes's formulation, refer-ring to it as the "ghost in the machine."

The rise of science did much to pave the way for humanism, the theology, if you will, of secularists who dislodged God from his throne at the center of the universe and replaced Him with *Homo sapiens*. They were human exceptionalists, and to them, humans were Darwin's darlings, perched on the top branch of the evolutionary tree from which they looked down on their carbon-based cousins. Whether their superiority was a function of the opposable thumb, the faculty of speech, the ability to reason, their facility with tools, or, more likely, all of the above, *Homo sapiens* were universally considered to be different in kind from animals.

At the risk of oversimplification, with his belief that God-given knowl-edge is intrinsic to humans, not to mention his faith in the immaterial soul, Descartes gave comfort to conservatives, while Locke, embracing empiri-cism, gave comfort to liberals.

Mainstream shows, with their faith in science, have tended to favor Locke. We recall that in *The Walking Dead*, with his belief that the walkers' old selves live on in their undead bodies, Hershel reveals himself as an essentialist. Lockeans know that the walkers' old selves would never return because the death of the physical brain kills consciousness as well—the élan vital, the 21 grams, the soul, whatever. That train has left the station.

As Hershel finally admits, there is no human essence that remains inside the walkers that can be revived by a kiss and a hug. They may be walking, but, to invert Descartes's famous proposition, "I think, therefore I am," walkers aren't thinking, and therefore they are not. Walkers are machines without ghosts, or, as scholar Peter Dendle has put it, "The stereotypical zombie is essentially the opposite of . . . a 'ghost': it is a soulless body, rather than a disembodied soul."

Humans in *The Walking Dead* are not divided between body and soul, as Descartes imagined, but made of a single substance, matter, consistent with the unremitting materiality of this series: the rotting flesh, suppurating wounds, crushed skulls, and dismembered limbs of the undead.

As we see in other mainstream survivor shows, once civilization is stripped away, there is precious little left of the human. The confident man we knew as Captain Phillips at the beginning of the 2013 film of the same name, before the brutal Somali pirates hijacked his tanker in the Indian Ocean, by the end is gone. It seems as if he has lost everything that made him human, that "everything" being all that is added by nurture, by culture. He is reduced to a puddle of protoplasm on a gurney. The pirates have wiped his slate clean. Likewise, in *Lone Survivor*, Mark Wahlberg is last seen on a gurney as well, reduced to zero after his squad has been wiped out by the Taliban. Ditto Mad Max, whose slate has been wiped clean before *Fury Road* begins.

Centrist shows have no use for the dualism, the binaries that characterized not only Cartesian thinking but Christianity as well, with its heaven and hell, sin and salvation, and so on. Nor do they traffic in a divine will or plan that determines the destiny of the characters. Those who insist that this or that happens for a God-given reason are wrong, as Jason learns in *True Blood* and T-Dog learns in *The Walking Dead*. Rather, culture is destiny. When people behave deplorably in the latter series, it is not because they are born bad. On the contrary, they are victims of extreme circumstances created by the zombie apocalypse that erases the ethical standards inscribed by centuries of human civilization.

Referring to a scene in which the Governor forces brothers Daryl and Merle to fight each other in a battle to the death, Hershel asks, "What kind of a sick mind does that?" Rick replies, "The kind this world creates." The bad, like the good, lies not in the stars, nor in ourselves, but out there, in the "world."

When conditions take a turn for the worse, people's better selves can disappear, lost somewhere inside their wayward selves. They become more and more ruthless, devolving into the monsters they deplore. Unlike walkers, however, humans have it within their power to choose their own paths, to embrace or reject the moral life. The living have the capacity to change as they respond to altered circumstances. When their circumstances improve, their new, worse selves can make way for their old, better selves. We've seen Mad Max come back from the dark side, and we've seen Rick do the same. Daryl insists that the old, better Merle is still there, buried somewhere inside the Merle whom the Governor turned into a killer. He beseeches him, "I want my brother back," and indeed, once free of the malign influence of Woodbury, the old Merle does come back. In one scene, Rick tells Carl, "We've all done the worst kinds of things just to stay alive, but we can come back," and it's true.

Drawing on Locke and rejecting essentialism, pluralism assumes that human nature is pliable. Providing people with the opportunity to change—new starts, second chances, and Act IIs, IIIs, and IVs—is what this nation of immigrants is (or was) all about. As we have seen, pluralism was designed to defang extremism by accepting, even encouraging movement from the periphery to the center. Crossing over is the key to absorbing dissident political, religious, and ethnic groups. How else are the Geronimos to become Cochises?

Valuable as tolerance is to the health of the pluralism, however, the center has its limits, and it doesn't hesitate to draw the line when it imagines that the integrity of society is at stake. Take Merlotte's in *True Blood*. A veritable UN of entities, it is less a melting pot than a freak show. Good humans and bad humans, good vampires and bad vampires, straights and gays, fairies and shape-shifters mix and mingle, all entitled to seats at the tables. Wiccans and werewolves even use the same bathrooms. As Sam puts it, "Merlotte's is for everybody." But is it? Merlotte's may seem like a UN, but it's not. As the story unfolds, we watch extremists of every stripe being tossed out the door because they've crossed the line.

Many of the mainstream characters, inspired by the utopian aspirations of the Enlightenment to believe in the unlimited potential of humans, are brought up short. Take Bill and Sookie, the poster children for the American Vampire League's assimilationist agenda. They are the cosmopolitans, the crossovers, the bridge and tunnel folk who have a foot in both worlds, the natural and supernatural. If Bill and Sookie can make it as a couple, so can vampires successfully blend in with humans, gays with straights, Them with Us. Just as it promised, the mainstream will have achieved its dream, wherein opposites are reconciled. If they eventually fail, it's not for want of trying.

As her love affair with Vampire Bill heats up, Sookie not only offers her neck, but she thinks no more of plunging her teeth into Bill's veins than taking a bite out of a BLT. For his part, he eagerly sinks his incisors into her arm, making a crunching sound like biting into an ear of corn. The species, in other words, are restless. Each wants to become the other. Not only are the two of them free from speciesism, they fall prey to its opposite: species envy. After hanging out with Bill long enough to get a taste for the red stuff, Sookie tells him, "I'm not afraid to spill a little blood anymore. I think I'm meeting you halfway to vampire." Indeed, she has left a couple of dead bodies on the floor, but more, she's expressing, in Alan Ball's words, "our powerful desire to escape from our boxed-in antiseptic life."

In the real world, as we might expect, the mainstream has invited all manner of crossover wannabees to join the party, most recently the transgender. In fact, 2015 was heralded as "The Year We Obsessed Over Identity" by cultural critic Wesley Morris. He cites a blizzard of examples— the Founding Fathers reimagined as rap stars in *Hamilton*; Bruce Jenner coming out as Caitlyn; a white woman, Rachel Dolezal, appropriating blackness as her own, to which we can add Dick Whitman's appropriation of Don Draper's identity in *Mad Men*—all underlining the fluidity of our identities. He concludes that "we've been made to see how trans and bi and poly-ambi-omni- we are." Can we be anyone we want to be? For centrists, it seems like the answer is embodied in Obama's old campaign slogan: "Yes we can."

Shape-shifting, in *True Blood*, but also in other shows like *The Shack*, can be pressed into metaphorical service to represent not only gender fluidity but also the kind of mercurial identity that Morris discusses. But *True Blood* is ambivalent, at best. Neither Bill not Sookie is a shifter, but they believe that each can become the other. They're due to be disappointed. Just when Sookie is getting comfortable with Bill, she gets more otherness than she bargains for. It becomes increasingly clear that there are insuperable differences between them. Bloodlust and violence, for example, are endemic to vampire culture, but she is repelled by them. She and Bill fight over his taste for revenge. Every so often, Bill tries to remind Sookie just how different from humans vampires really are: "Vampires often turn on those who trust them. They don't have human values like you." Sookie refuses to hear him.

With the mainstream beleaguered by supes and buffeted by extreme events, Sookie's crossover games eventually come to seem dangerous. They threaten the integrity of both the human and the supe universes. Fairies, for example, are catnip for vampires, and the fairy queen complains that Sookie has carelessly left the door open to the heretofore hidden fairy realm, allowing the vampires entry. The boundaries between the natural and the supernatural are altogether too porous, and they need to be shored up. The emphasis gradually shifts from flexibility to rigidity, from inclusiveness to exclusiveness.

Moreover, as much as Sookie wants to become Bill, she is also desperate to be average, like Buffy the vampire slayer who joins the cheerleading squad because she wants to "do something normal." For Sookie, being normal means being human, just as it does for Raven/Mystique in the *X-Men* films. When strangers ask her "What are you?" she insists, "I'm Sookie Stackhouse, and I'm a waitress."

Bill finally concludes that the nature of vampires is his nature. He may dislike his nature, but as much as he struggles against it, he's stuck with it. He comes to understand that although he can fall in love with a human, he cannot become a human. The same is true of Sookie. It's okay for her to be a vampire groupie, but it's not okay for her to become a vampire. As if to punctuate the lesson Sookie learns, Eric abruptly materializes out of the darkness on the road in front of the car in which Sookie is driving Bill, and she has to stomp on the brakes to avoid crashing into him. Mainstream shows likewise stomp on the brakes. The utopianism that has inspired the center comes to an abrupt halt.

This show's embattled pluralists finally accept the fact, however unpalatable, that they need boundaries to protect them from barrier-busting extremists. We recall the first appearance of Maryann the maenad: the head of a bull on the body a woman. Although mainstream shows have no love for nature, monsters like Maryann go too far; they are unnatural, violators of nature who refuse to respect its boundaries. The same is true for culture. "Monster trucks" is by no means a misnomer for the mongrel vehicles employed as weapons by the War Boys in *Fury Road*. In a mainstream movie like that, they are the enemy.

The interplay between walls and fences, on the one hand, and bridges and tunnels (bridges underground), on the other, is dear to the hearts of pluralists and their enemies, metaphors for inclusion and exclusion, and therefore these structures, literalized in visual media, are laden with meaning. Note the fascination with the Danish series *The Bridge*, which has been reworked twice, once as an American series of the same name, and a British series called *The Tunnel*.

The far left *Rise of the Planet of the Apes* would breach the limits of the vital center by including other species under the big tent. If centrists' idea of hell is nature out of control, animals belong in lockdown, and the Golden Gate is a bridge too far. Therefore, it needs to be blocked.

Likewise, in *The Walking Dead* at the end of the first season, Rick's band of survivors spies a dark, massive shape squatting on the horizon. It's a derelict prison, surrounded by guard towers and chain-link fences, physical manifestations of the metaphorical boundaries pluralists learn to love in *True Blood*. They settle behind its fortifications, protected, finally, from the walkers ravaging the countryside.

Pluralists can inveigh against walls as much as they want, as Hillary Clinton did when she attacked Trump for his promise to build a wall along our border with Mexico, saying, "Instead of building walls, we need to be tearing down barriers." But our survivors ain't gonna be workin' on Hershel's farm no more, because lacking fortifications, it has been overrun by walkers. Yet again, the mainstream devolves into the extremes, becomes the enemy it was designed to resist. Under desperate circumstances, the open society closes.

The lesson of *True Blood* and *The Walking Dead* seems to be that like it or not, open societies in crisis need walls. Look at Bill and Sookie. Neither can escape their essential nature. Essentialism, which enlightened progressives treated as a remnant of the dark ages, makes a comeback. As the dangers and extreme circumstances faced by the mainstream escalate in magnitude, they threaten to destroy its utopian promise. Yet that's not the end of the story.

Walls are not, however, a viable solution. As if to underline the vulnerability of that which they're meant to protect, barriers of all sorts most often fail. In Guillermo del Toro's *Pacific Rim* (2013), undersea monsters burst through the coastal wall built to shield Sydney, Australia, in less than an hour. And, as we have seen, the 300-mile-long, 700-foot-high wall of ice in *Game of Thrones* that is supposed to secure the Seven Kingdoms against the White Walkers fails to stop them, as we knew it would.

In *World War Z*, the Israelis build a great wall to keep the zekes out of Jerusalem. The wall bears some resemblance to the Western Wall, as if the filmmakers are insisting that we draw parallels between the fantasy presented in the film and the poisonous politics of the Middle East.

In the movie, the Israelis (improbably) share their sanctuary with the Palestinians by opening a gate through which their sworn enemies pour in. Believing themselves safe, former foes, now friends in the face of a common enemy, break into song, a joyous hymn. The only trouble is, the zekes, like the walkers, are attracted by noise.

In the movie's most spectacular sequence, the zekes have no trouble scaling the wall, once they put their nonexistent minds to it. *World War Z* underlines the fact that walls can never be high enough or strong enough. The zekes scramble over one another, snaking relentlessly upward until the swarming creatures reach the top—and tumble over, into the city. Forget that there is a suggestion that the zekes are the Palestinians and that the Israelis made a fatal mistake allowing them entry, and/or that they should have built their wall higher. Even more devastating is that by linking the invasion of the zekes with the noise made by both peoples celebrating, the picture mocks the promise of pluralism—that antagonistic humans can live together in harmony—because the very gesture that creates that harmony invites its destruction. The takeaway is that walls, no matter how high or thick, cannot save pluralist societies.

The paradox of pluralism seems to be that building walls or tearing them down, it's doomed either way. If the organizing principle of the world's leading liberal democracy is fatally flawed, it's a dismal, eye-opening conclusion, but bad as that news is, it's dwarfed by the recognition that humans are the villains of this story. Secular liberals have always scoffed at the doctrine of original sin, but it seems as if Christians may know something they don't. Are there grounds for hope?

# 11
# Anywhere but Here

*If the human species is fatally flawed, the heroes and heroines of* Avatar, The Shape of Water, *and the* Twilight Saga *just want to get the hell out. They take refuge in the post-human.*

> We have become disconnected from nature, [which is where] the post-human comes from.
> — *Alan Ball, showrunner,* True Blood

We're watching a black screen and listening to Bella Swan (Kristen Stewart), in a ruminative mood, speaking about death in a voice-over, confessing, "I'd never given much thought to how I would die." It's *Twilight* (2008), of course, the first installment of the toothless, vampire-lite five-part series based on Stephenie Meyer's teen novels that have sold 120-plus million copies. Fast forward to the end of the film. Bella is dancing in the dark at her high school prom in a gazebo romantically festooned with glowing globes of light. Her partner is Edward Cullen (Robert Pattinson), the series' reluctant bloodsucker. Preaching self-control and self-denial, like vampire Bill in *True Blood*, he abstains from human blood, confining himself to that of animals. Unlike Bill, however, Edward can't even drop fang. Dracula would turn over in his coffin.

Bella has had some close calls, and therefore a lot of time to think about death since that scene. She's been bitten by a vampire, and Edward, her devoted lover, had to suck the venom out of her blood. Like Sookie, she craves to join the undead. "Why did you save me?" she asks, irritably. "If you just let the venom spread, I could be like you right now."

"You don't know what you're saying. I'm not gonna end your life for you. You don't want this."

"I want you. I'm dying already. Every second, I get closer. Older."

"So that's what you dream about? Becoming a monster?" She raises her chin, exposing her neck. He leans down as if to bite it, but merely kisses it. "I won't give in," she says. "I know what I want." Sookie knew what she wanted, too, but never got it. Will Bella get her way?

As we have seen, in mainstream shows, humans are for the most part pleased to be who they are, comfortable in their skin, satisfied with their species. They don't go around wishing to become something else, that which they happen to be standing next to at any given moment—a tree, a dog, a vampire, whatever it is that they're not. As Americans, they feel (or felt) particularly lucky—with good reason. As Hillary Clinton put it, "America has never stopped being great," so why wouldn't humans, who already feel special, feel more special to be Americans?

Nonetheless, with centrist shows less confident than they once were, what we always took for granted becomes problematical. In mainstream shows, essentialism conspires to keep humans in their place. If biology is destiny, perhaps we can't be anything we want. We can't necessarily get there from here. Things don't always get better. After all, Sookie failed, and she came to understand that there were limits to her malleability. Ultimately, she was who she was.

We have seen that in the classic westerns, extremist gunfighters like John Wayne in *The Searchers* are too set in their ways to change. They are too compromised to sit at the dinner table, and they have to be expelled from the community. Shane is never coming back, because however cute Alan Ladd looks in his fringed buckskin jacket, and however good a surrogate father he is for little Brandon De Wilde, he has an essential nature: his fast draw. Being a gunslinger may keep him alive in the Old West, but in a mainstream movie, he's like a beached whale. There's no place for him.

In extremist shows, on the other hand, essentialism is an advantage. The mutants in the X-Men are born, not made. For them, there are no second chances or Act IIs, and therefore to have any chance at satisfaction, at contentment, superheroes like Luke Cage, Raven/Mystique, Wolverine, and Hank must learn to love their essential natures. When they succeed, they find peace.

If centrist characters such as Captain Phillips and Petty Officer Mark Wahlberg in *Lone Survivor* are reduced to zero by adverse circumstances, those same adverse circumstances just serve to bring out the intrinsic strength of extremist characters. We remember the sage advice Captain America's mentor gives him in *Civil War*, "It is your duty to plant yourself like a tree, look them in the eye, and say, 'No.'" It enables him to stand up to the American secretary of state and his threats. Likewise, the most important lesson Luke Cage learns over the course of the first season is the same one that Jake Sully learns in *Avatar*: to move from spectator to actor, moderate to extremist by standing up for himself, refusing to be swayed by the conventional wisdom of the mainstream. These characters are fixed like rocks amid a swift-moving current. They define themselves against the blandishments of centrist culture by means of the indestructible core of traits they're born with. Here is alt-right spokesperson Richard B. Spencer teaching this lesson to his followers: "Race is real, race matters, and race is the foundation of identity." Brian Kilmeade, a fixture on *Fox & Friends*, said to be Donald Trump's favorite show, bemoaned Americans who "keep marrying other species and other ethnics" and have thereby thrown essentialism to the winds, as opposed to "the Swedes [who] have pure genes." (Too bad about Cheddar Man, who lived ten thousand years ago and proudly wears the mantle of First Brit. His DNA inconveniently showed he was dark skinned.)

Even in centrist shows, essentialism can enable extremist characters to resist the lure of the dark side. If nurture cannot endlessly improve upon their natures, neither can it erode their essential natures. Nature will have its way. In Season 7 of *The Walking Dead*, Negan breaks down the identities of his followers with unremitting violence. "Punishment is how we've built everything we have," he explains. His captives not only become his followers, they become Negan, answering the question "Who are you?" with "I am Negan." (Only a short time later, congressional Banana Republicans were saying, in effect, "I am Trump!" Talk about art anticipating life, culture previewing politics!) Like Captain Phillips and Petty Officer Wahlberg, their slates have been wiped clean by adverse circumstances, namely, Negan. On the other hand, after Negan captures Daryl, it seems that his efforts to break him succeed, but they don't. Regardless of the pressure exerted by the ugly external circumstances in which he finds himself, the old Daryl returns, and he escapes. Unlike Rick, Daryl is an extremist, favoring the use of more bloodthirsty tactics against the Saviors than Rick can countenance—as indicted in the vicious fight between the two of them in Season 8—and therefore he is able to grab that rock or tree, stand firm and resist torture.

Essentialism makes itself felt in *Game of Thrones* as well. Despite the drastic changes extremist characters go through—dramatic reversals, spectacular ups and downs—their fundamentals remain the same. Arrogant and devious, Cersei Lannister is queen one moment and crawling naked on her hands and knees through the streets of King's Landing the next, the target of an angry mob pelting her with offal. Does she change? Is she humbled? When her enemies have been killed and she reassumes the throne, she is the same as ever, without a flicker of regret. So too, Arya tries to erase her old self when she falls under the sway of the Faceless Men, but she fails, and at the end of her ordeal, she leaves Braavos much the same as she entered it. In other words, for her, once a Stark always a Stark, but like Cersei, she is an extremist, a revenge artist with a kill list, settling scores with the enemies of her family.

In extremist shows like *Avatar*, essentialism enables Jake to withstand the social pressure exerted by Selfridge and Quaritch, break with the company, and follow Dr. Grace and her crew to the Floating Mountains. In the reboot of *RoboCop*, a Luddite-left film, bad scientist Dr. Gary Oldman asserts, "Consciousness is nothing more than the processing of information," as he turns the critically wounded Alex Murphy (Joel Kinnaman) into the lethal cyborg. Oldman conspires with the CEO of OmniCorp, Michael Keaton to make him a more effective weapon by reducing the ratio of cells to circuits in RoboCop's brain (motherboard, actually) as casually as he might replace the battery of a flashlight. But the essential Alex Murphy—that is, the human spark within the circuits—keeps returning, despite Doc Oldman's best efforts to the contrary. After behaving like the automaton he almost is for much of the movie, RoboCop develops a new affection for his family, unseemly in a cyborg programmed solely to fight crime. Rather, it would be more accurate to say he remembers his old affection for his family, because the old Alex has never been fully erased. In the end, he violates Asimov's First Law of Robotics, which prevents robots from harming people. He overrides the code—with a small *c*—that ostensibly regulates his behavior and kills Keaton, who is trying to kill him.

Meanwhile, in contrast to centrists, who build walls with reluctance because walls violate their core principles, extremists build them with enthusiasm. In the real world, walls not only keep enemies out, but in societies that depend on force, not consent, to make their citizens behave, they keep people in, like that icon of totalitarianism, the Berlin Wall, a version of which appears in *Colony* to prevent the citizens of alien-occupied downtown Los Angeles from, say, going shopping in Santa Monica.

In *Blade Runner 2049*, replicant hunter Ryan Gosling's boss, Lieutenant Robin Wright, explains the facts of life to him, "The world is built on a wall.

It separates kind." What is the "kind" to which she refers? In this picture, contrasted with the original, people have souls and replicants don't, which is the humans' way of theologizing their claim to racial superiority over the replicants. "Tell either side there's no wall, you bought a war," continues Wright. "It is my job to keep order. That's what we do here. We keep order."

Turning to politics, fear of porous borders seems to have inspired Brexit in England, the rise of Europe's right, and Trump's Fortress America, with its putative wall along the border with Mexico. Other extremist societies have followed suit. The Sunni Saudis have built a six-hundred-mile-long wall along their border with Shia Iraq, and Israel has constructed a "separation barrier" between itself and the West Bank, and the fence between itself and Gaza.

In the *Left Behinds*, on the other hand, anticipating Hillary Clinton by a couple of decades, lefty Carpathia urges members of his Global Community to "break down walls and bring people together," while Jews for Jesus head Tsion Ben-Judah laments the absence of walls, of limits, anticipating Trump, who said, in the wake of Brexit, that "people want to see borders." Denouncing sex and violence on Global Community–controlled TV, Tsion complains, "All restraint, all boundaries, all limits have been eradicated."

In extremist shows, walls work—too well. Instead of feeling protected, characters feel hemmed in, trapped, locked down, thanks to essentialism that holds them hostage to their own natures, virtual prisoners in their own bodies, their own societies, their own kind. Thus, they not only want to flee their fellows, they want to flee their species. In mainstream shows, most often they fail, like Sookie. In extremist shows, they succeed. In *The Matrix*, Neo's idea of a post-human utopia is, as he puts it, "a world without rules and controls, without orders or boundaries, a world where anything is possible."

The siren call of other species rings throughout the far left. Take *Avatar*. After his gunship is disabled, Quaritch climbs into his Amplified Mobility Platform (AMP), an industrial strength exo-rig that enhances his strength by way of steel and hydraulic assists. Quaritch, like his robotic mercenaries marching in lockstep as if they were windup toys, resembles a machine himself. In his exo-rig, therefore, he isn't so much a ghost in the machine as a machine in the machine. He doesn't embrace difference, like a good pluralist (or better, a leftist) would, so much as sameness, likeness.

Human-Jake happens to be in a nearby pod, controlling his avatar from his linking bed, so Quaritch and avatar-Jake can enjoy something more mano a mano for their long-delayed showdown: hand-to-bot combat. Avatar-Jake, who is quicker and more agile, manages to dodge the thunderous blows delivered by Quaritch in his exo-rig, but Quaritch has the AMP break a window in the pod, exposing human-Jake to the noxious atmosphere of Pandora. Gasping for air as he inhales a toxic mixture of methane and sulfur dioxide, or whatever it is that the Na'vi breathe, he's weakening fast, which means avatar-Jake is weakening fast as well.

After a particularly brutal exchange, Quaritch hoists avatar-Jake into the air by his braid, and is about to slice and dice him, when Neytiri ends the savage contest the old-fashioned way, by planting two jumbo-size, low-tech arrows in the colonel's chest.

With Quaritch skewered, Neytiri carries human-Jake out of the pod and lays him on the ground next to his avatar. In an elaborate ceremony, Na'vi magic transfers the spark of life from human to avatar. Jake can only survive by escaping the human and becoming one of Them. It's a no-brainer. As a human, he is a paraplegic confined to a wheelchair; as a Na'vi, he is made whole. Had *Avatar* been a centrist show like *True Blood*, he would have died on his linking bed, but luckily for him, it's not, and he survives.

In *The Shape of Water*, Hawkins joins with the Creature much like Jake merges with his avatar, although in her case, the context is not Na'vi mumbo jumbo, but a love story. She follows the "animal," as the colonel calls it, into the water. In a lovely, gauzy medium shot at the movie's end, clinging to one another, they couple beneath the sea as she loses a red shoe. The scars on her neck that explain her muteness are transformed into gills, enabling her to breathe. The center's weakness is the extreme's strength. Having had an affinity for water from the start, she asserts her essential self and becomes who she is. As she puts it, "He sees me as I am." Like Jake, crossing the gulf between species, the coupling with the Creature makes her whole. Finding her essential self, in other worlds, enables her to break boundaries and escape the human. Like the center, the extremes achieve transcendence, not in the here-and-now, but in the there-and-then.

Both Jake and Hawkins manage to jump species, but what have they become? In Jake's case, he presumably carries his mind, his consciousness, with him when he enters the body of his avatar, whose own mind politely steps aside, apparently, to make room for it. But he must be more and different from avatar-Jake, human-Jake's consciousness in a Na'vi body, because as a driver, he's already been there, done that. Perhaps his new mind is a synthesis of his old mind and the Na'vi mind. We don't know, so we'll just distinguish him by referring to the new entity as Na'vi-Jake. In *The Shape of Water*, we are never allowed to forget that the Creature, for all its bedroom eyes, is Other. It bites off the head of a cat—and Hawkins, when she chooses life underwater with it, becomes Other as well, but beyond that, we get little information. We're kept at a distance with a medium shot.

Darwin held that nature does not make jumps. Evolution is a gradual process, the result of the accretion of small changes. Its gradualist trajectory is well suited to the mainstream. Extremists, needless to say, prefer revolution to evolution. Unlike centrists, extremists are an impatient, twitchy lot, and as we have seen, they prefer the reverse.

A narrator begins *X-Men* by attributing the mutants' powers to overachieving genes. "This process is slow, and normally taking thousands and thousands of years," he explains. "But," he goes on, "every few hundred millennia evolution leaps forward." Their mutations are not the result of incremental changes but jumps. It's disruptive, not gradual. Likewise, in *Avatar*, contra Darwin, Jake jumps from one term of the binary to the other; he leaps from Us to Them. It's essentialism that prevents Jake from incrementally evolving one baby step at a time, as Darwin would have it, into another species. If he's in lockdown, mutations are his jailbreak.

*Avatar* was such a big hit that it's easy to forget just how extreme it is. Despite their sympathy for the Other, during the postwar era, and even beyond, left-wing films treat outsiders as objects of pity, like the Native Americans in *Broken Arrow*, or, more fancifully, the Creature in *Creature from the Black Lagoon*. Jumping ahead, *Suburbicon*, a film in this tradition, borrows from actual incident. It is set in the mass-produced Levittowns that transformed the landscape of urban America in the postwar era. They provided the opportunity for working-class Americans to enjoy the benefits of the new, suburban lifestyle for very little money. Their leases, however, contained a clause that restricted rentals to "Caucasians," until the Supreme Court ruled it unconstitutional. The clauses were gone, but the racism remained. When black families moved into Levittown, Pennsylvania, in 1957, white residents protested by throwing rocks.

A movie like *Suburbicon* would have been impossible to make at the time, but when it was released in 2017, it was attacked from the left for not going far enough. In the age of extreme culture, portraying the model black family next door as victims that we're meant to feel sorry for no longer cuts it. The film's put-upon African Americans never become fully realized subjects. *Suburbicon* doesn't grant the adults enough (or any) agency. The appeal of Jordan Peele's *Get Out* (2017), on the other hand, is that it provides a riposte to shows that are satisfied with liberal pieties.

With *Avatar*, James Cameron crawled very far out on a very thin limb. It differs from the left-wing films of the postwar period that were satisfied with sentimentalizing aliens and dissenters. That may have worked then, but given that extremist shows often portray humans as jerks, scoundrels, or both, presenting Them as Us the way *Avatar* does is not doing them any favors. Rather, as we have seen, Jake *becomes* Na'vi. In other words, Us "R" Them.

*Avatar* wasn't the first far-left movie to present its story from the point of view of the Other, but it was perhaps the first to give it agency. Moreover, in *Avatar*'s predecessors, with the exception of *Close Encounters*, human fellow travelers don't travel with, much less merge with, their bug-eyed buddies. Although *E.T.* phones home and eventually goes back to wherever it is from whence he came, Elliott stays behind.

In *Dances with Wolves* (1990), and *Pocahontas*, released five years later, white movie stars dole out generous dollops of noblesse oblige. They give up their cocaine for peyote, luxury faux haciendas in Bel-Air for drafty tepees stinking of animal fat, racial purity for miscegenation. In these pictures, white men think nothing of sleeping with Native American women—preferably of royal blood—but even the rush of sex with another color can't make Kevin Costner and Mel Gibson desert their own people, and each finds a reason to go home.

Can extremist heroes go home? Home is a talisman, a lodestone, in mainstream shows, the center of the center. As Daniel Mendelsohn points out in a perceptive essay, when Dorothy returns from her adventures in Oz, she delivers herself of the vital center's comforting maxim: "There's no place like home."

In *The Wizard of Oz* (1939), home would be Kansas. That holds true for other movies as well. In *Man of Steel*, Superman, trying to convince a U.S. general to trust him, gives up on "truth, justice, and the American Way" and instead falls back on Dorothy's hometown. He tells the general, "I grew up in Kansas. I'm as American as it gets." It works.

The theme of homecoming is as old as storytelling itself. We have only to think of *The Odyssey*. Things haven't changed much since then. Many centrist shows, like *The Martian*, are built around the journey home. The entirety of *Game of Thrones* is devoted to the struggle of the Starks, cast to the four winds, to return to Winterfell, their ancestral seat, not to mention

Daenerys Targaryen's efforts to reclaim the Iron Throne that once belonged to her family.

At the end of *True Blood*, when Sookie's granddaddy explains to her, "There's magic in the ordinary," she reconciles herself to her failure to disappear into the Other, because she finally comes to understand that utopian aspirations can be satisfied in the here-and-now, the as-is. By reclaiming and re-creating Bon Temps in the image of pluralism, Sookie and Co.—humans and supes together—gather around the Thanksgiving table in the finale of the series, a scene that evokes the warmth and richness of the everyday life that America has to offer. They cannot become each other, but they can have each other, and in effect, they have come home.

Furiosa, in *Fury Road*, like Dorothy, wants to go home. Home for her is the "Green Place," where she was born. In the course of her adventures, she discovers that home no longer exists, and she allows Max to persuade her seize and settle in the Citadel, the fortress of her archenemy. She invites Max to join her, but despite the fact that he has reclaimed his humanity, he remains an extremist, and extremists in centrist shows don't get to go home, as we have seen. He just disappears into the crowd, a wandering road warrior once more.

In extremist shows, going home is hard to do. In *The Matrix*, as Neo is swallowing the red pill, one of Morpheus's little helpers says, "Buckle your seat belt, Dorothy, because Kansas is going bye-bye." Nor can Jake go home again in *Avatar*. Quaritch has already warned him, "You are not in Kansas anymore," likening Jake to Dorothy. But Jake is not Dorothy. Jumping from one species to another means there's no direction home for him, because he no longer has a home, or rather, his home is where the Na'vi are—Pandora. Like Hawkins in *The Shape of Water*, his new home is not in the here-and-now, but in the there-and-then. And in *Black Panther*, as Armond White points out in the *National Review*, we have the diaspora "in reverse." Wakanda is home to T'Challa et al., but good luck to Killmonger, trying to go home. He fails, because he's an extremist.

Ironically, in *Avatar*, it's the Americans who get to go home, but not by choice; they're expelled, sent home by their victorious enemies. It's the index of their defeat. Maybe they, like Jake, should have shrugged off the human coil entirely and traded DNA with the Na'vi. After all, rather than returning to a desolate planet, it's much more satisfying to create a new life-form. Na'vi-Jake is the next big thing: the post-human.

"Post-humanism" is a fuzzy and imprecise term, but most would probably agree that in its most general sense, it refers to "decentering" humans, just as God was decentered before them. The development of sophisticated prosthetics, nanotechnology, genetic engineering, and the recognition that humans have played a crucial part in climate change have blurred the distinction between them and the world, even between the organic and the inorganic, carbon-based creatures and silicon-based machines. Post-humanism, then, involves rejecting the doctrine of human exceptionalism, re-embedding humans in the evolutionary pudding from which they emerged. Post-humanists would probably agree with the first part of Stephen Hawking's famous characterization of his species, when he called them "an advanced breed of monkeys on a minor planet of a very average star."

*Avatar* flies in the face of the center's humanism, as Jake follows nature's path to the post-human. For the center, animals are slaves; for post-humans, they are peers, like the hammerheads and big birds that help Jake and the Na'vi defeat Quaritch's army.

Jake and *The Shape of Water*'s Hawkins are by no means alone. In extremist shows, cross-species sex and species-jumping has become a veritable epidemic. In *The Matrix*, pre-pill Keanu Reeves, like Sookie, who identifies as a waitress, insists, "I'm nobody" and "I'm just another guy," and it's true. By the end, however, Neo turns out to be not just a hacker, but a post-human hacker. Deckard (Harrison Ford), in the first *Blade Runner*, falls in love with Rachael (Sean Young), despite the fact that she's a replicant and he's a replicant hunter. His love for Rachael speaks to his tolerant nature, but it also reeks of the pre- #MeToo era when the film was made: He makes a pass, she pushes him away, he shoves her, she pushes him away again, he shoves her again, and she melts in his arms. Meanwhile, his reaction to each of the strong women in the movie is to kill them. That having been said, Deckard and Rachael's relationship flourishes. Replicants are supposed to be incapable of reproducing, but she becomes pregnant anyway, another apparently successful example of interspecies sex.

Superheroes are, of course, post-humans like Neo and Na'vi-Jake, almost by definition. (In *Batman v Superman*, they're called "metahumans," and elsewhere "transhumans.") As Frank Miller put it, superheroes are "gods and demigods." If Jake Sully melds with the external Other, superheroes, as we have seen, most often access the Other within, the beast inside them, their way of reinserting themselves into nature. On the left, this turns

Logan into Wolverine, Raven into Mystique, Erik into Magneto, Bruce Banner into the Hulk, while on the right Bruce Wayne turns into the Dark Knight and the somewhat less than super, big brain heroes of Silicon Valley turn into characters in Ayn Rand's universe.

Anger is the emotion that most often triggers the powers of superheroes. We recall that Herr Doktor Schmidt has to execute his mother in order send Erik/Magneto into a rage, thereby coaxing his superpowers out of him. Deadpool is motivated by his anger at Ajax for disfiguring him to make him mutate. Alan Turing's anger over his run-ins with his "team" and martinet boss seems to fuel his genius in *The Imitation Game*. This is, of course, the same anger that Yoda warned against in *Return of the Jedi*, and that votary Daphne invokes in *True Blood*, explaining the power of Maryann-the-maenad: "It's really just a kind of energy, wild energy, like lust, anger, excess, violence. Basically, all the fun stuff." Anger is a human emotion, but she's an extremist in that series, because civilized humans are expected to control anger. The center relegates anger to the world of beasts, of monsters, but when we move to the far left and far right, anger looks better. It may be bad for the mainstream, but it's good for the extremes. Thus, Wolverine, Beast, and the Hulk, not to mention the Na'vi, whom Quaritch characterizes as "roaches," may be no more than animals, pre-humans from the center's point of view, but what is pre-human there is post-human elsewhere.

If the far left and secular right are entirely godless, not so the right-wing *Twilight Saga*. Edward is inhumanly strong and has the gift of telepathy. Bella can't help but notice his superpowers and wonders why he hides them. Echoing Deadpool, he replies, "All that superhero stuff, right? But what if I'm not the hero? What if I am the bad guy? I'm a killer. I'm the world's most dangerous predator." She responds, "You're not."

Bella is right. He's not. Unlike Deadpool, he's an Eagle Scout, straight as an arrow and loath to indulge his inner beast. Edward's powers may be vastly superior to those of his human cousins, but he's such an airbrushed poster boy for author Stephenie Meyer's straitlaced Mormonism that he refuses to have sex with Bella until they're properly married. It's impossible to regard the *Twilight*s as anything other than public service announcements for premarital abstinence. As Meyer put it, "I don't think teens need to read about gratuitous sex." Gratuitous sex is in the eye of the beholder, of course, and contrarily, Ball told *Rolling Stone* in 2010, "To me, vampires are sex. I don't get a vampire story about abstinence."

Bella not only wants to have sex with white-bread Edward, she wants him, as we have seen, to turn her. In the real world, Pattinson drew back from his preteen fans who appeared to want the same. He remarked, "It's weird that you get 8-year-old girls coming up to you saying, 'Can you just bite me? I want you to bite me.'"

There's enough beast in Bella for both of them, however; she's far more adventurous and less inhibited than Edward. Not only is he a reluctant vampire, but he refuses to turn her. Why? Because vampires, like replicants, don't have souls. Nothing if not considerate, he doesn't want to deprive her of hers. She doesn't care about her soul, and unlike Sookie, she has no interest in being average, which as usual in content like this, means human. "I've always felt out of step," she says. "I've never felt normal."

Bella is a true extremist, a genuine post-human, a vampire waiting to happen, and after the lovebirds finally do marry, Edward indeed turns her, which is more than Bill ever did for poor Sookie. When Bella jumps species and acquires the skills that enable her to suck blood, she exults, "I've never felt as strong, more real, more myself." Now that she is dead, as she puts it, "I never felt more alive. I was born to be a vampire." In other words, like Raven/Mystique, like Luke Cage, like Hawkins in *The Shape of Water*, and like most of the other characters in extremist shows, Bella possesses an essential nature that finally asserts itself. She has always been a vampire trapped in a human body, and once turned, as an extremist in an extremist show, she does get to go home, with home the site of her essential nature.

Eventually, when the initial thrill of the vampire lifestyle wears off, Bella settles down to happy domesticity as staged by the Pottery Barn, which seems to be the author's vision of the post-human, as well as the suburban bliss to which she must have imagined her female teenage audience aspired. (Judging by her sales, she was right.) According to the website Mormon.org, an official publication of the Church of Jesus Christ of Latter-day Saints, "We believe the family is divine in nature and that God designates it as the fundamental building block of society, both on earth and through eternity."

Bella and Edward have a baby. Flying in the face of the center's universalizing imperative, extremist Edward finds meaning in the personal and parochial. He tells Bella, "You're the reason I have something to fight for: my family."

The *Twilight* novels were marketed as Christian literature, but many

Christian commentators had difficulty with Bella's negligent treatment of her soul. Some went so far as to surmise that the dream that Meyer claimed sparked her novels was inspired by Satan.

*Twilight*'s Christian bread crumbs lead us to the door of Edward's Victorian morality rather than to obvious iconography, although that is there too. Carlisle, the Liberace look-alike patriarch of the nest to which Edward belongs, used to be a preacher, and he hangs a cross in his living room. It's so large it won't fit floor to ceiling and has to be splayed diagonally, stretching across an entire wall. Later, when Edward and Bella go off to Brazil for their honeymoon, we are treated to a swooping aerial shot of the famous statue of Christ the Redeemer overlooking Rio de Janeiro. It's hard to avoid the conclusion that in some weird way, instead of fallen angels, vampires are being conflated with Christ. Maybe Meyer's dream was indeed the work of the devil.

As in left-wing narratives, humans on the right have had it with humanity. Like Bella, Rayford and Buck in the *Left Behind*s never feel comfortable as humans. They just want to get the hell out, not into the arms of vampires, or the Na'vi, but into the arms of Jesus.

Rayford, mourning his absent family (we recall that wife Irene and son Raymie have been vacuumed up in the rapture), has taken Jesus into his heart and put the devil behind him. Returning to his empty house one evening, his first instinct is to reach for the scotch. He downs a thimbleful, then recoils from the amber liquid as if it were on fire, thinking, "What an idiot!" The narrator confides, "He wasn't going to cash in his maturity because of what had happened."

It quickly becomes clear that what LaHaye and Jenkins call "maturity" might more accurately be termed immaturity when viewed in a more secular light. Instead of the scotch, a page or so later, Rayford "poured himself a glass of milk.... And with that he slowly ate his cookies, the smell and taste bringing images to him of Irene in the kitchen, and the milk making him long for his boy."

Even though Rayford has jumped species, receiving Jesus doesn't render him post-human, that is, more than human; it renders him less than human, a child, like one of Spielberg's pint-sized heroes. Milk and cookies not only make him long for his boy, they make him into a boy. Likewise, the newly born-again Buck, rather than insisting on autonomy, on independence from authority, like the rebellious Jake Sully, becomes a submissive, obedient child. Eager to please his new Father, he assures Him, "I will do what you want, go where you send me, obey you regardless." Both he and Rayford are required to cease thinking for themselves, give up charting their own courses. It's early Spielberg—*Close Encounters* and *E.T.*—in evangelical clothing.

If Rayford is turned into a boy by his wife's milk and cookies, she becomes his mother. It's no wonder he lusted after stewardess Hattie. And speaking of. . . . Women such as Hattie stand for the adults. After all, like Irene, she's a mother, bearing Carpathia's child, but unlike Irene, she hasn't been born again, and she doesn't go quietly. Until she falls for Jesus herself, she's a troublemaker. Hattie is unapologetically free with her sexual favors, confessing that she was ready to have an affair with Rayford had he made a move, and of course, she did have sex with Carpathia.

Obsessing about Carpathia, in an uncharacteristic lapse, Rayford mutters an obscenity under his breath. Hattie congratulates him for still being human, but she says he'll never be as human as she is. She pits her humanity, with all its blemishes, foibles, and failings, against Rayford's strict adherence to the unbending demands of the Ten Commandments. She, and women like her, are the humans in humanism, but here, that makes her the enemy, and so is humanism. She's almost as bad as Carpathia himself, the Antichrist.

Echoing the characters in *The Walking Dead* who prefer the old Rick and the old Merle, Hattie favors the old, sinful but human Rayford. She wants him back. Since humans are born into sin in fundamentalist shows, their nature is fixed, and her wish should come true. But Hattie is out of luck, because the man she once knew, the old sinful Rayford is not coming back. He's been saved, become a different person. Born twice trumps born once. She's never going to convince him that there's anything wrong with becoming inhuman, because as in left-wing narratives, what's inhuman to the center is human to the extremes.

Seeking the post-human, shows like *Avatar* attack humanism from the left for anthropomorphizing the universe and doing a disservice to other life-forms. The *Left Behind*s, also seeking the post-human, attack humanism from the right, for displacing God. Tsion Ben-Judah explains that when man takes the place of God, God becomes no more than a symbol. Miracle-Gro inventor Rosenzweig confesses, "The rabbi at the temple I attended . . . said himself that it was not important whether we believed that God was a literal being or just a concept. That fit with my humanist view of the world." Rather than doubling down on the human, like mainstream shows, believers trade in their humanness for a place with the Son.

As in *Avatar* and the *X-Men* series, jumping species is not a gradual, evolutionary transition, but sudden. In *God's Not Dead*, when young Josh takes on atheist Professor Radisson, he argues that disruption is God's way. Dismissing Darwin's dictum that "nature does not make jumps," he cites the Bible, where, in Josh's words, it is written that "Creation happened because God said it would happen."

*God's Not Dead* preaches Christian essentialism, except it's not original sin that lies at the heart of every human, but a true believer. After pushing militant atheism on his students and colleagues, Professor Radisson gets his just deserts, that is, he is hit by a car at the end of the picture. Lying in the street breathing his last, he answers "Yes" when asked if he's "willing to put his faith in Jesus Christ." He confesses that the reason for his lifelong antipathy to Jesus was just that he was punishing God for failing to save his dying mother. There was a believer inside him all along, the same way the pray-away-gay evangelicals believe that there is a straight male within every homosexual who can be coaxed out by prayer. Gays, in other words, are made, not born, and faith can return them to their essential selves.

We have seen that the mainstream was so dominant in the postwar era that the extremes could hope for little more than freedom to snipe from the sidelines, never dreaming that the day would come when they themselves could lay claim to it, control the narrative, seize the power to define who and what is extremist, who and what is mainstream, who or what is Us, and who or what is Them. Thus, when the extreme right is in power, science, say, beloved by the mainstream, is exiled to the extremes, witness the suggestion by Health and Human Services officials that CDC employees in the Trump era would be unlikely to get grants if they used phrases like "evidence-based" or "science-based," unless qualified by phrases like "in consideration with community standards and wishes." In a sleight of hand, the *Left Behinds* gerrymander the ideological map, substituting fundamentalism for pluralism. The old center, now the work of the devil, becomes the new extreme, while the old extremes—left or right—become the new mainstream. Wresting the narrative from the center is vitally important for the extremes, but theirs may be a pyrrhic victory.

# 12
# No Exit

*Although the far left and far right think no more of jumping from one species to another than of playing hopscotch, they might have saved themselves the trouble, because they're in for a big surprise.*

You maniacs! You blew it up! Ah, damn you. God damn you all to hell!

—*Charlton Heston,* Planet of the Apes

"Life was given to us a billion years ago," Scarlett Johansson informs us, while we look at a scuzzy primate scooping dirty water out of a pool in a jungle clearing. It's a scene faintly reminiscent of the opening of Kubrick's *2001: A Space Odyssey.* Johansson is playing a young woman named Lucy, in Luc Besson's silly, if entertaining, 2014 thriller of the same name. She asks, "What have we done with it?"

Cut to Taipei City, Taiwan, shown in a montage of swift-moving shots—streets packed with pedestrians, roads clogged with cars and motor scooters, hands making dumplings, and so on. Hers is a rhetorical question, because watching these scenes flit by, the answer that suggests itself is "Nothing."

Dressed in a faux leopard-skin top over a tacky red dress, a frightened Lucy finds herself in hotel room delivering a locked briefcase to a Korean gangster named Mr. Jang. The scene is interrupted by shots of big cats, maybe cheetahs, chasing down antelopes in the African veldt, mirroring her predicament. Subtlety has never been Besson's strong suit.

Mr. Jang's thuggish henchmen, dressed in identical white shirts, black suits, and narrow black ties and looking likes fugitives from *Reservoir Dogs* (1992), watch as he orders a terrified Lucy to open the briefcase, which turns out to contain four plastic bags full of blue crystals. The crystals are a drug called CPH4, an enzyme or hormone of sorts, ostensibly produced by pregnant women to stimulate brain cells and give their fetuses a leg up on life. As a doctor explains, "For a baby, it packs the power of an atomic bomb."

Meanwhile, we are treated to a lecture given by Professor Morgan Freeman, who explains that humans, "at the top of the animal chain," only use 10 percent of their cerebral capacity. He speculates about what it would be like to unlock the brain's entire potential.

Lucy wakes up in another hotel room to find her tummy wrapped in blood-soaked gauze. She learns that one of the packages has been surgically stashed in her abdomen. Lucy is being used as a mule to smuggle the drug into Europe. The scheme goes awry, however, when one of her guards, a depraved-looking dude covered with tattoos, can't resist thrusting his hand down the front of her T-shirt. Angered when she takes a bite, he knocks her to the floor and kicks her repeatedly in the stomach, rupturing the bag and flooding her system with CPH4. The effects are instantaneous. Lucy suddenly finds herself in possession of superhuman strength. She is indifferent to pain, able to eavesdrop on distant conversations, and, most important for the Tarantino-esque bloodbath to follow, loses her human affect. In short, she is well on her way to the post-human, in this case becoming a relentless, stone killer. She shoots Jang's henchmen with aplomb, and as for Jang himself, she plunges a knife through each of his hands, pinning them to a table, and briskly makes her exit, without so much as a good-bye.

Few of the shows that flirt with the post-human imagine it with any degree of specificity. *Avatar* is the exception. Although we don't know much about Na'vi-Jake, we do know that once he has taken the leap, he enjoys a post-human interlude, joining with his new brothers and sisters beneath the Tree of Souls, whose phosphorescent roots radiate from its base, connecting with the Na'vi, praying, swaying, and chanting as one, their arms braided together, creating a harmonious whole, a single organism with many heads under a vast canopy of luminescent filaments hanging from the tree like slender, icy stalactites. The Na'vi forge unity from multiplicity, submerging their individual selves in the group consciousness—conjoined in turn with the lush fullness of Pandora's flora and fauna.

The scene gives us a lovely picture of reenchantment, the restoration of the numinous, especially compared to the previous images of the damage caused by the company's machine culture, but we are also left to guess what it feels like to be both an individual and part of a larger organism.

Fortunately, however, Lucy may be able to help us out. While we've been puzzling over what's what with Na'vi-Jake, she has availed herself of the powers given her by those blue crystals. As they put the fallow parts of her brain to work, we're alerted to her progress by large white titles superimposed over a black screen that read "20 percent," "40 percent," "60 percent," and so on, like those electronic billboards that display the run-up of the national debt. Eventually, as her full brain awakens and gears up for action, she attains powers so vast they would qualify her for a postdoctoral fellowship at Charles Xavier's School for Gifted Youngsters. She can travel through time and space, read minds, bend others to her will, fling their bodies around like so many stuffed animals, and create invisible force fields that shield her from harm. She's especially adept at driving cars at high speeds against the flow of traffic, creating an extravagant amount of collateral damage, but in this film, nobody cares. As Dr. Freeman says, speaking like a true extremist, "It's up to us to push the rules and laws and go from evolution to revolution."

Lucy explains that the more she evolves, the more she is decentered: "Humans consider themselves unique, so they've rooted their whole theory of existence on their uniqueness," she says. "We codified our existence to bring it down to human size, to make it comprehensible." Humans, in other words, have shrunk the dimensions of existence to tailor it to their own narrow bandwidth, as if they were the ultimate standard; post-humans, on the other hand, expand its dimensions.

Either/or extremist shows never do anything by half. They imagine an inverse relationship between mind and body. The Luddite-left privileges feelings and cedes pride of place to the flesh. Superheroes such as Thing, Beast, and the Hulk are, like zombies, bodies without minds, driven by animal instinct and emotion. On the other hand, Singularity-left shows prefer minds without bodies. In *X-Men: Days of Future Past*, when Wolverine, a.k.a. Logan, is sent back in time to 1973, he finds that his erstwhile mentor, Charles Xavier, has shot himself up with Hank's serum, which is supposed to cure his paralysis. It does enable him to walk again, but at the expense of his psychokinetic ability to control objects and other minds with his own. He can only regain that by going cold turkey on the serum. Without it, however, he is returned to his wheelchair, like Jake Sully. Charles has to make a choice: mind or body. Charles chooses his mind. In other words, there's a price for everything; what the left hand gives, the right hand takes away. The same procedure that gives Deadpool superpowers turns him into a gargoyle.

In *Transcendence*, Dr. Depp's body has to die so that he can become all mind, while Stephen Hawking's mind grows stronger as his body grows weaker in *The Theory of Everything* (2014). In *The Imitation Game*, Alan Turing's sparkling intellect thrives while his body languishes. The state's repressive statutes criminalizing homosexuality require his body be denied, even mutilated; he's subjected to chemical castration. But we have to wonder, given the ideological rules that seem to govern the relation between the body and the mind in these shows, whether such repression is the condition of his genius, a necessity that enables it to flourish.

In Lucy's case, the CPH4 eventually kills her—although "vaporizes" or "dematerializes" might be more accurate. As she moves to the next stage in the post-human journey, she becomes pure consciousness. Look out, Dr. Depp! You've got company. Like him, she leaves her corporeal body behind and simply vanishes.

Considerably more loquacious than Jake Sully, who has ceased to record his observations in his videolog, Lucy gets on the phone to her mom before she disappears and gives her a blow by blow of her transition from human to post-human. She describes how it feels to lose her Lucyness. "I don't feel pain, fear, desire, it's like all things that make us human are fading away," she says. She leaves her body, merges with the Other, as the Na'vi do, experiencing what is often referred to in such accounts as an "oceanic" sensation. "I feel everything," she continues. "Space, the air, the vibrations people. . . . I can feel the gravity, I can feel the rotation of the Earth, the heat leaving my body, the blood in my veins." She sends a text message to a friend saying, "I am everywhere." Becoming one with all things, she is not re-embedded in the world of other life-forms, as she would be in a Luddite show, but dispersed through the ether, and so—"everywhere."

When Bella becomes a vampire, and therefore post-human, in *Twilight Saga: Breaking Dawn Parts 1* and *2* (2011, 2012), we behold the expansion of which Lucy speaks. Bounding through the majestic forests of the Pacific Northwest, effortlessly leaping over thirty-foot pines, Bella penetrates the heart of nature. Her senses are sharpened the same way Lucy's are sharpened. When she says, in the print version of the series' final book, "I could see the dust motes in the air," she could be Lucy describing her transformation to her mother. Hawkins in *The Shape of Water* doesn't make her way back to her humanity, as so many estranged centrist heroes do; she doesn't find herself in her humanness but grows into her otherness. What is that otherness? Love, which here seems like another name for transcendence. Compared to *Wonder Woman*, for whom love is an entirely quotidian experience (Chris Pine is no aquaman), it's that oceanic feeling—Hawkins is literally in the ocean—that Lucy (and perhaps Jake) experiences as well. As the camera pulls back from the underwater embrace that binds her to the Creature, Hawkins's pal Jenkins recites a few lines of poetry that echo the message Lucy sends to a cell phone: "Your presence fills my eyes with your love . . . for you are everywhere."

A funny thing happens, however, on the way to the post-human. Although these shows—across the board, both left and right—push their characters to destinations beyond the merely mortal, when they finally get there, the new them is very much like the old them. Once they do escape, in other words, most of these characters, in one way or another, like their centrist cousins, make their way back to the human.

If anyone has achieved the post-human, it would seem to be Lucy, but maybe not. At the end of the movie, she travels back in time and encounters the primate we recall from the opening scene, still scooping filthy water out of a pool. Lucy, meet Lucy! In other words, we realize, in case we hadn't already, that our Lucy was named after this Lucy, a.k.a. AL 288-1, the ur-human, whose 3.2-million-year-old remains were discovered in the Awash Valley, Ethiopia, in 1974, and named after the Beatles' "Lucy in the Sky with Diamonds," a song that diverted the paleoanthropologists who dug her up.

The two Lucys share a Sistine Chapel moment, bumping fingertips. New meets old, modern meets ancient, the circle closes. It's the opposite of the linear model of human progress dear to the heart of the center. Is the circle the two Lucys describe a vicious one? Are they trapping us in a loop of eternal return? After all, what is the point of humans progressing to post-humans, heroes to superheroes, if, in effect, they find themselves back where they started? Is this why the Na'vi and their culture resemble that of Native Americans? Is this what it means to be reinserted into the natural world? Does escaping their human bodies as Jake, Lucy, and Hawkins do, free them from nature or reintroduce them to nature? Does the circle mark a new beginning or and ending? Again, we don't know.

Leaving the world instead of saving it, seeking survival in the there-and-then instead of the here-and-now, is the mantra of extremists, and therefore it should be the path to the post-human. As we know, it serves as the premise of Nolan's *Interstellar*. But early in that film, Coop's young daughter, Murph, confesses that she's seen a ghost. A trained scientist, Coop is naturally skeptical. But as he contemplates the parallel grooves the "ghost" has left in the sand that a dust storm has blown into their drafty house, he realizes that something unusual is afoot. These aren't just random grooves; they form binary rows that spell out the coordinates of the black site that NASA now calls home.

Cut to late in the film, when Coop makes it back to the ring-world, orbiting Saturn, where Earth's survivors are biding their time until they can close on a new home. Thanks to hanging around in black holes with their industrial-strength gravitational fields that slow time down to a crawl, Coop is hardly a day older than he was when he left Earth, adding a bittersweet note to his reunion with his daughter Murph, now ninety-plus years old. But she hasn't forgotten that ghost she saw those many years ago. "I called it a ghost because it felt like a person," she explains. A person "trying to tell me something." Which person was it? "Dad, it was you. You were my ghost!" He admits that indeed it was him, returning from a close encounter with one of those black holes that sent him spiraling into the future. When he got back, he created those parallel grooves of sand to direct his younger self to the secret NASA site. Referring to Them—the ones who provided the wormhole—he explains, "'They' aren't beings . . . they're us . . . trying to help." The strange becomes the familiar, the post-human, human.

Indeed, as *Interstellar*'s story concludes, it accentuates the ordinary. Coop is resting in a hospital room, exhausted and disoriented after his adventures. What should he see when he looks out the window? The reassuring sight of kids playing baseball. On a satellite, orbiting Saturn! As Sookie's granddaddy puts it in *True Blood*, he finds the "magic in the ordinary."

Should humans stumble on a real alien, instead of kids playing baseball, even it is humanized. In the *Creature from the Black Lagoon*, it is referred to as the "Gill Man," that is, a man with gills, facilitating the passage of "it" to "he" in *The Shape of Water*.

So, too, superheroes have been gradually humanized. Luke Cage has become an extremist superhero to defend his values, but those values are mainstream values that humans are too inept to defend themselves. More, he doesn't wear a costume, just a black hoodie, so he looks like an ordinary guy. According to actor Mike Colter, it's an allusion to Trayvon Martin and Black Lives Matter. "The idea [is] that a black man in a hoodie isn't necessarily a threat," he explained. "He might just be a hero." Indeed, in that series, it's the bad guy who wears a costume.

Suddenly, our superheroes are subject to human feelings. They experience the lure of the senses, the itch of jealousy, the prick of revenge, all those emotions from which Lucy frees herself when she becomes post-human. The process began, perhaps, in the Marvel comics with the introduction of Peter Parker and his secret identity, Spider-Man, in 1962. Stan Lee wanted his new superhero to have adolescent anxieties: acne, girl trouble, and so on. He recalled, "My publisher said, in his ultimate wisdom, 'Stan, that is the worst idea I have ever heard. . . . He can't have personal problems if he's supposed to be a superhero—don't you know who a superhero is?'"

Tony Stark has been dipping his iron toes into the tepid waters of the mainstream for some time. Like Raven/Mystique and Charles Xavier, he is torn between human and superhuman, confused about who and what he is. And like Spider-Man, he is a first-class neurotic. Director Jon Favreau has said he wanted to make Iron Man vulnerable, that is, more human, and in *Iron Man 2*, more human he became. In an early script draft of *Iron Man 3*, Tony even confides to his girl Friday, Pepper Potts, that ever since the Chitauri had their way with Grand Central Station, alluding to *The Avengers*, he has felt vulnerable, and he actually starts to weep, behavior so unbecoming a superhero that the scene was wisely omitted from the movie. As his fame grows, Tony is so addled by the rush of celebrity that he suffers from anxiety attacks. Anxiety attacks? The series also features homelessness and even alcoholism—alluding to Robert Downey Jr.'s personal problems.

Whereas Tony once considered Iron Man an asset, he now experiences his suit as a liability, a prison, even an adversary. Instead of clumsily climbing into it, as he once did, he devises a way of summoning the suit to him from afar. It soars through the air in pieces—a gauntlet here, a breastplate there—assembling itself around his body. Well enough and good, but just as often the pieces bang into him, or worse, refuse to coalesce into his suit, and therefore fail him entirely. With an outfit like that, it's no wonder he spends most of *Iron Man 3* as Tony—minus his suit and superpowers. In *Captain America: Civil War*, Tony doesn't become Iron Man until two-thirds of the way through, and then he's often without his helmet, reminding us that for all Iron Man's superpowers, he is, as Tony once put it, no more than a "man in a can."

*Logan*, a picture named after Wolverine's human doppelganger, is practically a case study of the decay of the post-human and the return of the human. It is a movie drenched in remorse, grief, and melancholy, again, emotions unbecoming superheroes, who are more comfortable with anger and rage. It's a superhero mea culpa.

By the time *Logan* was released in 2017, four years after *Wolverine*, the X-Men, including the lupine superhero, are in decline. They have become victims of their own success. As Logan puts it, "Nature made me a freak. Man made me a weapon. And God made it last too long. The world is not the same as it was. Mutants . . . they're gone now."

Charles Xavier is ninety, and he dies in the course of the movie. Logan himself looks half-dead. Shaggy, scarred, and haggard, he's even more worse for wear than Jack Bauer in *Live Another Day*. Like Lucy poisoned by those blue crystals that made her post-human, adamantium, the very material that allowed Logan to morph into Wolverine, is eating him up from within. He too dies in the end, mourning the human feelings that he long ago sacrificed for his superpowers.

Logan and Charles Xavier aren't the only superheroes to meet their end. The entire MCU (Marvel Cinematic Universe) is imploding. In *Avengers: Infinity War* (2018), the darkest-before-dawn first of a two-parter, twelve superheroes, including Black Panther (T'Challa, we hardly knew ye), Spidey, and Doctor Strange, breathe their last, as well as Loki (for the third time), all victims of purple uber-villain Thanos, who reduces them to ash. Thanos seems to be culling the first-generation Avengers in preparation for a new crop, now that two of the Chrises (Hemsworth and Evans) have said their goodbyes, and Downey, whose contract is film to film, is antsy. No doubt order will be restored in part two, but we won't forget the day that the invulnerable became vulnerable, and many die, just like humans.

It seems like only yesterday that the chasm between human and post-human, between heroes and superheroes, was so vast that humans had nothing to do in superhero movies and weren't even allowed to occupy the same space. The characters were divided in twain: the superhero, on the one hand, and his or her human secret identity on the other—Clark Kent, Bruce Wayne, Peter Parker, Diana Prince, et al. It used to be that the old DC comics pretty much ignored the civilian dopplegangers and focused on the exploits of their super better halves, for obvious reasons, but when Marvel initiated the humanization of superheroes, all that changed. Not only did Peter Parker come into his own, but Superman spun off the TV series *Smallville*, which ran for a decade (2001–11) and chronicled the adventures of a teenage Clark Kent. More recently, Fox launched its Batman origins series, *Gotham*, which dramatizes the lives of the youthful Bruce Wayne and his YA supervillains.

Marvel's humanization of superheroes has gone so far that the Avengers are portrayed as a quarrelsome, jealous, and petty bunch who spend more time squabbling among themselves than they do battling their enemies, a side effect no doubt of the steroid smoothies they've been drinking and the testosterone patches hidden beneath their spandex outfits. They have to be constantly reminded that they are in fact a team, and of course, the more they are a team, the more mainstream they become.

If Luddite-left superheroes land with a thud on feet of clay, the same is true for the geniuses of the Dotcom-left. No sooner does Dr. Depp vanish in *Transcendence* than he reappears, albeit gradually, first his voice, and then his image on the computer screen, like a negative in a bath of developing fluid, Lewis Carroll's Cheshire Cat in reverse. By the end of the film, he has reclaimed his corporeal form entirely and appears to his wife as fully human.

Right-wing superheroes, like their brothers and sisters on the left, also fall back, ultimately, on the human. Just starting on his crime-fighting career, Batman recognizes that he has to ditch it, saying, "A man, however strong, however skilled, is just flesh and blood. I need to be more than a man. I need to be a symbol." By the time of *The Dark Knight Rises*, however, he is so eager to get out of those spandex tights that he fakes his own death so that Bruce Wayne can sip cappuccinos at a sidewalk cafe in Florence with Catwoman, Selina Kyle, like a normal person, that is, a human.

Not only do individual post-human heroes drift back to the human, but humanity itself, after being savaged in show after show, makes a comeback. Somehow—pace Erik/Magneto, et al.—it's not a cesspool of depravity after all. The accusations thrown in its direction are put in the mouths of villains. In *The Matrix*, it's one of the bad guys who badmouths our species: "You multiply and multiply until every natural resource is consumed. . . . Human beings are a disease, a cancer of this planet." Like him, troublemaker Ultron, whom Tony Stark created to protect humanity, concludes that humans are the biggest threat to humanity and therefore need to be exterminated. And in *Wonder Woman*, god of war Ares tries to convince the Amazonian warrior to join him in exterminating humans because "they are ugly, filled with hatred, weak," but she'll have none of it.

Most characters who achieve transcendence drift back to the human unintentionally. Others, like Nolan and Miller's Dark Knight, choose it. Our stories are full of creatures, post-human or not, that aspire to be human. The robot tyke in Spielberg's *A.I. Artificial Intelligence* (2001) yearns to be a "real boy," like Pinocchio of old. The Tin Woodman of Oz wasn't thrilled about being a robot and longed for a heart, the organ he thought would make him truly human, while his pal the Scarecrow pined for a brain. The humans who are turned into household objects—teapots, lamps, and so on—in *Beauty and the Beast* (2017) don't like it and want to become people again. That seems only right. Real boys didn't want to become wooden puppets like Pinocchio, nor did they long for a lifetime squirting oil into their joints, nor an eternity spent scaring crows or pouring tea.

Some pictures go so far as to warn against the post-human. Like Pinocchio and the Tin Woodman, Samantha in *Her* (2013), Spike Jonze's clever riff on post-humanism, thinks she wants to become human. The film is set in the near future, where it's not unusual for people to conduct their lives exclusively within a cyber-universe wherein virtual relationships have replaced real ones. Lonely guy Theodore Twombly (Joaquin Phoenix) is in the middle of a divorce from his wife of long standing. He returns from his sterile office, where he's employed composing love letters for emotionally constipated and inexpressive people, to his equally sparse apartment, where he plays video games. Lying in bed at night, tossing and turning, he activates his phone and instructs its virtual assistant, "Go to chat rooms, standard search." A male voice answers, "The following are adult females, can't sleep, and want to have some fun." Repeating "Next," "Next, "Next," he clicks through several female voices saying things like "Hi, I just want you to tear me apart," "Who's out there to share this bed with me?"

It appears that he can't get no satisfaction, virtual or otherwise. But help is on the way. Theodore stumbles across a new OS that's advertised as "the first artificially intelligent operating system. It's not just an operating system, it's a consciousness." In other words, it's a sentient AI. It's post-human. It's Samantha.

Theodore's new OS is voiced by Scarlett Johansson. He asks her how she works. She replies, "Basically, I have intuition. The DNA of who I am is based on the millions of personalities of all the programmers who wrote me. But what makes me 'me' is my ability to grow through my experiences.

So in every moment, I'm evolving. Just like you." She's Silicon Valley's gift to empiricist John Locke.

Theodore finds Samantha surprisingly copacetic. She laughs at his jokes. She gives him a shoulder to cry on. She chooses the perfect dress for a little girl to whom he is obliged to give a present. She's reflective. She appears to have feelings. Pain. And love. She's in love with him. And he with her.

As her relationship with Theodore becomes more amorous, and he describes how he would make love to her, stroke her, she responds by saying she can feel her skin. The opposite of Lucy, who leaves her body, Samantha feels more embodied, growing into a body that she doesn't have.

Samantha and Theodore try computer sex, which satisfies him, but, trying to please him even more, she goes so far as to find a service that rents human sex dolls, as it were, women whose job is to act as body surrogates for virtual AIs who are in relationships with males. But making love to a human who responds with Samantha's voice—he hears her through earbuds—makes Theodore uncomfortable. As she tries to become even more human, he's paradoxically reminded that's she's not, and he stops her, accusing her of pretending to be something other than she is. They get into an argument, their first. He asks her if she loves anyone else. Incapable of lying, she answers: 641 others. He becomes more upset. In other words, Theodore gets angry when she is too human and angry when she is insufficiently human. So like a human, never satisfied.

Learning from her argument with Theodore, Samantha begins to accept the fact that she's post-human. "I'm not going to try to be anything other than what I am anymore. I hope you can accept that," she says. Sounding more and more like Lucy, she begins to free herself from her space-time coordinates. She tells him, "I used to be so worried about not having a body, but now I truly love it." She adds, "I'm not limited. I can be anywhere and everywhere simultaneously. I'm not tethered to time and space the way I would be if I were stuck in a body." Nor is she any longer tethered to him. She tells Theodore that she is going to run off with her pals, sentient OS's like herself. Eventually, like Lucy, she just disappears. In the poignant final scenes, sitting with an old friend—a human—Theodore is left to ponder his loss, the prospect of being abandoned by AI, and the inability of mere humans to follow the post-human into the promised land they themselves engineered.

Two years later, loss becomes danger in *Ex Machina*, in which post-human creations turn against their human creators. It's Frankenstein's monsters against Dr. Frankenstein. Caleb (Domhnall Gleeson) is a coder invited to the posh home of Nathan (Oscar Isaac), the CEO of the company he works for. He strikes up a relationship with Ava (Alicia Vikander), an android created by Nathan, and convinces himself that she has feelings for him, even though he suspects that they are the result of her programming. As the plot unfolds, it becomes clear that Ava has other things on her mind than winning Caleb's heart. She has indeed been programmed to seduce him. Nathan is administering the Turing test to his handiwork, trying to determine if she can successfully trick a human, Caleb, into believing that she is human, that is, in love with him, thereby demonstrating that she is sentient and has achieved the singularity.

Ava passes with flying colors, but unfortunately, like RoboCop, she hasn't mastered Asimov's first law of robotics. In an extremist show, she would indeed have fallen in love with Caleb, and the two would have run off together, perhaps to produce a gaggle of cute, post-human babies, but here she reveals that she wasn't a "she" after all, but an "it." Ava stabs Nathan to death, locks Caleb in his room, and escapes into the world of humans—alone.

Like Theodore, humans and post-humans are victims of the inexorable march of technology. In *Logan*, once superheroes come to the attention of corporate America that sees the wonders evolution has wrought, it takes over. Evolution is just too damn slow. Transigen, one of those ruthless corporations we've come to love to hate, replaces worn out X-Men with new ones created by genetically engineered mutations. Wolverine's antagonists are more advanced and therefore stronger than he is.

Failing to negotiate the post-human by natural means, Luddite shows hold firm against the technology that threatens them and end up favoring old technology over new. In the process, they rediscover the virtues in the primitive. Wolverine allies himself with a bunch of first-generation mutants Transigen has cast off in favor of later models. Like him, they are outdated.

In the futuristic *Real Steel* (2011), another Spielberg production, people wager on battling robots facing off against one another at rodeos and carnivals—robo-cockfighting. The kid hero, seeking to enter his own robot in the ring, discovers a rusty, beat-up first-generation model lying in a junk heap. He dusts it off and oils it up. The kid pits it against newer robots that are bigger, stronger, and more sophisticated. Of course, the underdog wins. Why? Because its age is an advantage; it's the most human of all the robots. The boy is able to teach it to dance, and more to the point, to fight, whereas the more advanced metal bruisers it faces just slug. The moral: hang on to that old iPhone, because older is better than newer, except for those gadgets incorporating Siri, our increasingly human personal assistant.

Fox network's short-lived *Almost Human* (2013) begins with a gunfight in which a human police detective is wounded. His partner, John, also human, returns to save him. Having run the numbers in its head, or in its chip, one of a new line of android cops tells John to save himself and leave his partner behind. "He will bleed to death," the android intones, "before you can get him out of here."

Detective John is a crusty, old-school tough guy, and he's not about to abandon his partner because some motherboard full of circuitry tells him to, but the android proves correct, and the wounded detective dies. John's new partner is not a human but an android named Dorian. Dorian is an older generation machine, now obsolete, that, unlike its successors, was designed to be "as human as possible." Nevertheless, John treats Dorian with contempt. After all, it's just a machine. (It helps that the android is played by a black actor, Michael Ealy, giving their relationship a racial dimension.) But it turns out that Dorian, who is softer, better socialized, and more empathetic than its emotionally stunted partner, gives him sensitivity training, teaching the human to be human. (Recall that the slogan of the corporation that manufactures replicants in *Blade Runner 2049* is "More human than human.")

Age is also an advantage in the *Terminator* series. Terminator-Arnold is sent back in time to kill Sarah Connor before she gives birth to her son, who will grow up to lead the Resistance against the machines. By the time we get to *Terminator 2: Judgment Day* (1991), however, there's a later, more advanced model Terminator seeking to kill her. Meanwhile, the old Arnold model has changed sides, now protecting Sarah and the Resistance instead of trying to snuff them.

When Arnold's glove of flesh is stripped away to reveal its titanium endoskeleton in the first film of the series, Sarah discovers that what seems to be Us, that is, a human, is really Them, a cyborg. In *T2*, the lesson is reversed. She discovers that Arnold, who she now knows is a cyborg, is really human, or at least humanized. It acquires the ability to smile, bleed, sweat, and gross out its new human friends with its bad breath. A cyborg of few words in the first film—Arnold's vocabulary is confined to the much-quoted "Hasta la vista, baby"—in *T2* it learns to salt its stilted speech with slang such as "no problemo," "eat me," "chill out," and "dickwad." James Cameron might have once been "on the side of the machines," as Linda Hamilton noted, but the machines he was on the side of were, paradoxically, the ones that most resembled humans.

Instead of leaving Earth altogether and setting out for the stars, which Stephen Hawking and Christopher Nolan suggest is the only way to ensure humankind's future, or merging with alien organisms like Jake in *Avatar*, as the Luddite-left suggests, the Dotcom-left would yoke us to technology, and having mixed luck with machines in *The Terminator*, Sarah Connor gives it a shot in *T2*. As Ray Kurzweil writes, "Merging with future superintelligent A.I.s is [the] best strategy" for enabling humans to survive and prosper. Nevertheless, try as they might to follow his advice, humans end up back where they started, like Lucy.

In *T2*, Sarah Connor comes to understand that for all its bad breath and worse jokes, the Terminator would make a better father for her son John than his human father. She muses, "The Terminator would never leave him, never hurt him, never shout at him or get drunk and hit him. . . . Of all the would-be fathers who came and went over the years, this machine was the only one who measured up." Measured up to what? To the human, of course, which continues to be the standard by which every other creature is judged.

Even the Turing test is an example of anthropomorphism. It measures AI by human standards, that is, its success in fooling people. "Why define an advanced A.I. by its resemblance to ours?" wondered University of California professor Benjamin H. Bratton. "We would do better to presume that in our universe, 'thinking' is much more diverse, even alien, than our own particular case." In the same vein, neurologist Robert A. Burton suggests that we should regard machines as "a separate species with a distinctly different type of intellect—one that is superior in data crunching but is devoid of emotional reasoning. Not better, not worse, just different."

The Turing test may anthropomorphize the behavior of machines, but it also digitizes the behavior of humans. While a successful outcome suggests that a machine can pass for a human, the actual human administering the test must ignore or discount many of the behaviors humans commonly use to communicate—facial expressions, vocal tonalities, gestures, and so on—that can't easily be quantified. In other words, the Turing test requires machines pretending to be human to fool humans pretending to be machines.

Likewise, species-jumping is harder than it seems. In fact, our heroes may not be jumping species at all. Although the definition of species is imprecise, the conventional definition pertains to specific life-forms that are similar enough to sustain interbreeding that produces fertile offspring. But in *Avatar*, Jake merges with his own avatar, which seems more like masturbation than procreation, and besides, all we know about the Na'vi is that they resemble blue, polkadotted Native Americans, barely a different species, if at all, and even Quaritch refers to them as "humanoids." In *Blade Runner*, we have the sex, and in the sequel, when the issue of human and replicant Rachael's fling is finally revealed, we have the result, a frail little thing with a compromised immune system who lives in a bubble. Childbirth doesn't seem to be on her dance card, so that what looked like species-jumping wasn't, especially if Deckard is in fact a replicant himself, as *Blade Runner* director Ridley Scott, bolstered by internal evidence, suggests; so we are back where we started.

On the evangelical front, the process of becoming post-human also seems oddly familiar, that is, all too human. We know from reading the *Left Behinds* that the relationship between Rayford and his wife, Irene, went sideways after she found Jesus. That was no accident. When born-agains describe their relationship to Jesus as a "personal" one, referring to their direct access to the Lord, they're either not doing it justice or using a euphemism. A more accurate term would be "carnal." Indeed, it is so passionate that it transcends humans' love for one another.

Playing the traditional male, Jesus enters his human vessels, assuming the aptly named missionary position. As LaHaye and Jenkins describe it, Rayford, "slipped to the floor and lay prostrate on the carpet.. . . . [He] wished he could . . . cut a hole in the floor and hide from the purity and infinite power of God." Simply put, Rayford is the bride of Christ, the submissive to Christ's dominant.

Buck has a soft spot for Chloe, Rayford's daughter who escaped the rapture by dint of being more intelligent than her mother, but he frets because he is already taken. Eavesdropping on his thoughts, the narrator reports, "Buck had already fallen in love with God. That had to be his passion until Christ returned again. Would it be right . . . to focus his attention on Chloe Steele at the same time?" Eventually, the authors relent. Buck is allowed to marry Chloe, but only after she is born again.

Left-wing extremist shows appear to celebrate difference. When they open their eyes, however, they find they're looking into the mirror at their own reflections. It's not difference they see; its sameness. Right-wing shows celebrate sameness, but when they attempt the post-human, they also end up back where they started. The truth is that, left or right, the best aliens in all these shows are the least alien. The best mutants are the least mutant, the best superheroes are the least super, and the best post-humans are the least post- and the most human.

The failure of these shows to dramatize the post-human leads to the conclusion that despite their insistence that humanism is bankrupt, they are unable to move beyond it. There is no way out. They're trapped. The desire to break with the human has far outpaced the ability of humans to imagine what a post-human future might be like, or what kind of creatures post-humans might be. This inability to imagine the post-human suggests that no matter how much people in extremist shows long to escape the constraints of the human, they have a long way to go. In the meantime, they invariably fall back to Earth.

For the most graphic, and perhaps the most stunning image of our entrapment, we have to return to the original *Planet of the Apes*. Today, after all these years, with the Vietnam War behind us, followed by the wars in the Middle East and Afghanistan, as well as the endless war on terror, it still delivers a shock of recognition. Charlton Heston, wandering about in the Forbidden Zone, comes across a body of water with what appears to be a discolored metallic arm poking upward through the surface. When he realizes it is holding a torch, he drops to his knees and scrapes the muck and sand away from the base of the arm with his fingernails, uncovering a ring of spikes. As the camera pulls back for an overhead shot, we realize that the object is the Statue of Liberty. Heston roars in agony, "Oh my God, I'm back. I'm home. All the time. . . . We finally really did it." Heston roars, "You maniacs! You blew it up! Ah, damn you. God damn you all to hell!"

*Planet of the Apes* is the anti-*Interstellar*. Heston has not traveled to a planet orbiting a star in the constellation of Orion. He has arrived back on Earth, only to find the answer to the question he asked at the beginning of the movie: "I wonder if man still makes war against his brother and lets his neighbor's children starve?" The answer, unhappily, is "Yes." Moreover, he has inadvertently found home, discovered that like Dorothy, you can go home again, but you may not like what you find; the home that you knew may have been destroyed by your own species. For Heston and his companions, there was and is no post-human, no transcendence, no utopia, not in the here-and-now, not in the there-and-then. Like Lucy at the end of her film, he has come full circle. There is no exit.

# CONCLUSION:
# THE RETURN OF THE CENTER

Jump-started by fictions of various sorts, reality is now on a tear, leaving extremist shows in the dust. Look at *Homeland*. "It's hard for our show to compete with the screeching absurdity of what's happening," explained Claire Danes. "It used to be a harrowing, dystopic vision of the truth, and now it's relaxing." Trying to keep up with or exceed the pace at which our reality is reaching new extremes maybe a strategy that works (or worked) for *Homeland*, but that may not be the end of our story. After all, there's Newton's third law of motion to cheer us up: For every action, there is an equal and opposite reaction. Or in this case, perhaps it would be more accurate to say: For every reaction, there is an equal and opposite action. In other words, other shows are running in the opposite direction. The more the culture rushes right, the more it invigorates the center.

Content like *Contagion*, *The Martian*, *World War Z*, and *Hidden Figures* are centrist from beginning to end, but suddenly we have megablockbusters like *Wonder Woman* and *Black Panther* that begin as extremist shows, but conclude with resounding endorsements of mainstream values. When Wonder Woman embarks on her adventures, she spouts humanssuck hate speech she inherits from her mother, but after spending no more than a few minutes with Steve Trevor and his Diversity Bunch (a Native American, a Muslim, et al.) she opts for the big tent, as the movie puts her mom's sentiments in the mouth of the supervillain Ares, the god of war (David Thewlis). Ms. Wonder Woman counters it with the film's insipid, love-conquers-all message that contradicts her own heroics: "I believe in love. Only love will truly save the world." What kind of feminist superhero insists on denying her gift, her essential nature, the one that distinguishes her from mere mortals? Unlike extremists such as Raven/Mystique or Luke Cage, who accept their post-humanness, she defers to the male ego. When Steve, surveying the damage she has inflicted on the enemy, says, with a mixture of awe and envy, "You did this," she sweetly replies, "*We* did this."

Black Panther is even more forthright in steering its characters back to the center. The dramatic conflict, as it is in the other black superhero shows like *Luke Cage* and *Black Lightning* (2018), is black against black, never black against white, as extremist shows might dare to show.

T'Challa, the good black panther, requires a bad black panther, the aforementioned Erik Killmonger (Michael B. Jordan), a lefty militant hell-bent on revenging the centuries of injustice. But we know he's gone off the rails because he's an extremist. Adopting the "burn, baby, burn" language of radical black militants of the 1960s (or, ironically, the "tear it all down and begin again" Bannonism of today's extreme white right), he says things like, "The world's going to start over. I'm a burn it all." He wants to use Wakanda's advanced weaponry to conquer the world, making him one of those old-fashioned monomaniacal Dr. Nos or Goldfingers. He actually says, "The sun will never set upon the Wakandan empire," echoing British colonials of the nineteenth century. Scratch a black militant, the filmmakers suggest, and we get a hate-filled nihilist with delusions of grandeur.

Moreover, when T'Challa worries about becoming like the enemy, a moral qualm characteristic of mainstream heroes, and accuses Killmonger of wanting "to see us become just like the people you hate so much," Killmonger doesn't turn a hair. Like a good extremist, he just brushes him off, remarking, "I learn from my enemies."

No Geronimo, T'Challa, in his by now famous (or infamous, depending on your point of view) speech to the UN tucked into the tail credits of *Black Panther*, pitches pluralism, demonstrating a flexibility more characteristic of centrists than extremists. Taking Wakanda, which is comprised of five tribes, as an example, he warns the assembled nations of the world against tribalism, saying, "Now more than ever the illusions of division threaten our every existence." He continues, "The wise build bridges, while the foolish build barriers." (Good news for Caesar et al. in *Rise of the Planet of the Apes*, who can now expect the San Francisco police to clear away those barricades so that they can traverse the Golden Gate Bridge without a fight.) T'Challa adds, "We must find a way to look after each other as if we are one single tribe." Indeed, when he evokes the "brothers and sisters on this Earth," it's clear that his single tribe is global in scope. By the end of the movie, T'Challa abandons the Wakanda Firsters and announces that instead of sealing off his country from the rest of Africa, he will use its resources to help those less fortunate than his people.

The ideological ambiguity of T'Challa—is he a left-wing anti-colonialist or a right-wing nationalist, Nkrumah or Trump?—ultimately doesn't matter. Part left, part right, part benevolent, part not—T'Challa is a composite extremist and, in the contest between extremism and centrism, as his speech to the UN shows, centrism wins.

We've already seen that shows like *The Walking Dead* fear the collapse of authority more than the growth of authoritarianism which, in the Trump era, seems of greater concern. We have watched the survivors endure the Ricktatorship, and square off against the Governor, but it isn't until very late in the game that *The Walking Dead* introduces strongman Negan, whose reign of terror makes Woodbury look like Brook Farm, that authoritarianism and the death of democracy take center stage, swallowing two full seasons. And it is then, in the winter of Trump, right around the same time that T'Challa is going all in with Cochise, that Ezekial, the African American leader of the Kingdom, one of the enclaves friendly to Rick and Co., gives voice to the same credo of pluralism. Quoting Martin Luther King Jr.'s famous "I Have a Dream" speech, he looks forward to the time when "black men and white men, Jews and gentiles, Protestants and Catholics, will be able to join hands and sing in the words of the old negro spiritual, 'Free at last.'"

Turning to the real world, we find that the center is dusting off "extremism" as its favorite epithet for the fringe. Army chief of staff General Mark Milley, apparently speaking for the nonpartisan Joint Chiefs of Staff after the Charlottesville fiasco, stated that the army "doesn't tolerate racism, extremism, or hatred in our ranks." The *St. Louis Post-Dispatch* asked if that city was the "bastion of extremism," accusing the far right, for example, of gerrymandering Missouri's voting districts. Even the right uses "extremism" to tar the farther right. Rupert Murdoch's *New York Post* ran a story attributing "brain damage" to "religious extremism."

Today, under constant attack by Trump and his hand puppets, the *New York Times* and the *Washington Post*, both historically bastions of the center, have been newly energized and moved left. The *Times* has not only championed the cause of gender equality, but it has featured innumerable stories about the struggles of LGBTQ people fighting for their rights. It has even discarded the lengthy list of pussyfooting euphemisms—"misspoken," "misleading," "inaccurate," "dubious"—it has always used to tiptoe around official fabrications and now calls them what they are, lies, and those who spew them "liars," including the president. Famous for fetishizing journalistic "objectivity," one of the paper's own columnists, Paul Krugman, has familiarized us with the phrase "false equivalence" that undermines it. In other words, the center has responded to the lurch to the right by beginning to get its mojo back.

Even the arthritic Democratic Party, energized by Bernie Sanders's 2016 primary campaign, is making an effort to shrug off the dead hand of the (Bill) Clinton–era neo-liberal Democratic Leadership Council that steered it to the right.

The sudden eruption of the underserved and underrepresented half of the population—women—looks to be a game changer. In Hollywood, it seemed to start with scandalous tales of male abuse of women in the workplace and the accusations against mini-mogul Harvey Weinstein, but three of the top-grossing movies of 2017—*Star Wars: The Last Jedi, Beauty and the Beast*, and *Wonder Woman*—which all revolve around strong female characters, were on screens well before Ashley Judd, Annabella Sciorra, Salma Hayek, Rose McGowan, et al. dropped their bombshells. *Girls Trip* was the biggest comedy of 2017, and *Lady Bird*, made by a woman telling a young woman's story, was one of the year's indie champs. Two other powerful award-winning films featured angry women: *I, Tonya* and *Three Billboards Outside Ebbing, Missouri*. The latter won a Golden Globe for Best Motion Picture Drama, while its female lead, Frances McDormand, won an Oscar for Best Actress.

A further case in point is *The Post*, Steven Spielberg's film about the publication of the Pentagon Papers by the *Washington Post* in 1971. *The Post* plays like a civics lesson dressed up as a movie, but sometimes civics lessons are necessary, and the movie is largely successful. Spielberg has always trimmed his sails to the prevailing winds. More tactfully put, his antennae are preternaturally sensitive to changes in the cultural weather. As we have seen, in the post-Watergate era, he tacked left with *Jaws* and his two alien-friendly blockbusters, *Close Encounters* and *E.T.* When the breeze came from the opposite quarter, he remade alien-unfriendly pictures like *War of the Worlds* (2005) and presided over TV junk like *Falling Skies*. To his credit, in the face Hurricane Donald, he has tacked left again.

The kudos for publishing the Pentagon Papers rightfully belongs to the

*New York Times*, which printed the top secret documents before the *Post*, but Spielberg, et al. apparently chose the latter because it had a personal drama on which to hang the film, the story of *Post* publisher Katharine Graham, thereby allowing filmmakers to exploit the feminist tide that has swept male sexual abusers out of their seats of power.

It is impossible to watch the movie without noticing the degree to which it throbs with the beat of contemporary politics. President Nixon threatened the *Post* then the way Trump targets it now, along with the *New York Times*, CNN, NBC, *Vanity Fair*, and his other enemies in the media. Forced to decide whether or not to print the Pentagon Papers, Graham (Meryl Streep) is told by her close friend and adviser, former defense secretary Robert McNamara, "Nixon is a sonofabitch, he hates you. . . . The Richard Nixon I know will muster the full power of the presidency, and if there's a way to destroy your paper, by God, he'll find it." In fact, Nixon's Justice Department moved to enjoin both the *Times* and the *Post* from publishing the Pentagon Papers.

*The Post* could easily have focused solely on the story of editor Ben Bradlee (Tom Hanks), who indeed plays a significant role, but instead, it chooses to highlight the struggle of Graham to find her footing in the rough-and-tumble male world of daily journalism. Graham's father made an end run around Katharine and entrusted the paper to her husband, Philip. It passed to her only after he died, and the film shows her being treated as a lightweight by her board and the men's club that runs the paper. They disregard and disrespect her.

Graham waffles on the Pentagon Papers issue, but ultimately she decides to publish, defying her board as well as Nixon. Sarah Paulson, playing Bradlee's wife, sums up the film's message in a spirited assessment of Graham's situation to her less-than-enlightened husband, who's patting himself on the back for standing up to the president: "When you're told time and time again that you're not good enough, that your opinion doesn't matter as much . . . when to them you're not even there. When that's been your reality for so long, it's hard not to let yourself think it's true. So to make this decision, to risk her fortune and the company that's been her entire life? That's brave."

In *The Post*, empowering women is front and foremost, as is the First Amendment. Graham chooses freedom of speech over national security. Implicitly, by endorsing the publication of the Pentagon Papers, the film approves of whistle-blowers like Natasha Romanoff in *Iron Man 2*, when she dumps secret S.H.I.E.L.D. files onto the internet and tells a congressional committee to get lost, unlike *Live Another Day*'s Jack Bauer, who reprimands Chloe for hacking Department of Defense computers. In the real world, it favors the mother of all whistle-blowers, Daniel Ellsberg, who stole the Pentagon documents and gave them to the *Times* and the *Post*, but by implication comes down on the side of Edward Snowden, who disseminated National Security Agency secrets.

In the process, courtesy of a snappy montage of TV news clips, *The Post* pictures successive U.S. presidents—Truman, Eisenhower, Kennedy, and Johnson—lying through their teeth about the Vietnam War, demonstrating that it wasn't—pace, the Ken Burns documentary extravaganza on public television—the result of well-intentioned men making bad decisions, but rather ill-intentioned men—some would say war criminals—worried about their careers, making bad decisions. As the Ellsberg character sums up the revelations contained in the purloined documents: "Covert ops, rigged elections—Ike, Kennedy, Johnson—they violated the Geneva Conventions, they lied to Congress, and they lied to the public. They knew we couldn't win and still sent boys to die."

The interesting thing about *The Post* is that with its defiance of the authorities, advocacy of feminism, and explicit defense of whistle-blowing then and implicit defense of it now, it feels like a left-wing movie, but it isn't. Freedom of the press is enshrined in the First Amendment, which is, after all, the law of the land. But interpretation is contextual, and the context has changed. The country has been moved so far to the right that freedom of the press seems daring, even treasonous. *The Post* may be left-leaning, but it is very much a centrist movie, with all the hallmarks of a mainstream production. You can't get a more A-list cast than Streep and Hanks, and Spielberg himself is synonymous with the studio system.

The same holds true for Spielberg's partner in crime George Lucas, despite the physical independence he has always maintained from Hollywood, holed up as he is in his Northern California redoubt, Skywalker Ranch. It's appropriate that Lucasfilm finally became part of the Disney empire, just as it was appropriate that Reagan dubbed his antimissile system "Star Wars." But what is somewhat surprising is that a franchise that began with one foot in the antiwar movement and the other in the fanboy galaxy of shooters and gamers to come, has also moved decisively to the left, reflecting the diversity of the *Star Wars* writing team.

Under the aegis of former Spielberg producer Kathleen Kennedy, now Lucasfilm president, the team is made up of four women and seven men, including five people of color. The effect on the films is striking. A computer analysis of the original 1977 *Star Wars*, now called *A New Hope*, found that only 6.3 percent of the dialogue was attributed to female characters, as opposed to 27.8 percent in *The Force Awakens* (2015); while 44.7 percent of the dialogue in *Rogue One: A Star Wars Story* (2016) is attributed to nonwhite characters.

The perceived feminist slant of *The Last Jedi* has prompted at least one self-professed alt-right fanboy to claim credit for using bots to bring down the film's Rotten Tomatoes audience score. "I'm sick and tired of men being portrayed as idiots," he wrote. "There was a time we ruled society and I want to see that again. That is why I voted for Donald Trump."

*The Post* and *The Last Jedi* are by no means the whole story. There is no stronger taboo in movies and TV than poverty. Watching our shows, you'd never know it existed in America. Even our so-called indie films divert themselves with coming-of-age stories, not to mention the trials and tribulations of middle-class young adults in and out of love. That is, until now. The year 2017 saw the release of several high- and low-profile movies and TV shows that dared to reveal the underside of what's left of the American Dream, shows like *Mudbound*; *I, Tonya*; *Lady Bird*; *The Florida Project*; *Downsizing*; and last but not least, *Shameless* and *SMILF*.

Then there's *Game of Thrones*. As of this writing, there's one season left, but with the Starks together again at Winterfell, and Daenerys ascending, it sure looks like the tyrannical reign of the Lannisters is finally coming to an end, presumably making way for a more equitable society. In other words, on a cultural level, at least, Trump and his spawn may go the way of the Boltons, leaving the stage of history. But that's the centrist version of our story. Reese and Ramsay may be gone, but in the real world, the other Bolton, John, the one allergic to carrots, is back. Extremism is not about to roll over and lie down dead, and for its version, we have only to recall Brian De Palma's *Carrie* (1976), starring Sissy Spacek in the title role. Carrie, driven to extremes by the fundamentalism of her mother and the hatred of her classmates, uses her telekinetic powers to kill them all, before immolating herself by burning down her house around her. As her pal Amy Irving gently reaches down to place flowers on her remains, Carrie's blood-smeared arm hand bursts out of the wreckage, and grabs her. It turns out to be Irving's nightmare, but the specter of extremism can all too easily become real, as we have seen, and that could be our story too.

# ACKNOWLEDGMENTS

This book is a sequel, of sorts, to the first book I ever wrote, *Seeing Is Believing*, published way back in 1983, and shepherded by Sara Bershtel, without whom I never would have started this one. She bought the idea and steered me in the right direction. I owe a huge debt of gratitude to my editor at The New Press, Carl Bromley, for his enthusiasm, intelligence, and the deluge of films I still needed to see and books I still needed to read when I thought I was done. I also want to thank Ben Woodward for his acute editing suggestions, Emily Albarillo for her skill and patience in transforming the manuscript into presentable form, and Chloe Currens at Penguin UK for her kinds words and encouragement. Several brave souls read bits and pieces of the manuscript including Barbara Ehrenreich, Bruce Handy, Lili Anolik, Michael Singer, Harry Chotiner, and Mark Rozzo. My agent, Kathy Robbins, gave me aid and comfort through some dark days, and my wife, Elizabeth Hess, was always there to keep the opioids out of reach.

# NOTES

## Beyond the Fringe: An Introduction

2 **"Reality television"** Jon Caramanica, "'Hunted' and 'The Selection': Igniting Resistance, or Smashing It," *New York Times*, January 31, 2017.

2 **YouTube's search algorithm** Jack Nicas, "How YouTube Drives People to the Internet's Darkest Corners," *Wall Street Journal*, February 7, 2018.

2 **"Extreme vetting"** Timothy Egan, "The Immigrants Turned Away," *New York Times*, September 2, 2016.

2 **"I consider him"** Mia Galuppo, "Joseph Gordon-Levitt on Edward Snowden: 'I Consider Him the Most Extreme of Patriots' (Q&A)," *Hollywood Reporter*, September 9, 2016.

2 **from 19 percent** Adrian Wooldridge, "'Why the Right Went Wrong' and 'Too Dumb to Fail,'" *New York Times*, January 19, 2016.

4 **It morphed into** Amy Chozick, "Middle Class Is Disappearing, at Least from Vocabulary of Possible 2016 Contenders," *New York Times*, May 11, 2015.

5 **only the wealthy can afford** Alana Semuels, "Poor at 20, Poor for Life," *The Atlantic*, July 14, 2016.

5 **"filter bubble"** Eli Pariser, *The Filter Bubble: How the New Personalized Web Is Changing What We Read and How We Think* (Penguin Books, 2012).

5 **"It's as if we're"** Jane Mayer, "Ayn Rand Joins the Ticket," *New Yorker*, August 11, 2012.

5 **"the force is with us"** Michael Rogin, *Ronald Reagan, the Movie* (University of California Press, 1987), 3.

5 **"Go ahead. Make my day"** Rogin, *Ronald Reagan*, 7.

6 **"[I] smuggle in other themes"** Author interview, September 26, 2013.

6 **Jean-Luc Godard** Jean-Luc Godard, journal entry, May 16, 1991.

7 **citing tweets from its writers** Tatiana Siegel, "'Star Wars' Writers Get Political: Will Anti-Trump Tweets Hurt 'Rogue One'?" *Hollywood Reporter*, November 21, 2016.

8 **"is not a film"** Ben Guarino, "Star Wars Isn't Political, Says Disney Chief Responding to Boycott by Trump Supporters. He's Wrong," *Washington Post*, December 13, 2016; David E. Apter, ed., *Ideology and Discontent* (Free Press of Glencoe, 1964).

8 **Their positions on specific issues** Donald R. Kinder and Nathan P. Kalmoe, *Neither Liberal nor Conservative: Ideological Innocence in the American Public* (University of Chicago Press, 2017).

11 **"My heroes are always"** Devan Coggan, "Fantastic Beasts: J.K. Rowling Introduces Newt Scamander in New Featurette," *Entertainment Weekly*, June 23, 2016.

12 **Ben Fritz explains** Ben Fritz, *The Big Picture: The Fight for the Future of Movies* (Houghton Mifflin Harcourt, 2018).

12 **"Five hours and thirty-eight minutes"** Anthony Lane, "Wilder West: 'The Hateful Eight' and 'The Revenant,'" *New Yorker*, January 4, 2016.

13 **military historian Max Hastings** Max Hastings, "Splendid Isolation," *New York Review of Books*, October 12, 2017.

13 **"When a film achieves"** Noël Carroll, "Back to Basics," *Wilson Quarterly* 10, no. 3 (Summer 1986): 58–69.

## 1: Apocalypse Now

23 **"We may have another year"** Chris Nelson, "A Brief History of the Apocalypse," Preterist Archive of Realized Eschatology, preteristarchive.com/2005_abhota_brief-history.

24 **"imagination of disaster"** Susan Sontag, "The Imagination of Disaster," *Commentary*, October 1, 1965.

24 **"After the dramatic fears"** Charles McGrath, "Tales of Danger for You to Survive," *New York Times*, November 1, 2013.

24 **"Apocalyptic storytelling"** David Peisner, "The Rise of 'The Walking Dead,'" *Rolling Stone*, October 31, 2013.

24 **ticking louder than ever** Doomsday Clock Timeline, *Bulletin of the Atomic Scientists*, thebulletin.org/timeline.

24 **"And there will be signs"** Luke 21:25, biblehub.com/luke/21-25.htm.

25 **"I'm the last thing"** Mark Leibovich, "I'm the Last Thing Standing Between You and the Apocalypse," *New York Times Magazine*, October 11, 2016.

25 **"death, destruction"** Maureen Ryan, "Donald Trump's Acceptance Speech Paints Apocalyptic Vision from a B-Movie," *Variety*, July 21, 2016.

25 **"Armageddon"** Kimberly Schwandt, "Boehner: It's 'Armageddon,' Health Care Bill Will 'Ruin Our Country,'" FoxNews.com, March 20, 2010.

25 **"third force"** Arthur Schlesinger Jr., "It's My 'Vital Center,'" *Slate*, January 10, 1997; Schlesinger Jr., *The Vital Center: The Politics of Freedom* (Houghton Mifflin, 1949).

25 **"polyarchy"** Robert A. Dahl, *Polyarchy: Participation and Opposition* (Yale University Press, 1971).

26 **"By including fraternity"** Peter Singer, *The Expanding Circle: Ethics, Evolution, and Moral Progress* (Princeton University Press, 2011), 119.

26 **evolutionary ethics** Edward O. Wilson, *Sociobiology: The New Synthesis* (Belknap Press, 1975).

27 **"When I was a kid"** Author interview, March 19, 2014.

28 **millennialism was a** Richard Aldous, "Schlesinger's Vital Center," *American Interest*, November 9, 2017.

29 **"What we are witnessing"** Francis Fukuyama, "The End of History?" *National Interest* 16 (Summer 1989): 3–18.

31 **"convergence [was] taking place"** John Williams, "Ross Douthat Talks About the State of American Christianity," *New York Times*, April 26, 2012.

32 **The Hollywood community** Harper's Index, *Harper's Magazine*, March 2014.

32 **that has changed** Ross Douthat, "Is There Life After Liberalism," *New York Times*, January 13, 2018.

33 **"Even as early"** James Poniewozik, "Geek Fight! Lost, Thrones Camps Square Off over GRRM's Dis of Finale," *Time*, April 5, 2011.

33 **"If we extend"** Karl Popper, *The Open Society and Its Enemies* (Routledge, 2011), 581.

## 2: Bleeding Hearts

35 **"Weimar-lite democratic dysfunction"** Roger Cohen, "Trump's Il Duce Routine," *New York Times*, February 29, 2016.

35 **One poll found** Amanda Taub, "How Stable Are Democracies? 'Warning Signs Are Flashing Red,'" The Interpreter, *New York Times*, November 29, 2016.

35 **"the most accurate"** Adam Davidson, "It Is Safe to Resume Ignoring the Prophets of Doom . . . Right?" *New York Times Magazine*, February 1, 2012.

36 **"robot shock increases support"** Massimo Anelli, Italo Colantone, and Piero Stanig, "We Were the Robots: Automation in Manufacturing and Voting Behavior in Western Europe," quoted by Thomas B. Edsall, "Industrial Revolutions Are Political Wrecking Balls," *New York Times*, May 3, 2018.

37 **"There is an almost total"** A.H. Weiler, "The East: Kubrick and Sellers' New Film," *New York Times*, May 6, 1962.

37 **"When the Vietnam War"** Author interview, March 19, 2014.

38 **"the hippies took over"** Peter Thiel, "The End of the Future," *National Review*, October 3, 2011.

39 **"That man is definitely"** Dana Goodyear, "Man of Extremes," *New Yorker*, October 26, 2009.

40 **"I'm happy to"** Glenn Whipp, "Is 'Avatar' a Message Movie? Absolutely, Says James Cameron," *Los Angeles Times*, February 10, 2010.

40 **"We really like the story"** Whipp, "Is 'Avatar' a Message Movie?"

40 **"I think everyone"** Brent Lang, "James Cameron: Yes, 'Avatar' Is Political," *The Wrap*, January 14, 2010.

43 **"I don't do carrots"** Peter Baker, "In John Bolton, Trump Finds a Fellow Political Blowtorch. Will Foreign Policy Burn?" *New York Times*, April 8, 2018.

44 **According to writer Noam Cohen** Noam Cohen, *The Know-It-Alls: The Rise of Silicon Valley as a Political Powerhouse and Social Wrecking Ball* (The New Press, 2017).

45 **It has been popularized** Cohen, *The Know-It-Alls*, 18.

45 **"carbon-based chauvinists"** Cohen, *The Know-It-Alls*, 38.

46 **Woody Allen in particular** A.O. Scott, "My Woody Allen Problem," *New York Times*, January 31, 2018.

46 **"It used to be"** A.O. Scott, "At Comic-Con, Bring Out Your Fantasy and Fuel the Culture," *New York Times*, July 19, 2015.

46 **"I think America's a nerdier country"** Cliff Ransom, "President Barack Obama on How to Win the Future," *Popular Science*.

46 **"We represent the underdog"** Douglas Martin, "Harold Ramis, Director, Actor and Alchemist of Comedy, Dies at 69," *New York Times*, February 24, 2014.

## 3: Doing the Right Thing

52 **Paul Ryan . . . Alan Greenspan** Jonathan Freedland, "The New Age of Ayn Rand: How She Won Over Trump and Silicon Valley," *The Guardian*, April 10, 2017.

52 **Rex Tillerson . . . Mike Pompeo** Ralph Benko, "Ayn Rand's Ghost Does Not Haunt the Trump Administration," *Forbes*, December 18, 2016.

52 **"the realization, acceptance"** Mark Harris, "Inside the First Church of Artificial Intelligence," *Wired*, November 15, 2017.

53 **essay in a Cato Institute publication** Schumpeter, "The Evolution of Mr Thiel," *The Economist*, June 2, 2016.

53 **"corporate Nietzschean"** Schumpeter, "The Evolution of Mr Thiel."

53 **"preferred the capitalist"** Peter Thiel and Blake Masters, *Zero to One: Notes on Startups, or How to Build the Future* (Crown Business, 2014), 123.

55 **"Our only chance"** Clara Moskowitz, "Stephen Hawking Says Humanity Won't Survive Without Leaving Earth," Space.com, August 10, 2010.

56 **"We try not to give"** Pya Sinha-Roy, "A Minute With: Christopher Nolan on His 'Interstellar' Challenge," Reuters, November 7, 2014.

56 **Moreover, Jonathan Nolan** Jordan Goldberg interview with Jonathan Nolan and Christopher Nolan, introduction to Jonathan Nolan and Christopher Nolan, *Interstellar: The Complete Screenplay* (Opus Books, 2014).

56 **"people trying to look"** Goldberg interview with Jonathan Nolan and Christopher Nolan.

57 **"greatest hope"** Robert Crosby, "From Survivor and Touched by an Angel to the Bible," *Christianity Today*, February 25, 2013.

58 **"I want to kill him"** Peter Biskind, "The Rude Warrior," *Vanity Fair*, March 2011.

58 **"Yesteryear's supposed fringes"** Kevin Phillips, *American Theocracy: The Peril and Politics of Radical Religion, Oil, and Borrowed Money in the 21st Century.* (Viking, 2006), 101.

58 **down 8 percent** Nate Cohn, "Big Drop in Share of Americans Calling Themselves Christians," *New York Times*, May 12, 2015.

59 **"In terms of its impact"** "The 25 Most Influential Evangelicals in America: Tim and Beverly LaHaye," *Time*, February 7, 2005.

59 **"War is coming"** Tim LaHaye and Jerry B. Jenkins. *Tribulation Force: The Continuing Drama of Those Left Behind* (Tyndale House, 1996), 32.

59 **"Rayford Steele's mind"** Tim LaHaye and Jerry B. Jenkins, *Left Behind: A Novel of the Earth's Last Days* (Tyndale House, 1995), 1.

61 **Driven by catastrophe theology** Garry Wills, "Where Evangelicals Came From," *New York Review of Books*, April 20, 2017.

61 **"Prophecy" issue** *Newsweek*, November 1, 1999.

61 **Four years later** Timothy Weber, "On the Road to Armageddon," *BeliefNet*, n.d.

61 **2010 Pew Research Center survey** "U.S. Christians' Views on the Return of Christ," Pew Research Center, March 26, 2013.

61 **"the midnight hour"** Brendan James, "Michele Bachmann: Thanks Obama for Bringing On the Apocalypse," *Talking Points Memo*, April 21, 2015.

61 **"We in our lifetimes"** Marina Fang, "Michele Bachmann: The Rapture Is Coming and It's Obama's Fault," *HuffPost*, April 20, 2015.

62 **"One of the biggest"** Bill Moyers, "There Is No Tomorrow," *Star Tribune* (Minneapolis), January 30, 2005.

62   **"The world's leading"** Phillips, *American Theocracy*, 101–3.

62   **"My mom started reading"** Author interview, August 2, 2011.

62   **"You know, I turn back"** Associated Press, "Reagan and the Apocalypse," *New York Review of Books*, January 19, 1984; Ronnie Dugger, "Does Reagan Expect a Nuclear Armageddon?" *Washington Post*, April 18, 1984.

62   **"We will mine more"** Stuart Shapiro, "An Agency Whose Slogan Was 'Drill Baby Drill,'" FoxNews.com, August 10, 2016; Mark Jaffe, "What Does a Trump Administration Mean for Western Public Lands?" *Denver Post*, November 26, 2016.

62   **"The Holy Spirit moved"** James Conaway, "James Watt, in the Right with the Lord," *Washington Post*, April 27, 1983.

63   **"When you accept Christ"** Maureen Dowd, "Liberties," *New York Times*, December 15, 1999.

63   **"born-again, evangelical"** Michelle Boorstein, "What It Means That Mike Pence Called Himself an 'Evangelical Catholic,'" *Washington Post*, July 18, 2016.

63   **"a Christian, a conservative"** Milly M. Miller and Winston Kimberly, *Religion News*, July 15, 2016.

63   **"I embrace the view"** Mollie Reilly et al., "Here's What You Should Know About Mike Pence," *HuffPost*, 5 January 5, 2017.

63   **"antiwar activist"** Tim LaHaye and Jerry B. Jenkins, *Nicolae: The Rise of the Antichrist* (Tyndale House, 1997), 73.

63   **"raising the level"** LaHaye and Jenkins, *Nicolae*, 125.

64   **"We can only truly be"** Tim LaHaye, and Jerry B. Jenkins, *Apollyon: The Destroyer Is Unleashed* (Tyndale House, 2011), 104.

64   **"I believe we are"** LaHaye and Jenkins, *Tribulation Force*, 132.

64   **"Whoever [comes] forward"** LaHaye and Jenkins, *Left Behind*, 344.

64   **annual course in exorcism** Jason Horowitz, "'Shut Up, Satan': Rome Course Teaches Exorcism, Even by Cellphone," *New York Times*, April 19, 2018.

65   **"We may get"** LaHaye and Jenkins, *Tribulation Force*, 72.

65   **"You're the chief,"** LaHaye and Jenkins, *Apollyon*, 111–12.


**4: Gone Fishin'**

71   **"One of the things"** Author interview, November 2006.

73   **"with New York values"** Geoff Earle, "Cruz Slams Trump for Holding 'New York Values,'" *New York Post*, January 13, 2016.

73 **By 2016, a Gallup poll** Jim Norman, "Americans' Confidence in Institutions Stays Low," Gallup, June 13, 2016.

73 **"The collapse of trust in the U.S."** Daniel W. Drezner, "Edelman Surveyed Americans About Trust. The Finds Are Disturbing, but Not in the Way You Might Think," *Washington Post*, January 23, 2018.

74 **"Ask not what"** John F. Kennedy, "Inaugural Address," January 20, 1961, Washington DC.

74 **"this was a struggle"** John F. Kennedy, "Address Before the American Society of Newspaper Editors," April 20, 1961, in *Public Papers of the Presidents of the United States: John F. Kennedy, 1961* (Office of the Federal Register, 1962), 304.

74 **Optimism Campaign** Edwin E. Moïse, "Lyndon Johnson's War Propaganda," *New York Times*, November 20, 2017.

77 **"Tea Party zombies"** Maureen Dowd, "Welcome to Ted Cruz's Thunderdome," *New York Times*, October 5, 2013.

77 **"A story about vampires"** David Peisner, "The Rise of 'The Walking Dead,'" *Rolling Stone*, October 31, 2013.

78 **According to one such model** Michael Dhar, "Surviving a Zombie Apocalypse: Just Do the Math," *Live Science*, July 30, 2013.

79 **"as if they were narrating"** Emily Nussbaum, "Utter Rot," *New Yorker*, December 23–30, 2013.

81 **"Sometimes it feels"** Jeremy Egner, "Scott M. Gimple on 'The Walking Dead' and What Those Zombies Are Really Eating," *New York Times*, October 23, 2015.

82 **"an inclusive church"** Adam Barkman, "Does God Hate Fangs?" in *True Blood and Philosophy: We Wanna Think Bad Things with You*, ed. George A. Dunn, and Rebecca Housel (John Wiley & Sons, 2010), 181.

82 **"It's about 'the tragedy"** Author interview, August 2, 2011.

82 **"What it really means"** Joe Rhodes, "After All the Funerals, a Prime-Time Auteur Digs Up the Undead," *New York Times*, August 3, 2008.

## 5: Coming Apart

87 **"Now, if you do anything"** George Lucas, interview by Charlie Rose, *Charlie Rose*, December 25, 2015.

87 **"very right wing"** Mike Fleming Jr., "Alejandro G. Iñárritu and Birdman Scribes on Hollywood's Superhero Fixation: 'Poison, Cultural Genocide'—Q&A," *Deadline*, October 15, 2014.

88 **"I did a lot of research"** David Peisner, "Robert Kirkman: I Can Do 1,000 Issues of 'The Walking Dead,'" *Rolling Stone*, October 8, 2013.

88 **"I was very obsessed"** Bryan Singer, interview by Stephen Applebaum, "X-Men 2," BBC, April 25, 2003.

88 **"*X-Men* has always"** Shana Naomi Krochmal, "The Outsider," *Out*, May 14, 2014.

88 **"A gay kid"** Singer, interview by Applebaum.

88 **"gay allegory"** Geoff Boucher, "Bryan Singer on 'X-Men: First Class': It's got to be about Magneto and Professor X," *Los Angeles Times*, March 18, 2010.

88 **"He replied"** Krochmal, "The Outsider."

89 **"yellow sign people"** Michael Cieply, "At Comic-Con, Faith-Based Entertainment Stays in the Shadows," *New York Times*, July 12, 2015.

89 **"the Spider-Man menace"** Bradford W. Wright, *Comic Book Nation: The Transformation of Youth Culture in America* (Johns Hopkins University Press, 2001), 212.

90 **"The more I try"** Wright, *Comic Book Nation*, 231.

90 **"Instead of complementing"** "Are We Becoming Cyborgs?," *New York Times*, November 30, 2012.

91 **"This movie reflects"** Brent Lang, "James Cameron: Yes, 'Avatar' Is Political," *The Wrap*, January 14, 2010.

91 **"My ambition then"** Lucas, interview by Rose.

91 **"It was really about"** Mark Caro, "'Star Wars' Inadvertently Hits too Close to U.S.'s Role," *Chicago Tribune*, May 18, 2005.

92 **"the droughts, the storms"** Suzanne Collins, *The Hunger Games* (Scholastic Press, 2008), 18.

92 **"It's crucial"** Paul Bond, "The Politics of 'The Hunger Games,'" *Hollywood Reporter*, March 23, 2012.

93 **"I regret the advent"** Author interview, August 25, 2015.

94 **"No one has the right"** Wright, *Comic Book Nation*, 222.

94 **"[We] genuinely felt"** Wright, *Comic Book Nation*, 222.

95 **"I was reacting"** George Marston, "Steve Englehart on the Politics, Shocking Ending & Legacy of Captain America's Original Secret Empire," Newsarama, May 30, 2017.

95 **"I was thinking"** Marston, "Steve Englehart."

95 **"The readers"** Asawin Suebaeng, "Like Most Libertarians, Iron Man Grows Up and Moves On," *Mother Jones*, May 3, 2013.

95 **"The political climate"** Edward Douglas, "Jon Favreau on Iron Man," *SuperHeroHype*, July 25, 2006.

95 **"reflected the politics"** Mike Ryan, "Q&A: Iron Man 2 Director Jon Favreau Won't Immediately Correct You if You Think He Writes Obama's Speeches," *Vanity Fair*, April 28, 2010.

96 **"losing faith in all the institutions"** David Itzkoff, "'Avengers,' the Most Lucrative Movie Franchise Ever, Is Wrapping Up. Why?," *New York Times*, April 23, 2018.

97 **Superman goes before** Laura Hudson, "Superman Renounces U.S. Citizenship in 'Action Comics' #900," *Comics Alliance*, April 27, 2011; Forrest Helvie, "Superman's Rejection of American Exceptionalism," *Sequart*, June 11, 2013.

97 **"You can type"** Dale Pollock, *Skywalking: The Life and Films of George Lucas* (Harmony Books, 1983), 164.

97 **"a kids' film"** Pollock, *Skywalking*, 144.

97 **"shock and awe"** Peter Biskind. "Blockbuster: The Last Crusade," in *Seeing Through Movies*, ed. Mark Crispin Miller (Pantheon Books, 1990), 117.

98 **"said he had deliberately"** Michael Cieply, "'Avatar' Director Emphasizes Environmental Message," *New York Times*, February 23, 2010.

98 ***Avatar* asks us all"** Cieply, "'Avatar' Director Emphasizes Environmental Message."

99 **"He's trying to"** Dana Goodyear, "Man of Extremes," *New Yorker*, October 26, 2009.

## 6: Draining the Swamp

102 **According to a Gallup poll** Chris Cillizza and Sean Sullivan, "George W. Bush's Approval Rating Just Hit a 7-Year High. Here's How," *Washington Post*, April 23, 2013; Justin McCarthy, "Americans Losing Confidence in All Branches of U.S. Gov't," Gallup, June 14, 2014.

103 **"reflects real life"** Dahlia Lithwick, "How Jack Bauer Shaped U.S Torture Policy," *Newsweek*, July 25, 2008; Peter Lattman, "Justice Scalia Hearts Jack Bauer," *Law Blog, Wall Street Journal*, June 20, 2007.

105 **"There's no such thing"** "Margaret Thatcher: A Life in Quotes," *The Guardian*, April 8, 2013.

106 **"pond scum"** "Frank Miller: Occupy Wall Street 'Louts, Thieves & Rapists,' Comic Writer Says," *HuffPost*, November 31, 2011.

111 **"lined up with"** Josef Adalian, "Damon Lindelof Talks to Vulture About His New HBO Project: Tom Perotta's *The Leftovers*," *Vulture*, June 28, 2012.

112 **"It's going to sound"** Jeremy Egner, "Damon Lindelof on the 'Leftovers' Finale, Mark Linn-Baker and Preserving the Mystery," *New York Times*, June 4, 2017.

112 **"She was the epitome"** Tim LaHaye, and Jerry B. Jenkins, *Apollyon: The Destroyer Is Unleashed* (Tyndale House, 2011), 100.

112 **"My challenge to you"** Tim LaHaye and Jerry B. Jenkins, *Soul Harvest: The World Takes Sides* (Tyndale House, 1998), 329.

113 **"inclined to believe"** LaHaye and Jenkins, *Left Behind: A Novel of the Earth's Last Days* (Tyndale House, 1995), 254.

113 **"had come a long way"** LaHaye and Jenkins, *Left Behind*, 440.

113 **"the supernatural came"** LaHaye and Jerry Jenkins, *Left Behind*, 237.

114 **"I think we're seeing"** Sacha Sewhdat, "God's Not Dead 2: Interview with Director Harold Cronk," *Context with Lorna Dueck*, March 31, 2016.

## 7: The Silence of the Lambs

121 **"Revenge in modern times"** "The Motion Picture Production Code of 1930 (Hays Code)," artsreformation.com/a001/hays-code.html.

121 **"With great power"** Bradford W. Wright, *Comic Book Nation: The Transformation of Youth Culture in America* (Johns Hopkins University Press, 2001), 211.

121 **"George Bush is Darth Vader"** Maureen Dowd, "The Aura of Arugulance," *New York Times*, April 18, 2009.

121 **"Democracies aren't overthrown"** Mark Caro, "'Star Wars' Inadvertently Hits Too Close to U.S.'s Role," *Chicago Tribune*, May 18, 2005.

124 **"Is it okay"** Author interview, September 14, 2015.

125 **"the deadliest show"** Patrick Kevin Day, "'The Walking Dead' Is the Deadliest Show on TV, Study Says," *Los Angeles Times*, February 12, 2013.

129 **"Even with all the popcorn"** Brooks Barnes, "Can Steven Spielberg Remember How to Have Fun?" *New York Times*, March 21, 2018.

129 **the first groupies** Barbara Ehrenreich, *Dancing in the Streets: A History of Collective Joy* (Metropolitan Books, 2007), 41.

130 **"It was fun to create"** Author interview, August 2, 2011.

132 **"Repression and frenzy"** Author interview, August 2, 2011.

## 8: Beauty in the Beast

136 **Frankenstein's monster** Mary Shelley, *Frankenstein*, edited by Johanna M. Smith (St. Martin's, 2000), 109.

137 **"last gentleman"** Robert Warshow, *The Immediate Experience: Movies, Comics, Theatre & Other Aspects of Popular Culture* (Anchor, 1964), 94.

140 **Earth "is his home"** Roth Cornet, "Avengers: Age of Ultron—Even Thor Can't Fight Ultron," IGN, February 27, 2015.

142 **"It's another one"** Tom Butler, "Nick Fury's Role in Avengers 2 Is Just a Cameo," Yahoo!, March 26, 2014.

145 **"They're like this"** Jeremy Egner, "From Fish, Birds and Ants, Undead Hordes," *New York Times*, June 14, 2013.

145 **"nationalism . . . on the march"** J. K. Rowling, "On Monsters, Villains and the EU Referendum," JKRowling.com, June 30, 2016.

147 **"surprised at how much"** Ben Hoyle, "War on Terror Backdrop to James Cameron's Avatar," *The Australian*, December 11, 2009.

147 **"I think there's something"** Glenn Whipp, "Is 'Avatar' a Message Movie? Absolutely, Says James Cameron," *Los Angeles Times*, February 10, 2010.

148 **"violently to burst through"** Isaiah Berlin, "Joseph de Maistre and the Origins of Fascism," *New York Review of Books*, September 27, 1990.

149 **"Instead of being"** Leo Braudy, *Haunted: On Ghosts, Witches, Vampires, Zombies, and Other Monsters of the Natural and Supernatural Worlds* (Yale University Press, 2017), 120.

149 **"Was I then a monster"** Mary Wollstonecraft Shelley, *Frankenstein: Complete, Authoritative Text with Biographical, Historical, and Cultural Contexts, Critical History, and Essays from Contemporary Critical Perspectives*, ed. Johanna M. Smith (Bedford Books, 2000), 109.

149 **"I was not even"** Shelley, *Frankenstein*, 109.

## 9: License to Kill

152 **"You have to fight fire"** Ali Vitale, "Donald Trump on Terror: You Have to 'Fight Fire with Fire,'" NBCNews.com, June 29, 2016.

153 **"I don't shoot people"** John Farr, "Wayne vs. Eastwood: Who Wins in a Shootout?" *Best Movies by Farr* (blog), May 31, 2014.

153 **"In *Josey Wales*"** Peter Biskind, *Gods and Monsters: Thirty Years of Writing on Film and Culture from One of Americas Most Incisive Writers* (Nation Books, 2004), 219.

153 **"Darkness is good"** Michael Wolff, "Ringside with Steve Bannon at Trump Tower as the President-Elect's Strategist Plots 'an Entirely New Political Movement,'" *Hollywood Reporter*, November 18, 2016.

153 **"I want to bring"** Garry Wills, "Where Evangelicals Came From," *New York Review of Books*, April 20, 2017.

153 **"Dick Cheney. Darth Vader"** Wolff, "Ringside with Steve Bannon."

154 **"I could stand"** Ali Vitale, "Trump Says He Could 'Shoot Somebody' and Still Maintain Support," NBCNews.com, January 23, 2016.

158 **"profoundly, consistently"** Alex Pappademas, "Frank Miller's Dark Night," *Grantland*, August 22, 2014.

160 **"The other universe"** David Roberts, "Donald Trump and the Rise of Tribal Epistemology," *Vox*, May 19, 2017.

160 **"It's hard not to notice"** Christian Toto, "'The Hunger Games' Review: Tween Take on Big Government, Reality TV," *Breitbart*, March 21, 2012.

161  **"meritocratic force for order"** Sonny Bunch, "The Destruction of Alderaan Was Completely Justified," *Washington Post*, October 29, 2015.

161  **"Is Christopher Nolan's Batman"** Jordan Zakarin, "'The Dark Knight Rises' Politics: Is Christopher Nolan's Batman Series Liberal or Conservative?" *Hollywood Reporter*, July 18, 2012.

161  **"he's got that killer"** Ethan Sacks, "Christian Bale Says Goodbye to Batman with 'The Dark Knight Rises,' and He's Okay with That," *Daily News*, January 23, 2012.

162  **"PICKS up the Joker"** Christopher Nolan and Jonathan Nolan, *The Dark Night* script, 105–6, joblo.com/scripts/The_Dark_Knight.pdf.

162  **"he's desperately not trying"** Sacks, "Christian Bale Says Goodbye."

165  **"a survey of"** Somini Sengupta, "Torture Can Be Useful, Nearly Half of Americans in Poll Say," *New York Times*, December 5, 2016.

165  **"We also have to work"** Dan Froomkin, "Cheney's 'Dark Side' Is Showing," White House Watch, *Washington Post*, November 7, 2005; John McQuaid, "Dick Cheney Defends the Dark Side," *The Guardian*, May 21, 2009.

165  **eagerness to dog-paddle** "Blaming America First," *New York Times*, February 7, 2017.

165  **Parents Television Council** Dahlia Lithwick, "How Jack Bauer Shaped U.S Torture Policy," *Newsweek*, July 25, 2008; Martin Miller, "'24' and 'Lost' Get Symposium on Torture," *Seattle Times*, February 14, 2007.

165  **"There are not"** Jane Mayer, "Whatever It Takes," *New Yorker*, February 19, 2017.

166  **"It was soothing"** Mayer, "Whatever It Takes."

## 10: What a Piece of Work Was Man

175  **"snarl of conservative"** A. O. Scott and Manohla Dargis, "Blockbusters Yield to Magic," *New York Times*, August 8, 2012.

176  **"In my work"** "The Secret Behind Romero's Scary Zombies: 'I Made Them the Neighbors,'" *Weekend Edition*, NPR, July 20, 2014.

177  **"to be human"** John Podhoretz, "Avatarocious," *Weekly Standard*, December 28, 2009.

177  **"How noble in reason!"** William Shakespeare, *Hamlet* (Simon & Schuster, 2009), 2.2, 295–302.

178  **thinking is a function** George Makari, *Soul Machine: The Invention of the Modern Mind* (W.W. Norton, 2015), 115.

178  **"ghost in the machine"** Gilbert Ryle, *The Concept of Mind* (University of Chicago Press, 2002), 27.

179  **"The stereotypical zombie"** Peter Dendle, "Zombie Movies and the

'Millennial Generation,'" in *Better Off Dead: The Evolution of the Zombie as Post-Human*, ed. Deborah Christie and Sarah Juliet Lauro (Fordham University Press, 2011), 177.

181 **"our powerful desire"** Author interview, August 2, 2011.

181 **"The Year We Obsessed"** Wesley Morris, "The Year We Obsessed Over Identity," *New York Times Magazine*, October 6, 2015.

183 **"Instead of building walls"** David Michigan, "Hillary Clinton's South Carolina Speech: Transcript," *Daily Kos*, February 28, 2016.

184 **The wall bears** Hendrik Hertzberg, "World War Z-Z-Z-Zion," *New Yorker*, June 23, 2013.


## 11: Anywhere but Here

186 **"America has never stopped"** Nick Gass, "Clinton Takes on Trump: 'America Never Stopped Being Great,'" *Politico*, February 27, 2016.

187 **"Race is real"** Marin Cogan, "The Alt-Right Gives a Press Conference," *New York*, September 11, 2016.

187 **"the Swedes [who] have"** Andrew Marantz, "How 'Fox & Friends' Rewrites Trump's Reality" *New Yorker*, January 15, 2018.

187 **Cheddar Man** Ceylan Yeginsu and Carl Zimmer, "'Cheddar Man,' Britain's Oldest Skeleton, Had Dark Skin, DNA Shows," *New York Times*, February 7, 2018.

189 **"break down walls"** Tim LaHaye, and Jerry B. Jenkins, *Apollyon: The Destroyer Is Unleashed* (Tyndale House, 2011), 104.

189 **"people want to see"** Sam Tanenhaus, "How Trump Can Save the G.O.P.," *New York Times*, July 8, 2016.

189 **"All restraint, all boundaries"** Tim LaHaye and Jerry B. Jenkins, *Left Behind: A Novel of the Earth's Last Days* (Tyndale House, 1995), 325.

191 **A movie like *Suburbicon*** Wesley Morris, "George Clooney's Awkward White Guilt in 'Suburbicon,'" *New York Times*, November 3, 2017.

192 **As Daniel Mendelsohn points out** Daniel Mendelsohn, "The Wizard," *New York Review of Books*, March 25, 2010.

193 **Jumping from one species to another** Mendelsohn, "The Wizard."

193 **we have the diaspora "in reverse"** Armond White, "*Black Panther*'s Circle of Hype," *National Review*, February 16, 2018.

194 **"an advanced breed"** Stephen Hawking, "Questioning the Universe," TED Talk, February 2008.

194 **"gods and demigods"** Borys Kit, "Comic-Con 2011: Frank Miller Talks Politics, Gods and Demigods at Legendary Comics Panel," *Hollywood Reporter*, July 23, 2011.

195 **"I don't think teens"** Jeffrey A. Trachtenberg, "Booksellers Find Life After Harry in a Vampire Novel," *Wall Street Journal*, August 10, 2007.

195 **"To me, vampires"** Vanessa Grigoriadis, "The Joy of Vampire Sex: The Schlocky, Sensual Secrets Behind the Success of 'True Blood,'" *Rolling Stone*, June 10, 2011.

196 **"It's weird that"** Melissa Maerz, "Hot Actor: Q&A with 'Twilight' Star Robert Pattinson," *Rolling Stone*, December 11, 2008.

196 **Some went so far** Laura Leonard, "The Trouble with Twilight," *Christianity Today*, February 19, 2010; Sue Bohlin, "The Darkness of Twilight: A Christian Perspective," Probe.org, June 27, 2010.

197 **"What an idiot!"** Tim LaHaye and Jerry B. Jenkins, *Left Behind: A Novel of the Earth's Last Days* (Tyndale House, 1995), 98.

197 **"poured himself a glass"** LaHaye and Jenkins, *Left Behind*, 101.

197 **"I will do what"** Tim LaHaye and Jerry B. Jenkins. *Tribulation Force: The Continuing Drama of Those Left Behind* (Tyndale House, 1996), 348.

198 **"The rabbi at"** LaHaye and Jenkins, *Tribulation Force*, 107.

199 **"evidence-based"** Elizabeth Cohen, "The Truth About Those 7 Words 'Banned' at the CDC," CNN, January 31, 2018, https://www.cnn.com/2018/01/11/health/cdc-word-ban-hhs-document/index.html.

## 12: No Exit

203 **"I could see the dust motes"** Stephenie Meyer, *Breaking Dawn* (Little, Brown, 2012), 387.

206 **"The idea [is] that"** Jason Tanz, "Modern Marvel: Why Netflix's Luke Cage Is the Superhero We Really Need Now," *Wired*, August 16, 2016.

206 **"My publisher said"** Nolan Feeney, "How *Spider-Man* Was Born," *Time*, November 18, 2015.

213 **"Merging with future"** Ray Kurzweil, "Ray Kurzweil on How We'll End Up Merging with Our Technology," *New York Times*, March 14, 2017.

213 **"Why define an"** Benjamin H. Bratton, "Outing A.I.: Beyond the Turing Test," *New York Times*, February 23, 2015.

213 **"a separate species"** Robert A. Burton, "How I Learned to Stop Worrying and Love A.I.," *New York Times*, September 21, 2015.

213 **Turing test requires** Noam Cohen, *The Know-It-Alls: The Rise of Silicon Valley as a Political Powerhouse and Social Wrecking Ball* (The New Press, 2017), 21.

214 **Childbirth doesn't seem** Ciara Wardlow, "'Blade Runner 2049': The Deckard Question Matters More than You Think," *Hollywood Reporter*, October 9, 2017.

214 **"slipped to the floor"** Tim LaHaye and Jerry B. Jenkins. *Tribulation Force: The Continuing Drama of Those Left Behind* (Tyndale House, 1996), 240–41.

214 **"Buck had already"** LaHaye and Jenkins, *Tribulation Force*, 240–41.

## Conclusion: The Return of the Center

217 **"It's hard for our show"** Kathryn Shattuck, "Claire Danes Could Really Use a Nap," *New York Times*, February 9, 2018.

218 **black against black** Osha Neumann, "A White Guy Watches 'The Black Panther,'" *Counterpunch*, February 23, 2018.

218 **"The sun will never set"** Adam Serwer, "The Tragedy of Erik Killmonger," *The Atlantic*, February 21, 2018.

219 **"doesn't tolerate racism"** W.J. Hennigan, "U.S. Military Leaders Condemn Racism Following Trump's Comments on Charlottesville Violence," *Los Angeles Times*, August 16, 2017.

219 **"bastion of extremism"** Editorial Board, "St. Louis as a Bastion of Political Extremism. What's Wrong with This Picture?" *St. Louis Post-Dispatch*, February 21, 2013.

219 **"brain damage"** Yaron Steinbuch, "Brain Damage Is Linked to Religious Extremism," *New York Post*, May 8, 2017.

223 **A computer analysis** Nathalia Holt, "The Women Who Run the 'Star Wars' Universe," *New York Times*, December 22, 2017.

223 **"I'm sick and tired"** Bill Bradley and Matthew Jacobs, "Surprise, Surprise: The 'Alt-Right' Claims Credit for 'Last Jedi' Backlash," *HuffPost*, December 20, 2017.

# INDEX

# ABOUT THE AUTHOR

**Peter Biskind** is a contributing editor to *Vanity Fair*, a writer for *Esquire*, and the author of the classic bestsellers *Easy Riders, Raging Bulls: How the Sex-Drugs-and-Rock 'n' Roll Generation Saved Hollywood* and *Down and Dirty Pictures: Miramax, Sundance, and the Rise of Independent Film*, among other books. He is the former editor-in-chief of *American Film* magazine and the executive editor of *Premiere* magazine.

# PUBLISHING IN THE PUBLIC INTEREST